THE SEVEN
DAYS' BATTLES

THE SEVEN DAYS' BATTLES

The War Begins Anew

Judkin Browning

Battles and Leaders of the American Civil War
John David Smith, Series Editor

 PRAEGER

AN IMPRINT OF ABC-CLIO, LLC
Santa Barbara, California • Denver, Colorado • Oxford, England

Library of Congress Cataloging-in-Publication Data

Browning, Judkin.
  The Seven Days' Battles : the war begins anew / Judkin Browning.
      p. cm. — (Battles and leaders of the American Civil War)
  Includes bibliographical references and index.
  ISBN 978-0-313-39271-9 (hardcopy : acid-free paper) —
ISBN 978-0-313-39272-6 (ebook)   1. Seven Days' Battles, Va.,
1862.   I. Title.
  E473.68.B76   2012
  973.7'32—dc23   2012005043

ISBN: 978-0-313-39271-9
EISBN: 978-0-313-39272-6

16   15   14   13   12   1   2   3   4   5

This book is also available on the World Wide Web as an eBook.

Visit www.abc-clio.com for details.

Praeger
An Imprint of ABC-CLIO, LLC

ABC-CLIO, LLC
130 Cremona Drive, P.O. Box 1911
Santa Barbara, California 93116-1911

This book is printed on acid-free paper ∞

Manufactured in the United States of America

To my brother,
Jeremy Browning

Contents

A photo essay follows page 84

Series Foreword

In October 1864 Confederate president Jefferson Davis sought to rally increasingly demoralized Southerners, declaring "by fighting alone can independence be gained." Months later, in his Second Inaugural Address, President Abraham Lincoln reminded Northerners that "the progress of our arms, upon which all else chiefly depends, is as well known to the public as to myself; and it is, I trust, reasonably satisfactory and encouraging to all."

Though historians have debated endlessly about the causes of Union victory and Confederate defeat in the American Civil War, the North proved triumphant on the battlefield not because of its population advantage, its manufacturing superiority, or because of internal divisions in Dixie. Above all else, Southern hopes for independence and European recognition hinged on battlefield victories; Northern success ultimately resulted from combat victories and superior leadership.

The books in Praeger's *Battles and Leaders of the American Civil War* series focus closely on key Civil War battles and the leaders who led their men into the fight. The books treat major battles and examine minutely how the outcome of the battles depended on the abilities, skills, triumphs, and failures of commanders who orchestrated the campaigns. Each book underscores the nexus between military outcome and command decisions, including political implications, supply, tactics, and strategy. The authors emphasize contingencies that influenced battle outcomes. They also consider the social, political, and geographic context of each battle and the background and personalities of the commanders.

With more than 620,000 deaths, the Civil War was the bloodiest conflict on American soil. Books in *Battles and Leaders of the American Civil War* interpret the war's combat and its leadership as central to its meaning. Readers will find the volumes fast-paced, up-to-date, well-researched, and valuable guides as they ponder the war's triumphs and tragedies.

John David Smith

Charles H. Stone Distinguished Professor of American History
The University of North Carolina at Charlotte

Acknowledgments

I have always been drawn to the Seven Days' battles, ever since I was a teenager discovering the Civil War. The first article that I ever published—written while I was an undergraduate—was of one Georgia regiment's disastrous experience at the battle of Mechanicsville. I have always been fascinated by the stakes involved in the battle—the fact that it was the first major battle for a majority of its participants, and yet could have ended the war if things had turned out differently. As a result, it has been a great pleasure to research and write this book. I would like to thank John David Smith, the series editor, for suggesting that I write a volume for this series and for encouraging me to write on this campaign. I also thank the editorial and production staff of Praeger Press for the professionalism with which they handled the process. Finally, I owe a debt of gratitude to Dr. James P. Jones, my mentor at Florida State University, who took an interest in my work, encouraged me to pursue graduate study in this field, and guided me in that first article that I ever published.

I have benefited from the sage advice, comments, criticisms, and suggestions from several friends and colleagues in writing this manuscript. I thank Michael Thomas Smith and Steven Nash for reading every word of every chapter of the manuscript very thoroughly and sharing their criticisms and suggestions with me. I am grateful that Keith S. Bohannon took time out of his busy schedule to offer a close reading of chapter six and made sure that I did not get things too wrong. I thank my colleague, Tim Silver, who was genuinely interested in engaging in a lengthy discussion of the Seven Days during a long drive to Washington, D.C., in the summer of 2011. He allowed me to bounce my ideas off him and articulate my conclusions about certain aspects of the campaign that I had not yet committed to paper. He also shared with me a conference paper he had written on the environmental effects of the campaign. Any mistakes or errors in the book are in spite of, rather than because of, the input of these individuals. I also wish to extend my profound thanks to Brian Wize, the Appalachian State University Geography graduate student who agreed to create the maps for this volume despite the short time frame I provided, limited funds that I could offer, and the mountain of his own graduate work that he still had to complete. This book would not have been the same without his excellent maps.

Battles are inherently chaotic and confusing events. There truly is no substitute for walking the ground in order to understand the geography, terrain, and even occasionally weather conditions that participants experienced. To that effect, I have visited the Seven Days' battlefields outside Richmond more than a dozen times through the years—finding myself drawn to them nearly every time I pass through Richmond. I have taken many friends and family members to those battlefields to share my passion. My good friend, Chris Hoch, has been with me on many of those trips, and together we have covered nearly every inch of the battlefields and, if truth be told, plenty of ground that is not on Park Service property as well. One particular excursion stands out as Chris joined me in late June 2010 to spend all day in the 100-plus degree heat tromping all over the Gaines Mill battlefield and surrounding private property environs. I hope that we may continue our excursions to the hallowed grounds of the Civil War for many years to come.

Introduction

While not studied nearly as heavily as some other major campaigns—such as Antietam, Gettysburg, or the 1864 Overland campaign that matched Robert E. Lee and Ulysses S. Grant against each other—the Seven Days' battles were perhaps the most important battles of the Civil War. If they had turned out differently, then the three famous campaigns mentioned above likely would never have occurred. In the spring of 1862, General George B. McClellan took the largest army in American history, more than 100,000 men, to the eastern peninsula of Virginia and marched, inexorably it seemed, toward Richmond. He intended to defeat the Confederate army and capture the capital city of the rebellious South. Had McClellan accomplished his objective, it is very possible that the war would have ended in that summer of 1862. There is no guarantee of that result, of course, and Southerners' nationalism may have survived the dispiriting capitulation of their political capital, but there are strong indications that such a decisive and demoralizing defeat in the second year of the war could have stimulated an anti-war sentiment in the South and compelled many Southerners to rejoin the Union, thereby undermining the Confederacy's attempts to achieve its independence. Had the war ended in the summer of 1862, the United States that emerged from the brief war would have looked much like the United States of antebellum days. There would have been no emancipation, little confiscation of property, and only modest physical or social devastation to have to reconstruct after the war. But McClellan was not successful; he was defeated by a combination of his own strategic errors and the relentless attacks by Lee's Confederate army. As a result, the war began anew, and much more radical policies and physical destruction accompanied this new phase of conflict.

Though several wartime participants and observers wrote memoirs of the campaign in the years following the war, the first scholarly studies of the Seven Days' battles—the campaign that first introduced Robert E. Lee into the Confederate pantheon—occurred in the 1930s, when Douglas Southall Freeman wrote his magisterial, comprehensive, and hagiographic four-volume biography of Lee. The Seven Days' battles take up a large chunk of volume two in that series. Nearly a decade later, Freeman complemented his study of the Southern messiah with a three-volume study of his disciples. Nearly the entirety of the first volume of *Lee's Lieutenants* is dedicated to analyzing the positive and many negative contributions of Lee's subordinate officers, who in Freeman's opinion, foiled Lee's well-crafted plans.

Two decades later, the centennial of the war led to many histories of the conflict, which introduced great numbers of people to the Seven Days' battles and to the quirks of many of the commanders involved. Bruce Catton produced not one, but two trilogies of the war. In *Mr. Lincoln's Army*, the first volume of his Army of the Potomac trilogy, Catton brings out the eccentricities of Stonewall Jackson, the crippling caution of McClellan, and the thwarted genius of Lee. In *Terrible Swift Sword*, the second volume of his American Civil War trilogy, Catton elaborates on these themes in greater detail. Southern author and raconteur, Shelby Foote, joined the centennial party with his massive three-volume history of the war. The first volume presents more than 100 pages about the Peninsula campaign and the Seven Days. Foote is a masterful storyteller with a flair for the dramatic and a witty writing style. He also cannot conceal his pro-southern attitude and he idolizes Lee, as all good Southern boys are supposed to do. Like Catton, Foote's work introduced many to the war, including this author, who, as a teenager, enjoyed Foote's works (many years after they were published).

While Catton and Foote brought histories of the war to lay readers (though in Foote's case, not quickly, as he took nearly two decades to complete his trilogy), Clifford Dowdey specialized in Lee's first campaign. His book, *The Seven Days: The Emergence of Lee*, appeared in 1964 during the centennial celebration of the war and was itself a celebration of Lee, as was his biography of "Marse Robert," which appeared the following year. Dowdey is perhaps the most gifted writer of all the historians to cover this campaign—his storytelling skills are unmatched. Dowdey is also pointed in his criticisms and goes to elaborate lengths to craft alibis for the Confederate military legends, such as Jackson and Lee. Lesser lights of the Confederate galaxy do not fare nearly as well. Dowdey is unsparing of those he viewed as subpar, but is critical in such articulate and clever prose that it is a pleasure to read him tear apart Lee's subordinates.

After Dowdey, nearly three decades passed before another quality interpretation of the campaign emerged. Though some historians wrote forgettable volumes, it was not until Stephen Sears's *To the Gates of Richmond* appeared in 1992 that those interested in this pivotal first campaign had something substantial to sink their teeth into. Sears sanded off many of the worshipful edges of Lee and presented a more balanced, critical commentary on the battle. He did not spare Jackson as others had, and he credited Lee with some mistakes that others had not. Sears also bucked the historical trend by placing General George McClellan at the center of his volume, and pointed out that the Southern success was primarily due to McClellan's mistakes. This is not surprising as Sears had written a detailed and analytical biography of the "Young Napoleon" a decade earlier. By shining the light more on McClellan, Sears did not alter the negative opinion of McClellan's performance during the battle, but painted a much fuller picture of why McClellan made the strange and defeatist decisions that he did.

The final worthy entry into the history of these battles is Brian K. Burton's *Extraordinary Circumstances* (2001), whose title is a play on Lee's much-quoted summation of the campaign: "Under ordinary circumstances the Federal Army should have been destroyed." Burton points out that Lee was reading his future success back into his previous experience, arguing instead that a close analysis of all the factors in the battle—and Burton does a very close and occasionally tedious analysis—reveals that Lee was fortunate to accomplish what he did. Burton also provides a more forgiving tone than most authors. He views the campaign from the individual commanders' perspectives and largely absolves Lee's subordinate commanders (especially Jackson) from their frequently criticized decisions. He also tends to give McClellan and his subordinates a little more credit than other historians have, pointing out the skillful change of base that McClellan completed successfully, and providing more understanding as to why the general felt compelled to make the decisions that he made.

Thus, the history of Lee's first campaign—and the last greatest chance for the Union to end the war quickly with the country largely unchanged—has gone through several permutations. The initial histories were paeans to Lee's prowess, suggesting that his lack of decisive results was due to the flaws of his many subordinates. Later histories focused the lens on

Union commanders, high command decisions, and the view from the bottom—the enlisted men—and the complex nature and effects of military decisions. Much of the bright sheen on Lee's statue has been dulled, while some of the muck staining the monuments of McClellan and others has been scraped away. Yet, for the average American who knows anything about this battle (and admittedly that is a very small number), the basic story that remains reified to this day is that Lee aggressively sought to destroy the Union army and developed a skilled plan to do so, but was thwarted from realizing his plan by the mistakes of his subordinates. McClellan was too cautious and retreated too readily, even though he outnumbered his foe. In summation, McClellan lost his nerve and Lee was let down by his underlings.

Those with more knowledge of Civil War history will perhaps find remarkable similarities to the Southern rationalizations for the defeat at Gettysburg. That myth suggests that Lee made all the right moves, but was forced to suffer defeat because of the failings of his subordinates, primarily A. P. Hill, James Longstreet, Richard Ewell, and Jeb Stuart (all major players in the Seven Days' battles as well). The major difference between those two campaigns was that, after the defeat at Gettysburg in July 1863, Lee openly acknowledged his failure even if no one else would. After the Seven Days' battles, however, Lee never publicly admitted that he had made any mistakes. Instead, he quietly made changes, many of which reflected that he believed his subordinates had been the reason for the less than spectacular success he had desired.

* * *

This book synthesizes the historical scholarship on the campaign and offers a detailed synopsis of the battle, while putting forward some new arguments. I analyze the standard interpretations of many of the officers involved, the decisions they made, and the actions they took. I explain why the conventional wisdom is problematic in many cases, and on occasion I concede that some interpretations cannot be improved. However, I do challenge many scholars for their conscious or unconscious defense of Lee and persecution of McClellan. While I find it difficult to rehabilitate McClellan (and the few historians who have tried have failed), I find much fault with Lee's performance as commander during the week of June 25–July 1, 1862.

Rather than caricaturing McClellan as incompetent and warming in the glow that is Lee's brilliance, I argue that both sides committed many errors and that Lee was far from masterful. Lee did not manage any of the battles well, employed too many complicated maneuvers, had a poor grasp of the terrain and what was even possible to accomplish with the army he had, and he made exceptionally poor decisions at key moments during the week. Lee won the campaign, even though he scored a clear victory in only one of the five major battles during the week, while he unambiguously lost two of them. McClellan inflated Confederate numbers to illogical levels, failed to commit his troops to offensive action at key moments, and refused to develop a respectful relationship with his civilian superiors, which greatly hindered his campaign. In many ways, the seeds of the Seven Days' campaign were planted in the acidic soil of Union military politics in Washington, D.C. and watered with distrust. McClellan believed in a limited, enlightened form of warfare in which victory could be obtained without much bloodshed. His defeat and President Lincoln's subsequent order of his army's retreat from the peninsula in August 1862 presaged the end of this limited war phase of the conflict and ushered in a much more destructive phase.

NOTES ON SOURCES

In order to reduce the number of intrusive note references in this volume, I have limited myself to citing direct quotes and specific anecdotes. All other notes are general suggestions for where the interested reader can learn more about the specific topic referenced. The narrative is synthesized from approximately 10 different campaign histories or biographies that refer prominently to the campaign, and each source has not been cited in full. I recommend the interested reader consult the Bibliographic Essay at the end of the book for further reading suggestions. Unless otherwise noted, all biographical information about officers has been distilled from Ezra Warner's *Generals in Gray* (1959) and *Generals in Blue* (1964), as well as from the *Encyclopedia of the American Civil War* (5 vols., 2000). Similarly, the maps in this volume owe a great debt of gratitude to the cartographic efforts of Stephen Sears, Matt Collins (who created the excellent maps in Brian Burton's work), and the 19th-century U.S. army cartographers, who generated the magnificent maps in the *Battles and Leaders* series. Each offered inspiration for the maps in this book.

1

—∞∞∞—

The Road to the Seven Days

On August 3, 1862, while his army was camped at Harrison's Landing, where it had been languishing in the oppressively humid heat for a month since the end of the Seven Days' battles, General George B. McClellan received an order, the opening line of which stunned and angered him: "It is determined to withdraw your army from the Peninsula." McClellan admitted that the message "caused me the greatest pain I have ever experienced," but he protested to no avail.[1] The government was showing that it no longer had faith in either the commander or his campaign in eastern Virginia. McClellan had set off on the campaign that would end the war with the largest army in American history, more than 100 siege guns to pound the Confederate capital to rubble, and an enviable martial reputation. He faced an outnumbered foe, whose beloved commander had been so severely wounded in the campaign's first consequential battle that the Confederate army was entrusted to a heretofore disappointing general who generated very little confidence in his soldiers or his nation. By June 25, McClellan had pushed the enemy to the very doorstep of Richmond—the end of the war was in plain sight through the sultry summer haze. Now, just six weeks later, McClellan was being asked to abandon the campaign as a failure. How had it come to this disgraceful end after such a promising start? It all began in the summer of 1861, only 100 days into the war.

* * *

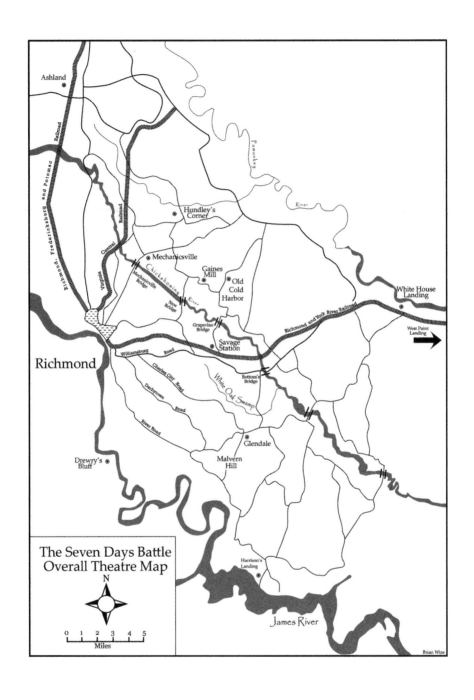

Ashland

Railroad

Richmond, Fredericksburg and Potomac

Central

Railroad

Virginia

Pamunkey

River

Hundley's
Corner

Mechanicsville

Chickahominy

Mechanicsville
Bridge

New
Bridge

River

Gaines
Mill

Old
Cold
Harbor

White House
Landing

Richmond and York River Railroad

West Point
Landing

Grapevine
Bridge

Savage
Station

Richmond

Williamsburg   Road

Charles City   Road

Bottom's
Bridge

White Oak Swamp

Darbytown

Road

River Road

Glendale

Drewry's
Bluff

Malvern
Hill

The Seven Days Battle
Overall Theatre Map

N

Harrison's
Landing

0   1   2   3   4   5
Miles

James River

Brian Wize

The dashing 34-year-old general arrived in the nation's capital on July 26, 1861, just five days after the Bull Run debacle, and witnessed signs of demoralization and disorganization in the dazed soldiers loitering around the city. McClellan had been appointed commander and he immediately set about saving the nation, as he saw it. He requested more of everything—more volunteers, more supplies of every kind, and more time to organize the army into a force that could win the war. President Abraham Lincoln had chosen McClellan because of some very small but greatly inflated victories in the mountains of western Virginia. He initially tolerated McClellan's exhaustive preparation and training of the Army of the Potomac, which grew larger and better equipped every day in the late summer and autumn of 1861, but Lincoln expected military action in a reasonable period of time.

McClellan certainly came with a military pedigree that suggested he was the perfect man for the job. Born to a distinguished family in Philadelphia in 1826, he had finished second in his class at West Point 20 years later. Immediately after graduating, McClellan served with the Army Corps of Engineers in the Mexican War, where he worked closely with Captain Robert E. Lee, 17 years his senior. In 1855 he was sent to Europe by then Secretary of War Jefferson Davis to report on the Crimean War, and his resulting reports led the army to adopt a new style of saddle and update their cavalry tactics. Due to limited prospects for advancement, McClellan resigned in 1857 and became chief engineer and later vice president of the Illinois Central Railroad, where he got to know one of the railroad's lawyers, Abraham Lincoln. McClellan was neither socially impressed with nor politically sympathetic to the gangly attorney. McClellan would never entirely abandon his initial negative views of the rustic and homely Lincoln.[2]

In fact, McClellan had a much closer bond to several of his opponents than he did to his president. While serving in the old army, McClellan had developed a close friendship with Joseph E. Johnston, the man who would be the initial commander of the Confederate army opposing McClellan. Johnston's second in command, General Gustavus W. Smith, had been McClellan's engineering instructor and friend at West Point and had served as his immediate superior in the Mexican War. McClellan liked Smith immensely and Smith certainly thought highly of his former pupil. Of the other Southern generals he would face, McClellan had worked alongside John B. Magruder in Mexico, had graduated from West Point in the same class as Thomas J. "Stonewall" Jackson (who finished 17th), and George Pickett (who finished dead last in his class), and had won the hand in marriage of Ellen Marcy—the same woman that Confederate General

Ambrose Powell Hill had once courted. Even his first cousin, Henry B. McClellan, would serve as Confederate General James Ewell Brown (Jeb) Stuart's chief of staff. In fact, McClellan's connection to Confederate officers and his conservative philosophies for prosecuting the war were so extensive that some later came to fear that he was secretly a Southern sympathizer.

In August 1861 McClellan submitted a plan of action that called for 300,000 more soldiers for the Army of the Potomac alone. McClellan was straightforward in his reasoning: "I understand it to be the purpose of this great nation to reestablish the power of the Government and restore peace to its citizens in the shortest possible time."[3] Amassing an overpowering army was the safest and surest way to accomplish this. Lincoln did not believe that so large an army was needed, but he did not publicly oppose it. He did not want to rush McClellan into disaster as he had General Irvin McDowell at Bull Run, and he gave McClellan all the support he could possibly desire. When the "Young Napoleon," as McClellan was sometimes called, felt hindered by the 75-year-old corpulent General-in-Chief Winfield Scott, whom he considered an "incubus" from a bygone era of American military success, Lincoln allowed McClellan to ignore Scott. When the insulted Scott abruptly retired, Lincoln did not attempt to dissuade him.[4] Lincoln then conferred the general-in-chief title on his self-important young general. When Lincoln expressed concern that the simultaneous duties of general-in-chief—in which McClellan was to oversee and coordinate Union army strategy nationwide—and commander of the Army of the Potomac might be too much for one mortal to handle, McClellan informed him confidently, "I can do it all."[5]

Almost from that moment of anointing McClellan the most powerful military man in the country in November 1861, Lincoln began to have misgivings. More than three months had passed since McClellan took the reins of the army and nothing of military significance had occurred. McClellan was preparing his army for a grand campaign that appeared to be perpetually occurring soon but never occurring now. Lincoln's gentle prods for McClellan to get moving and his occasional unsolicited suggestions were always met with a polite (at least initially) but firmly negative response. What Lincoln was slow to realize was that these suggestions and prods were not welcome at headquarters.

McClellan had taken on a messianic complex when he became General of the Army of the Potomac and his apotheosis grew with each passing day. McClellan felt (and wrote frequently to his wife) that he had been called on to save the nation—an enormous responsibility that he found very flattering, very satisfying, and very crushing. He resented the fact that an amateur like Lincoln would dare to offer advice to a professional military man about matters of tactics and strategy. The young general would not countenance such interference by his inferiors, and McClellan's personal tone in his references and dealings with Lincoln began shifting markedly in the fall of 1861. His actions spoke volumes, as he ceased explaining to Lincoln the reasons for his delays and simply began asking for more men and more supplies. Perhaps the culmination of his detachment from the president and his own sense of self-importance came one autumn evening when Lincoln and Secretary of State William Henry Seward paid a visit to the general's house to chat. Upon arriving, they were informed that the general was out and would return shortly. While the president and secretary of state waited in the parlor, McClellan returned home by the back door and chose not to meet his distinguished guests. When Lincoln later asked the orderly when McClellan was due, he was informed that the general had returned and gone to bed. The president and secretary of state departed humiliated. Seward was incensed, but Lincoln took it in his long stride, though he never again paid a social visit on his general.[6]

The relationship between McClellan and Lincoln began to fray when it became apparent to McClellan that Lincoln was not going to allow him to move on his own timetable and when it became apparent to Lincoln that his commanding general showed neither comprehension of nor sympathy for the political considerations in which the military was involved. Lincoln wanted McClellan to move sooner rather than later in order to drive the Confederate army away from Washington. Every day the Confederate army remained, shadowing the capital and reminding everyone that they had won the field in July 1861, was another day the administration looked impotent and unprepared to meet the demands of the contest. Lincoln expected McClellan to drive the Confederate army away by autumn, and he certainly expected McClellan to realize that he had to do something toward that end. He was disappointed in both regards and slowly came to lower his expectations for his general.

McClellan expected Lincoln to trust him to do the right thing with the army. Based on Lincoln's early efforts to strike a genuine friendship with the general, McClellan believed that he and Lincoln shared a common view on how to win the war and thought Lincoln would allow him to conduct it as he saw fit. Like Lincoln, McClellan was disappointed in his initial expectations, and came to expect nothing but opposition, negativity, and interference from Lincoln. For his part, Lincoln attempted on several occasions to repair the rupture and bring the general to understand his point of view. But once McClellan decided that Lincoln was not to be trusted, he refused to maintain a respectful attitude toward the president.

Such a poisoned relationship did not harbor promising outcomes in the military campaign McClellan would eventually embark on. McClellan needed to suppress his disdain for his superiors in order to get the job done, but he would have a difficult time achieving that necessary state of enlightenment.

Late in 1861 Lincoln began taking a much more direct involvement in the actions of the army, tentatively flexing his muscles as commander-in-chief as a means to, if nothing else, force McClellan to either move or at least communicate his military plans. Lincoln, known for his diplomacy and skillful handling of many different situations, was rather tactless with his handling of military affairs regarding McClellan. Lincoln had publicly defended McClellan for nearly five months, but had grown frustrated with his general's sluggishness and silence about future plans. Lincoln feared that McClellan would never move unless compelled. Therefore, in December 1861, Lincoln began maneuvering to get McClellan to finally put the army to use and drive away the enemy.

Though Lincoln was dismayed by McClellan's seeming lack of initiative, the fact is that McClellan had likely intended to move the army into action as early as October 1861. At that time, he ordered Major General Charles P. Stone to make a "slight demonstration" against the Confederates at Leesburg, Virginia, northwest of Washington, in order to compel them to fall back and create room for the Union army's right flank to maneuver. In this demonstration, one of Stone's brigade commanders, Colonel Edward Baker, a former senator who was a personal friend of Lincoln's and had no military training, too eagerly advanced with little knowledge of either the ground or the enemy's strength. Baker crossed the Potomac River, took up a poor defensive position, and was fiercely attacked by General Nathan "Shanks" Evans's troops, who decimated the Yankee force and killed Baker, causing a humiliating defeat at what became known as the Battle of Ball's Bluff. McClellan's first foray as commander was inauspicious, and the fallout was immediate and lacerating. Newspapers ridiculed the Ball's Bluff debacle, and the Joint Committee on the Conduct of the War—led by radical Republicans in Congress—vilified Stone, who they felt had been too lenient on Southerners. Stone, a well-respected professional soldier who had been instrumental in maintaining order in the nation's capital during the secession crisis, was imprisoned for six months and his military career was ruined. McClellan internalized the high cost of failure. The Ball's Bluff fiasco only increased McClellan's caution and renewed his determination not to commit his army to battle until he knew that he had such an overwhelming force that victory was the only possibility. Of course, waiting for the day when success is guaranteed in war would commit one to a wait without end.

Lincoln did not have that kind of time. In December 1861 McClellan came down with typhoid fever and was bedridden for several days. Lincoln took this opportunity to act. He called McClellan's senior generals to the White House to discuss potential strategies for an upcoming campaign. McClellan learned of this and, in humor as ill as his body, ventured to the White House and interrupted the meeting to announce that he was developing a plan that he would submit to Lincoln soon. Lincoln acquiesced. But when McClellan did not follow through with his promised plan, Lincoln started issuing orders on his own with the encouragement of his new Secretary of War, Edwin Stanton. A prominent Ohio lawyer and lifelong Democrat who came to champion the radical cause largely because of his antislavery convictions, Stanton was irritated by McClellan's arrogant and dismissive manner. The secretary urged Lincoln to assert his powers as commander-in-chief, which Lincoln did. After the war, McClellan blamed his bad relationship with Lincoln on Stanton's interference. After Stanton's appointment to the War Department McClellan wrote: "The impatience of the executive immediately became extreme and I can attribute it only to the influence of the new Secretary, who did many things to break up the free and confidential intercourse that had heretofore existed between the President and myself."[7]

On January 27 Lincoln issued General Orders No. 1, which stated that McClellan and his army would attack General Joseph E. Johnston's Confederate army at Manassas on February 22. The date was chosen for no other reason than because it was George Washington's birthday. On January 31 Special Orders No. 1 stated the different routes the various troops would travel to attack Johnston. McClellan read these orders for the first time in the newspapers, which did nothing to build trust with the president. McClellan begged to be allowed to submit his counterproposal, and did so on February 3.

McClellan called not for an overland approach but for a waterborne route that would take the army to Urbanna, Virginia, on the Rappahannock River to the rear of Johnston's force. Lincoln was not impressed. He could not understand why such a plan was better than a direct march. Lincoln even suggested a move to the Occuquan Creek, which would still be waterborne but of a shorter distance and still on the enemy's flank. McClellan refused this as much because the amateur Lincoln suggested it as for any sound military reasons. McClellan adamantly stood by his proposal, laying out its benefits and dismissing the other plans as too flawed. Lincoln grudgingly accepted, though he tried other ways of getting support to refuse the plan.

Lincoln had a meeting with McClellan in the White House on March 7 in which he stated that McClellan's plan appeared to leave Washington unprotected and claimed that some considered it traitorous. According to McClellan's description of the meeting, he bolted up immediately and demanded the president rescind the charge. Lincoln assured the general they were not his words, but he admitted that the plan did have "an ugly look" about it. McClellan declared he would call a council of war and allow his generals vote on the merits of the plan. If his generals disapproved the plan, McClellan would stand by their judgment. Lincoln accepted and undoubtedly hoped the majority would vote against the plan.

The president was visibly dismayed when the 12 generals composing the council of war came to the White House late that afternoon to deliver an 8–4 verdict in favor of McClellan's plan. General Irvin McDowell— who along with the other senior generals Edwin V. Sumner and Samuel P. Heintzelman and the army's chief engineer John Barnard, opposed the plan—recorded that Lincoln could not mask his disappointment when the vote was announced. After Secretary Stanton came in and cross-examined the generals in his legendarily aggressive lawyer-like way, Lincoln dismissed them and told them to return the next morning when he would render his decision. At that next meeting, on Saturday, March 8, Lincoln announced to the generals that he approved McClellan's grand plan and encouraged the generals to all commit to it. Lincoln then asserted his powers as commander-in-chief and named the four corps commanders for the army—Sumner, McDowell, Heintzelman, and Erasmus Keyes. None were McClellan loyalists and all but Keyes had voted against McClellan's plan. Now, they would be leading the army on the plan they opposed.[8]

McClellan did not think highly of the 43-year-old McDowell, who had taught tactics at West Point when McClellan was an underclassman, or the 56-year-old Pennsylvanian Heintzelman, but he absolutely despised the white-bearded 65-year-old Bostonian Edwin Vose Sumner, whom "Little Mac" considered imperious, ignorant, and incompetent. Keyes, the fourth corps commander and a favorite of General Winfield Scott's, had been McClellan's artillery instructor at West Point and had stated that he had never had "a pleasanter pupil."[9] McClellan later was able to add two more corps commanders of his own choosing. He picked Fitz-John Porter and William Franklin, men who had overlapped with McClellan at West Point—Franklin had finished first in the class of 1843, McClellan's plebe year—and who were loyal to their friend. While McClellan later complained about the corps commanders Lincoln chose, at the time he expressed pleasure that the president had approved his plan. For all intents and purposes, March 8 was the green light for the plan that would ultimately put McClellan on the eastern side of Richmond in the morass between the Chickahominy and the James; the future Seven Days' battles were born on that Saturday in Washington, D.C.

On that same Saturday, General Johnston began removing his men from the Manassas lines they had been defending for eight months and retreated south to Fredericksburg. Johnston retreated because he mistakenly believed that McClellan was going to attack him. When word arrived that the Confederates were gone, McClellan blustered about "pushing the retreat of the rebels as far as possible," and advanced his army into the abandoned Confederate works. There, they found logs painted black to look like artillery, which the media acerbically dubbed "Quaker guns." Though McClellan had actually known about the ruse for some time and was unconcerned, the news reports added to his blemishes. Attorney General Edwin Bates believed that McClellan "has no plans but is fumbling and plunging in confusion and darkness." On the heels of this movement, Lincoln removed the title of general-in-chief from McClellan's duties. Lincoln attempted to explain it to McClellan directly, but McClellan refused to return to Washington to meet with him. Therefore, he read about the demotion in the newspapers, further souring his relationship with his commander-in-chief. He wrote to his wife: "I regret that the rascals are after me again."[10]

Johnston's retreat had forced McClellan to amend his plan. Instead of landing at Urbanna, McClellan would now transfer his army to the peninsula at Fort Monroe, flanked by the easily navigable York and James Rivers. However, access to the latter was denied to him thanks to a Confederate naval experiment that enjoyed great success in early March—the CSS *Virginia* (which had been laid on the hulk of a previous ship named the *Merrimac*, and hence is almost always referred to as the *Merrimac*), an ironclad ship. On March 7 the *Merrimac* had steamed out of Norfolk and wreaked havoc on the wooden-hulled Federal blockading fleet, causing panic both among the naval commanders on site and in the highest levels in Washington. Stanton was particularly paranoid that the *Merrimac* might be unleashed in the Potomac and shut down the nation's capital. Thanks to uncanny foresight, a Union ironclad, the *Monitor*, arrived the next day to duel the *Merrimac* to a draw, but the presence of the Confederate ironclad inhibited unfettered Union access to the James River. The navy informed McClellan that they could not protect the James River route as long as the *Merrimac* was lurking; so, McClellan had to settle for a single approach along the York River. Norfolk would later fall to Union forces and the *Merrimac* would be scuttled, but by that time McClellan had already committed his army and his advance to the York and was not inclined to expand to the James.

In addition to having to adjust his plans on the peninsula, he received more unwelcome news from the president. Lincoln's major condition in approving McClellan's waterborne assault was that the commander had to leave enough troops behind to guarantee Washington's security. McClellan promised as much and began embarking his troops in late March and early April, headed toward Fort Monroe. On April 1 McClellan hastily wrote out a report of all the troops available to guard the capital, sent it to the War Department, and immediately set off down the Chesapeake for Fort Monroe even before Lincoln or Stanton had an opportunity to read it. So fed up was McClellan in dealing with the administration that he declined to meet with the president to explain the troop dispositions. He also probably realized that even he could not make the math work satisfactorily, but presumed instead that once the army was in motion, Lincoln would not have the temerity to alter the grand campaign designed to end the war in its second summer. This was the first of many times McClellan would misjudge Lincoln. When Lincoln and Stanton computed the numbers, they felt they had been played false by McClellan, who claimed more troops were available than actually existed. As a result, Lincoln sent a message to McClellan saying that he was ordering McDowell's I Corps, which had not yet embarked, to remain behind to guard Washington. Unaware of these developments, McClellan began moving his army slowly forward to scout the Confederate forces blocking his path to Richmond. With a swift movement, Little Mac could still make rapid advances to Richmond before Johnston could seize control of the situation. As he moved forward, he encountered a force of undetermined size in front of him, under the command of Major General John B. Magruder.

A native Virginian, Magruder—known as "Prince John" because of his fondness for dress parades, fancy parties, and partiality for living in a higher style than his pay allowed—was liked more for his charming and gentlemanly personality than for his military prowess. Though graduating only one year behind Lee and Johnston at West Point and serving with distinction during the Mexican War, he had advanced in rank more slowly. While much of the major military action during the Civil War had occurred elsewhere, Magruder had commanded 12,000 troops in a defensive line that stretched 12 miles from Yorktown to the James River over marshy land. In fact, he protected a line that had been established by General Robert E. Lee in May 1861 in one of Lee's first actions as commander of Virginia's state forces before they had been incorporated into the Confederacy. Magruder had been the commander who partook of the first real fighting of the war, the Battle of Big Bethel, when he successfully defended the line against a poorly planned and executed Union attempt to threaten Richmond from Fort Monroe. By all accounts, Magruder enjoyed his year in this sector, but now he had a real opportunity to employ the dramatic flair and theatricality for which he was known. As Stephen Sears has stated, "No one could match Prince John at stretching limited resources into plausible illusions."[11]

From the tip of the peninsula—where the York and James Rivers come together and meet the ocean at Hampton Roads—Yorktown is situated about 15 miles away over flat land, intersected by creeks, swamps, and marshes. McClellan moved his army over these 15 miles quickly, apparently not anticipating any serious resistance by Magruder. He set his army over the two main roads, traversing the distance to the Yorktown line. The northern road led directly to the city and ran parallel to the York River, and the second road, about five miles south, halfway between the two rivers, led to a village called Warwick Court House, with Lee's Mills a couple of miles beyond. Lee's Mills sat astride the Warwick River, a sluggish stream that drained into the James, and had many branches feeding into it. Magruder took advantage of the terrain and cleverly dammed up some creeks and part of the Warwick River, thereby flooding most of the fordable sections of the river and forcing any opponent to march along the narrow roads. A former artillerist, he had trained cannons on each of the available crossings and had divided his 12,000 men to guard these batteries and the crossings they dominated. He would not be able to hold out forever, but he would be able to make a strong showing against whatever McClellan brought against him.[12]

McClellan had stepped off rapidly on April 5—so rapidly that only about 60,000 of his 100,000 men had even disembarked. Little Mac's intelligence on the size of Magruder's force was quite accurate, perhaps the only time in the ensuing three months that it would be. McClellan expected to face about 15,000 men near Yorktown, and he decided that a quick approach would brush the enemy aside and get him to the location he most coveted: West Point—a stop on the Richmond and York River Railroad that would serve as his main supply line on his drive to Richmond. The problem was that McClellan's intelligence had not been able to discover Magruder's Warwick River line. As McClellan advanced, a report from Keyes, in command of the corps on the southern road, painted a grim and overstated picture of Magruder's defenses. Keyes's statement that "no part of his line as far as discovered can be taken by assault without an enormous waste of life" derailed McClellan's quest for a quick and decisive action. As historian Clifford Dowdey sardonically commented, "Had [Keyes] been placed in that position by Stanton solely for the purpose of drenching McClellan's offensive flair, he could not have been more effective."[13] At this first hint of an obstacle, McClellan abandoned the quick strike, on which the entire plan had been predicated, and decided to conduct a siege against an opponent that he outnumbered five to one. McClellan froze because suddenly everything was not going according to his plan. This was the first sign of an intense caution that was to characterize the remainder of McClellan's time in eastern Virginia. The march from Hampton Roads to Yorktown was the only rapid advance McClellan was to make during the entire campaign.

Conventional wisdom has it that Magruder's theatricality influenced McClellan not to attack. But actually it was Keyes's dour note overstating Magruder's forces and the disheartening news, which arrived by wire that night, that Lincoln was holding back McDowell that shaped McClellan's actions. McClellan began a rationalization process later that disingenuously blamed all the flaws of the campaign on the withholding of McDowell. He fabricated uses for McDowell that he had not contemplated until long after he learned he would be without him. Instead, the Young Napoleon began his preferred tactic and one that he likely intended to employ all along—a siege. He preferred it, in the words of military analysts, because of "its slow, deliberate execution, and small loss of life."[14] The fact that he had brought so many heavy weapons indicated that his real strategy was a war of posts, gaining ground foot by foot if necessary until he could maneuver his behemoth siege guns into place. He intended to do to Richmond what the Continental army had done to Cornwallis at Yorktown in 1781. Only he would give his siege gunners their first practice for the main event at Yorktown as well.

McClellan believed that Magruder's line had filled with reinforcements and was simply too strong to be taken by storm. McClellan had begun this campaign with the intention of getting to Richmond ahead of Johnston. However, his commitment to a siege meant that he would face the very army he claimed to be trying to avoid by taking this route. Of course, once McClellan believed that Johnston had brought his army down to reinforce Magruder, he could justify a siege as the only proper action anyway.

* * *

When Joseph Johnston received word that a Yankee army was marching east of Yorktown, he discerned what was afoot and promptly moved his army to the eastern peninsula in order to oppose the advance. When Johnston got to Magruder's line, however, he did not see the daunting fortifications and legions of Prince John that Keyes and McClellan had. He saw that Magruder was using smoke and mirrors to buy time, and he was not impressed. He felt that Magruder had not done enough and he considered the line absurdly weak. He wrote to Lee: "No one but McClellan could have hesitated to attack."[15] Never satisfied with anything short of divinely ordained perfection, Johnston's criticisms ruffled Magruder and led to a strained relationship between the two. During the army's retreat toward Richmond, Johnston did not entrust Magruder with any important assignments. After reviewing Magruder's position, Johnston immediately called a conference with the president and went to Richmond to explain why the Confederates had to retreat.

This conference was unusual, primarily because Johnston's highly distrustful attitude toward the president consisted mainly of *ignoring* his commander-in-chief. At 55, Johnston was nearly two decades older than the Young Napoleon, but nevertheless shared a great many characteristics with his friend. Like McClellan, Johnston was extremely cautious, beloved by his soldiers, and had a dysfunctional relationship with his commander-in-chief. A short, wiry, erect, gray-haired man who looked the part of a general, Johnston had graduated from West Point in 1829, the same year as Lee. He advanced rapidly in the old army and had distinguished himself as a colonel in the Mexican War, with five wounds amply demonstrating his valor. His commander, Winfield Scott, had wryly commented that though a "great soldier," Johnston's main flaw was an "unfortunate knack of getting himself shot in nearly every engagement."[16] But Johnston was a proud man, fussy, and given to finding fault. Johnston had felt insulted when he was not named the highest ranking Confederate general and carried that slight with him for the rest of the war. His admirable performance at the battle of Bull Run had brought him admirers and earned him command of the army, but his actions since then had not endeared him to the president. He had not adequately prepared a secondary defensive line south of Manassas even when he admitted that the army must fall back. He had destroyed many tons of supplies against the wishes of President Davis, when he did fall back. He had taken to completely ignoring Davis's inquiries and suggestions, to the point that the president was largely in the dark as to his commander's thoughts and actions. His sour relationship with the president was not going to sweeten once he shared his opinion that the Confederates had to abandon Yorktown and fall back on Richmond.[17]

For the April 14 meeting, Davis had invited his military advisor Lee and Secretary of War George Randolph to join him in order to help him counter what he feared Johnston would tell him. Johnston also arrived

with support, bringing with him his second in command, Major General
Gustavus W. Smith, and his trusted division commander, General James
Longstreet. Both men were stout fellows flanking the diminutive and wiry
Johnston. For 14 hours, the 6 men debated strategy. Finally, arguing that
the Peninsula was suitable for defense and that they needed to protect
Norfolk and buy time for the strengthening of the army and the defenses
around Richmond, Davis ordered Johnston to defend the Yorktown line.
Johnston obeyed, but never seriously expected to hold for long. Johnston
later wrote that he knew the government would eventually see that he
had to fall back on Richmond and this knowledge "reconciled me some-
what to the necessity of obeying the President's order."[18]

While Johnston was chafing that he had to defend a line he considered
indefensible, McClellan was preparing his siege and growing more confident every day as his army grew larger and the guns moved into place
all around him. McClellan ordered the occasional minor skirmish to prevent the Confederates from doing more to fortify their lines, but he was
focusing on the moment of blasting through the Southern lines. To that
effect, and to make sure he was following the proper European playbook,
McClellan asked his wife to send him his books on the British siege of
Sebastopol during the Crimean War, of which McClellan had been an
observer.[19]

* * *

One must be careful to distinguish the myth of the campaign that
McClellan later created from what his actual plans were in real time. At the
time, McClellan always intended to launch a siege of Richmond, pounding it into submission with his heavy ordnance. He spoke of rapid movement and brilliant strokes, but primarily because that was what the public
wanted to hear. It also helped alleviate pressure from the administration.
Despite his constant telegrams to the contrary, McClellan envisioned a
successful campaign that cost very few casualties from combat. He believed strongly in the military philosophy articulated by Baron Antoine
Henri de Jomini, the French Napoleonic military theorist, who argued
that wars could be won by capturing decisive strategic points (i.e., the
capital) without unnecessary fighting or bloodshed. Jomini heavily influenced the strategic theories taught at the U.S. Military Academy, and
all American officers were well versed in his treatises. Scott's successful
campaign to capture Mexico City during the Mexican War in 1847 basically adhered to Jominian principles all the way through the campaign.
In many ways, Scott's campaign served as the model for McClellan's peninsula campaign. Scott had landed at Vera Cruz and marched west to

capture the enemy's capital. Scott spent more time maneuvering around his enemy to avoid battles; his army suffered far more deaths to yellow fever than it did to enemy bullets. The capture of the capital led to the end of the war. McClellan was attempting to replicate that feat—capture the capital and end the war with as little bloodshed as possible. Only, McClellan was doing it with a much larger army and many more heavy guns than Scott had been able to carry, and, of course, he was fighting against fellow Americans.[20]

McClellan's Jominian principles applied to civilians as well. Jomini argued that armies should not inflict unnecessary destruction or hardships on civilians. McClellan was the chief proponent of the policy known as conciliation—the idea that the North should show kindness and benevolence to Southerners, protect their property, and not interfere with their social institutions, such as slavery. McClellan believed that the conciliatory approach would win back far more Southerners than the harsh approach that radicals preferred. After all, the only way to prevent this from becoming a remorseless revolutionary struggle was to win the war quickly and magnanimously. Lincoln had initially believed the same thing, but as the war dragged on, he began to shift his opinions. If McClellan was going to preserve the Union he wanted, he needed to end the war in this campaign and using the Scott/Jomini playbook was how he intended to do it.[21]

As such, McClellan allowed Southern forces to retreat up the peninsula without aggressively pursuing them or trying to cut them off. After reaching the West Point Railroad Station on the York River, he moved 10 miles west up the railroad and established his supply base at the White House landing on the Pamunkey River. He put a guard on the house to demonstrate his protection of Southern property, even if the property, in this case, was home to a rebel officer, Colonel "Rooney" Lee, son of the future army commander. McClellan sent his different corps up the railroad and surrounding roads toward Richmond at a careful pace. When Johnston crossed over the Chickahominy River, McClellan moved his forces up the north bank to within five miles of Richmond and crossed the river following the line of the York River Railroad due west toward the city. McClellan did not allow his forces to engage in unnecessary combat. He spent most of his time requesting more reinforcements to combat the overwhelming forces that he claimed opposed him. But he never explained why such a large enemy army was *retreating* in front of him rather than contesting every inch of ground to prevent Richmond from falling. Perhaps he believed the enemy thought as highly of him as he did. Certainly, the six Confederate leaders who met in Davis's office on April 14 did, as each shared their high praise of McClellan, reaffirming to all the difficulty of their task. However, any unexpected development could break McClellan's brittle psyche. Lincoln, Johnston, and Lee would all provide surprise disruptions to McClellan's plans at different times.[22]

One of the reasons Little Mac was so sure that a siege was the only practical route to victory was that he grossly overestimated the enemy's numbers. McClellan had always shown a propensity for giving his opponent too much credit. He frequently justified his inaction by claiming the Confederates outnumbered him. Many historians have blamed McClellan's hand-picked intelligence chief, Allan Pinkerton, former director of the Pinkerton Detective Agency in Chicago, for bad intelligence. Certainly, the intelligence techniques necessary for civilian detective agencies do not translate precisely to military scenarios. However, Pinkerton's original estimates to McClellan were generally accurate, but they did not satisfy his general. McClellan had overstated the rebel army from the day he took over, listing them as 100,000 strong in his very first accounting. He certainly never would admit that the rebel army had *declined* in strength from that initial report. Pinkerton, realizing the Confederates could not number nearly as many soldiers as McClellan estimated, had the impossible job of trying to reconcile McClellan's numbers with the facts that his intelligence agents had gathered. Eventually, Pinkerton would submit to McClellan's outlandish expectations and tell his general what he wanted to hear, which was that he was greatly outnumbered at all times.[23] Few people outside of McClellan believed these numbers. The president, his cabinet, and even many of McClellan's fellow generals did not believe the outrageous figures. General Samuel P. Heintzelman, commander of the III Corps, was unable to accept some of McClellan's ludicrous estimates and professed that the general "was in the habit of overestimating the rebel forces."[24]

The fact is that McClellan *wanted* to believe there was more of his enemy. From the very beginning, McClellan tried to control the narrative of the campaign. He could justify his methodical movements to the Lincoln administration and the public if they knew what odds he faced. If he managed to win the climactic victory and capture the rebel capital, his glory would be all the greater for having overcome such daunting odds. However, as McClellan repeatedly stated in his dispatches, if he suffered defeat, he would be blameless because no general could hope to overcome such incredible odds as he faced. At every opportunity, McClellan sought to increase the strength of his opponent. This would further justify his constant request for more troops. He claimed that Johnston opposed him with 150,000 men, even though he outnumbered Johnston nearly two to one. On June 25, he claimed that Lee had 200,000 troops, more than twice the size of Lee's actual army and almost as many men under arms throughout the entire Confederacy.[25] Ironically, though McClellan believed many Southerners opposed the rebellion, he seemed to think that nearly 100 percent of the population between the ages of 18 and 40 had already enlisted by the spring of 1862. Therefore, facing hordes of Confederate soldiers (who strangely never seemed inclined to attack their weaker opponent), McClellan prepared to fire his siege guns, which would level the playing field and give him an advantage against the superior foe. McClellan scheduled the siege gun symphony for the dawn of May 5.

Johnston would not let McClellan enjoy the music of his heavy artillery. Divining that McClellan was preparing an attack, Johnston sent word to Richmond in late April that the day he warned about had come. After a few delays, he ordered the army to withdraw on the night of May 3. To cover the withdrawal, Johnston ordered a massive, though unfocused, artillery barrage of his own. Under the distraction of these impressive fireworks that lit up the night sky, Johnston's army quietly retreated. Throughout the month of May, Johnston fell back rapidly, constantly fearful of being flanked by a Yankee force steaming up the York River. Along the way, he fought a couple of delaying skirmishes, the largest of which was at Williamsburg on May 5. The Williamsburg fight was intense, considering the small numbers involved. Longstreet's division checked Edwin Sumner's pursuing Union forces, though some Confederate regiments were badly mauled in the process.

Yorktown was approximately 60 miles from Richmond. In nine days, Johnston had moved his army 40 miles closer to the city. Some soldiers had managed to get all the way to the city itself, spreading their bleak tales of misery and gloom and generally appearing demoralized. All Johnston could tell President Davis was that he had to wait and react to McClellan's movements. This was not a plan to inspire much confidence in the nation's leader or its people. War Department clerk, John B. Jones, wrote in his diary on May 14: "Much anxiety is felt for the fate of the city. Is there no turning point in this long lane of downward despair?" Another despairing resident lamented, "It is almost universal opinion that the city will be in possession of the Yankees in a few days."[26]

On May 7, General Benjamin Huger abandoned Norfolk and eventually crossed the James River and joined Johnston's army near Richmond, while the *Merrimac* was scuttled on May 11. Union gunboats immediately began steaming up the James River toward Richmond. Johnston believed that now McClellan would utilize that watercourse as a conduit to Richmond, and on May 15, he ordered his army to retreat across the last river in front of Richmond, the Chickahominy. However, on that same day,

Confederate defenders managed to stop the Union flotilla at Drewry's Bluff, a sharp bend in the James River, a few miles downriver from Richmond. This gave Johnston some security that he would not be flanked on his right. Johnston had always wanted to take a defensive position closer to Richmond. He could not be flanked easily and he had the interior lines, meaning he could move units to threatened sectors more quickly and easily than his enemy. However, he also had precious little room left to retreat. In some places, his lines were only three miles from the city. Once McClellan caught up with him in front of Richmond, he did not have very far to go to bring his siege guns to bear. And once those guns opened up, the Confederate army and Richmond likely could not hold out for long. Johnston needed to find some way to turn the tables on his old friend. He needed some assistance as well, because by late May he was aware that McDowell's I Corps, which had been held back by Lincoln, was now at Fredericksburg, only 50 miles from Richmond and presumably marching south to join McClellan any day now, increasing the daunting odds against the Confederates. At this moment of darkness, light came from the Shenandoah Valley, and its consequences emboldened Johnston to do something that he almost never did during the entire war—launch an attack.[27]

* * *

On May 24, General "Stonewall" Jackson's success in the valley prompted President Lincoln to once again suspend McDowell's march to Richmond and order that general to send his forces into the valley to try to trap Jackson's army.[28] Those rebel forces had been wreaking havoc, thanks to orders from Lee. As the president's military advisor, Lee had viewed the union of McDowell's forces with McClellan's as potentially fatal for Richmond. In desperation, he began encouraging Jackson in late April to take the initiative in the Shenandoah Valley and disrupt the Yankees. On April 25, Lee implored Jackson to strike the dispersed Union forces. He gave him full authority to decide when, where, and who to attack, but emphasized, "The blow wherever struck, must, to be successful, be sudden and heavy."[29] That was the impetus Jackson needed, and he began to unite the 20,000 Confederate forces in the valley and deliver a series of blows that sent the Union forces reeling.

Jackson got into trouble in the Valley earlier in the spring because of his aggressive instincts. He had launched a couple of haphazard attacks in the lower Shenandoah Valley near Maryland and had been soundly defeated when he attacked a larger Union force at Kernstown on March 23. However, under Lee's authorization, Jackson's Valley Campaign would prove to be a model of how to move quickly and use maneuver to confound an enemy. After defeating a small Yankee force at the village of McDowell west of the Valley on May 8, Jackson turned north and headed down the valley (going north is going down the Valley because of the decline in elevation in that direction). He befuddled Union commanders by winning battles at Front Royal and Winchester, driving the enemy before him.[30]

McDowell who was at Fredericksburg with the I Corps had been informed by Union generals in the Valley that Jackson was in retreat. On May 17, McDowell received orders to march to the peninsula as soon as a division under General James Shields reached him to increase his numbers. A later order stated that McDowell would begin his march to McClellan on May 26 and join that commander by the end of the month. McDowell had stated that it would only take four days of easy marching to join McClellan. On May 24, McClellan's army had advanced to Mechanicsville, only five miles northeast of Richmond, and could hear the city's church bells ringing. McClellan seemed to have everything going his way. But that night the telegram arrived saying that Lincoln had again halted McDowell's march. Jackson's success had sent General Nathaniel Banks's army retreating down the valley and Lincoln both wanted to capture Jackson and protect the capital. He ordered McClellan to either carry out his attack or give up and come back to guard Washington. Although McClellan was not prepared to attack (especially with the enervating news that McDowell's large corps would not be joining his), Johnston felt ready to launch an offensive in order to try to finally do what Jackson had done in the Valley—reverse the course of the Union forces and relieve pressure on Richmond. It would lead to the Battle of Seven Pines, or Fair Oaks, which began on May 31.

When Johnston set out to attack the Union forces facing Richmond, he saw that McClellan had arranged his forces in such a way as to allow for an opening. To protect his White House base on the Pamunkey River and to prepare for a junction with McDowell, McClellan had placed more than half his army—three of his five corps—north of the Chickahominy River. This was a strange disposition of his troops, because McClellan was preparing to bring his siege train within firing distance of Richmond and would need the railroad line to transport those enormous weapons. Little Mac, for all of his fears of being hopelessly outnumbered, was moving on Richmond as if he expected the Confederates to allow him to dictate the tempo throughout the campaign. Ever since he first encountered Confederate forces outside Yorktown, they had not attacked him—except for a minor delaying action at Williamsburg on May 5—lulling him into the belief that he could continue to call the shots.

With the corps of Porter, Franklin, and Sumner all north of the river, Johnston crafted a plan that would attack the advanced positions of Keyes's IV corps (with Heintzelman's III corps behind him) south of the Chickahominy River. Heavy rains in the last 10 days of May had saturated the river, flooded the countryside around it, and threatened to wash away the bridges linking the army across it. Johnston explained the plan in detail to James Longstreet, whom he authorized to execute the attack. Johnston intended a two-pronged attack on the Union position at Fair Oaks Station. While Major General D. H. Hill's division engaged the Federals in front of Seven Pines with the support of Benjamin Huger's division on his right, Longstreet would lead the flank attack from the left at Fair Oaks Station down the Nine Mile Road. Together, these assaults should overwhelm the Union position and force them to draw back. When Longstreet left the meeting on the evening of May 30, Johnston was confident that the Southern attack would lead to a significant change of events the next day. Indeed, one of Johnston's staff officers later recalled that "it was an excellent & well devised scheme, & apparently as simple as any plan could be."[31]

However, Johnston should have written out explicit orders of his simple plan, because whatever Longstreet heard from Johnston, it was not the plan that Johnston had envisioned. The next morning, Longstreet marched his men to the wrong location, defanging most of Johnston's plan. Instead, Seven Pines was a badly botched battle in which the Confederates under D. H. Hill drove back some Union forces through sheer determination, but gained nothing substantial to alter the campaign. What did result from the battle was that Longstreet unjustly blamed the day's misfortunes on Huger in order to cover his own failures. The Confederates suffered nearly 5,000 casualties to little purpose. One of those casualties was the army's commander. Late on the afternoon of May 31, as he belatedly tried to fix what Longstreet had bungled, Johnston was hit by a bullet and a shell fragment nearly simultaneously, resulting in a grievous shoulder wound that would take him out of action for several months.[32]

On June 1, unimpressed with General Gustavus W. Smith's efforts and judging that no other senior officer was capable of handling the pressure of command, Davis appointed Lee to be commander of the Army of Northern Virginia, as it was then being called. No one knew at the time that this appointment would change the war and lead to a new type of revolutionary conflict. Lee's appointment would result in the war lasting longer and ushering in major social changes that likely would not have occurred if McClellan had captured Richmond in the summer of 1862.[33]

2

~∞~

Lee Takes the Initiative,
June 26

McClellan did not immediately learn that Johnston had been wounded, and would not discover until around June 10 that Lee had assumed command of the army.[1] Had he known earlier, however, he likely would not have been concerned. "I prefer Lee to Johnston," McClellan remarked to President Lincoln. Lee was "too cautious & weak under grave responsibility . . . wanting in moral firmness when pressed by heavy responsibility & likely to be timid and irresolute in action." McClellan even concluded later that "Lee will never venture upon a bold movement on a large scale."[2] Rarely has a commander so badly misjudged his opponent.

When Lee took command of the army that he would make famous, his Northern opponents were not the only ones who doubted his ability to lead the Confederates to victory. Newspaper editors, politicians, civilians, fellow officers, and enlisted soldiers each had strong misgivings about this staff officer being given such a weighty responsibility during the nascent nation's existential crisis. Newspapers compared Lee unfavorably to the successful Jackson, especially when Lee's first orders were to dig fortifications outside the city. Soldiers grumbled about this menial labor, better fitted for slaves, and referred to Lee as the "King of Spades." He had even more derogatory nicknames in some circles because his previous experience of leading Confederate troops in 1861 had not gone well. Johnston's officers grumbled about their new leader. Gustavus Smith felt he should have been left in charge; General Jeb Stuart, who would go on to great fame under Lee, initially commented that he had been "disappointed" by his former West Point superintendent as a general. Even Lee wrote the day after his appointment: "I wish that [Johnston's] mantle had fallen upon an abler man."[3]

Yet, through the initial gloom and complaints associated with any change in military affairs, especially the replacement of an officer as popular with the public and his soldiers (if not his president) as Johnston, a few prescient folks saw advantages in Lee as commander. Foremost among them was Johnston, who recognized the value of Lee's appointment. From his hospital bed, Johnston honestly admitted: "The shot that struck me down is the very best that has been fired for the Southern cause yet. For I possess in no degree the confidence of our government, and now they have in my place one who does possess it, and who can accomplish what I never could have done—the concentration of our armies for the defense of the capital of the Confederacy."[4] John B. Jones, a clerk in the Confederate War Department, wrote in his diary on June 3 that Lee's appointment "may be hailed as the harbinger of bright fortune," and three weeks later would declare, "I predict a career of glory for Lee, and for our country."[5] An officer who had served with Lee earlier in the war supported his commander. When asked by Colonel E. Porter Alexander if Lee was bold enough to lead the army, Colonel Joseph C. Ives responded heatedly, "If there is one man in either army, Confederate or Federal, head and shoulders above every other in audacity, it is General Lee! His name might be Audacity."[6] No one, not even Alexander who related the story, knew how Ives was able to form such an accurate estimate of Lee's abilities, but these anecdotes do convey the sense that at least a few folks were optimistic that Lee would bring about a positive change.

Certainly, Lee had not lived up to his antebellum acclaim during the first year of the war. Born in Virginia in 1807 to Henry "Light Horse Harry" Lee, a Revolutionary war hero but an absentee and fiscally reckless father, Robert E. Lee had graduated second in his class at West Point in 1829, the same year as Johnston (who was 13th) and a year after Jefferson Davis. He had served in the engineers in various capacities, helping construct several forts dotting the eastern seaboard. In the Mexican War, Lee had earned lasting fame for his many daring scouting exploits that allowed General Winfield Scott to bypass strong defensive positions on his way to capturing Mexico City in 1847. Within the army, no officer emerged from that conflict more well-regarded than Lee (even though General Zachary Taylor won the presidential election of 1848 based on his inflated wartime reputation). Lee served as superintendent of West Point in the mid-1850s, then with the cavalry out west before transferring to Washington, D.C., in the late 1850s. As such, he was the officer who led the response to John Brown's infamous raid at Harpers Ferry in October 1859. When war broke out in 1861, Scott persuaded President Lincoln to offer his protégé command of the Union Army of the Potomac, but Lee declined and resigned his commission to serve the recently seceded state of Virginia. Thus, everyone expected great things from this consummate soldier.

Lee's journey to command the Army of Northern Virginia was a circuitous one, riddled with disappointment. In May 1861 he was placed in command of all Virginia troops and had established a defensive line east of Richmond, near Yorktown, to prevent any assaults from Union-controlled Fort Monroe. That summer, Lee was ordered to take command of troops in western Virginia to win back control of that fractious territory and reverse the successes that McClellan had gained. Several weeks of bad weather, bad roads, bad morale, and bad decisions led to Lee's ultimate failure in the Cheat Mountain region of western Virginia by October 1861. After this embarrassment, Lee was reassigned to the decidedly inglorious task of erecting and improving coastal defenses in South Carolina and Georgia. In March 1862 Davis called Lee to Richmond. The president valued Lee as a military thinker and wanted Lee nearby to discuss strategy, so he named him his principle military adviser. However, Davis, who had been a West Point graduate, a colonel in the Mexican War, and a secretary of war, took a more active role as commander-in-chief than did Lincoln, thereby relegating Lee to a relatively powerless position as little more than chief of staff for Davis. Johnston's wounding prompted Davis to give Lee field command again, and now Lee was tasked with developing a plan to turn back McClellan's army. Lee knew he did not have much time to justify the faith that Davis had in him. If he failed this time, the capital would fall and the war may very well end in Southern defeat.

The weather was Lee's strongest ally that first week of June. Many Southerners in the years following the war elevated Lee to the status of a favored son of God, but if Lee did have a direct line to the Almighty, he likely would have asked for the heavens to open up in order to buy him more time. This they did, flooding much of the Chickahominy River bottom, washing away bridges that McClellan's engineers had constructed, and making it impossible for the Yankees to move any heavy artillery closer to Richmond. Even Lee may have thought the Lord was too generous, for he commented to Davis on June 5, "You have seen nothing like the roads on the Chickahominy bottom."[7] Lee used this delay to formulate a plan to drive McClellan away from Richmond. Lee knew that a direct assault on McClellan's lines was suicidal, because the Union army had the advantage in manpower and artillery. If he could threaten McClellan's line of supply, he could force the Union commander to leave his defenses and engage in battle in open ground. That was the only chance the Confederates had for success. If they did nothing but dig in and react to McClellan's movements, they would eventually be defeated by McClellan's overwhelming weight of artillery. Lee knew he had to take the initiative and force McClellan to dance to the tempo that Lee set.

In order to successfully attack McClellan's flank, Lee would have to weaken his center to provide enough troops to give his offensive punch some power. As a result, Lee immediately ordered his chief engineer to establish a line of fortifications in front of the city between the Chickahominy and the James. Once these fortified lines had been completed, Lee could hold that line with a relatively small number of troops and move the rest to be involved in the flank attack. Over the next three weeks, there would be much digging in the hot and humid June days and much complaining by the soldiers and the uncomprehending elements of the press. The editor of the *Richmond Examiner* angrily argued that an ounce of Stonewall Jackson's aggressiveness was "worth all the ditches and spades that Gen. Lee can display on this side of the Chickahominy."[8]

Lee was amazed at the resistance, but did not try to reason with his critics. There was no time and it would have availed nothing. He did vent his frustration to Davis: "Our people are opposed to work . . . All ridicule and resent it," but kept his mind on the task at hand.[9] Davis was delighted to just be in the loop. Compared to the figurative deaf–mute Johnston, Lee was refreshingly candid and informative with the president. Lee did not share Johnston's (or McClellan's) supreme distrust of the government, and the result was that Lee had a much better working relationship with his commander-in-chief. Lee would find his employment relatively unfettered by presidential intrusion, thanks in large part to the steps he took in his first weeks in command to establish an open dialogue.

As the embryo of Lee's plans developed, he needed to know exactly what the Union dispositions were north of the Chickahominy. Despite the Union and Confederate armies' marginal attempts at balloon reconnaissance in this campaign, the major reconnaissance force in any 19th-century army was cavalry, and Lee turned to his 29-year-old cavalry commander, Jeb Stuart. Lee wished Stuart to ride out beyond the Chickahominy as if he was going to join Jackson's forces in the Shenandoah Valley, but then to turn back east and scout McClellan's army. Lee expected a detailed description of McClellan's forces, their location, the quality of the roads, and the strength of his supply line. Lee wanted Stuart to pay particular attention to a ridge north of the Chickahominy that he was considering as cover for a potential flank attack by Jackson's Valley army. Stuart, excited by the possibilities and never too modest to have his name splashed in the papers for heroic deeds, suggested that perhaps he could ride around McClellan's army rather than merely return the way he set out. Although Lee did not forbid such an action, he strongly cautioned Stuart "not to hazard, unnecessarily, your command."[10] Lee was not interested in Stuart's headlines, but he absolutely demanded to know what McClellan had north of the river.

Stuart set off with 1,200 cavalry troopers and officers, including Lee's son, Colonel "Rooney" Lee, on June 12, heading north toward Ashland before swinging back east to get around McClellan's flank. As Stuart brushed aside enemy cavalry patrols and gathered the information that Lee needed, he faced his own crossroads on June 13. He could return the way he came, easily outrunning his pursuers, or he could push on and cross the river and ride around the rear of the Army of the Potomac. There never was really any doubt in Stuart's mind which route he would take and he pressed on, even though he was aware that he was being pursued by Union cavalry. Stuart may even have known that the commander of the pursuit force was General Philip St. George Cooke, and if so, he undoubtedly took a particular delight that many husbands might envy. Stuart had married Cooke's daughter seven years earlier, and he was now riding around (and perhaps laughing at) his father-in-law. June 13 was Cooke's 53rd birthday no less, and he spent that special day trying to kill his son-in-law. Cooke's pursuit was not very rapid or threatening because Cooke insisted on having infantry supports for his cavalry, so he could only move as fast as the accompanying infantry regiments. Even a regiment of Olympic sprinters could not win that race with Stuart's horsemen.[11]

Stuart sent a courier ahead of his column once he crossed the Chickahominy, and on June 14 the courier reported to Lee what they had learned. The next day, Stuart's force arrived back in Richmond and the weary, bedraggled but adrenaline-fueled cavalry leader reported personally to Lee with further details on his discoveries. Lee liked everything he heard: the ridge was not guarded, McClellan had weak and unprotected flanks, and the roads were even worse in McClellan's lines than they were in Lee's, which meant McClellan's movement would be delayed even longer than Lee had hoped. Therefore, Lee decided to bring Jackson's army secretly back from the Valley and have them lead the flank attack north of the Chickahominy. He would leave four divisions under Generals Magruder and Huger south of the river behind the fortifications and move the remaining divisions north to supplement Jackson's force. He sent word to Jackson to begin moving his army to Richmond.

Through the first two weeks of June, Lee had contemplated several possible scenarios for Jackson's army. Jackson had been in regular communication with Lee for several weeks, and in early June proposed being reinforced up to 40,000 men, so that he could lead an invasion of Maryland or Pennsylvania. Lee liked the idea, but the difficulty of getting that many reinforcements nixed it. His second idea was to send Jackson at least some troops and allow him to drive the Yankees in the Valley before breaking off and coming to aid Lee in Richmond. To this end, Lee sent General William H. Whiting's division and General Alexander Lawton's large brigade of new troops to Jackson. Knowing he could not prevent Union scouts from discovering the movement, Lee decided to be rather ostentatious about it and let it be clear to all who cared to look that approximately 10,000 Confederate troops were leaving Richmond for the Valley. That may, perhaps, cause the Federal authorities more concern about Jackson in the Valley and tie down more troops that might otherwise come to McClellan's aid. Some historians have mistakenly concluded that this movement was a deliberate deception. Although that movement certainly added to McClellan's mental calculations—why would Lee send 10,000 troops *away* from Richmond unless he already had more than he needed—Lee was in earnest when he sent the troops to Jackson. He hoped Jackson would use them to strike a sharp blow against the Union forces in the Valley before returning to Richmond. As it turned out, circumstances dictated that these units merely got to see the same countryside twice, because before they could be used in the Valley Jackson turned them around and started marching them back toward his rendezvous with Lee at Richmond.[12]

Jackson's victory over Union forces under General John C. Fremont at Cross Keys on June 8 and General James Shields at Port Republic on June 9 had already caused those Union forces in the Valley to pull back and break off engagement. Jackson wrote to Lee on June 13 that he doubted he could do much more in the Valley to disrupt the Union armies unless he had substantial reinforcements. Lee decided no material improvement to the Richmond front would be gained by having Jackson fight in the Valley any longer. So, he decided to bring Jackson eastward to Richmond to begin his plan to discomfit McClellan. On Monday, June 16, Lee wrote to Jackson to keep a cavalry screen between him and the Union troops in the Valley and to begin marching his troops to Richmond. He cautioned Jackson that "the movement must be secret."[13] That was not a warning he need have issued, because Jackson was already legendary for his penchant for absolute secrecy—so absolute that he rarely informed his senior commanders of his plans, even while they were marching toward a battle.

Jackson began moving his units by rail toward Richmond on June 20. The Virginia Central Railroad only had about 200 cars and the troops would cram onto them and ride down the line for a while before being unloaded so the cars could venture back up the track to pick up another load of soldiers. It was a slow process of transporting an army, but it saved the men some wear and tear on their legs. On Sunday, June 22, Jackson reached Fredericks Hall and decided to rest his men and do no marching that day. It would prove to be the first of many poor decisions that Jackson would make over the next 10 days.

Many contemporaries claimed that it was common for Jackson to take the Sabbath to rest, and only rarely did he fight or march on Sundays. However, evidence shows that the devout Jackson must have been adept at asking the Almighty for forgiveness, because in the recently completed Valley campaign Jackson had not only marched, but also fought no fewer than three battles on the Lord's Day. When military circumstances required it, Jackson had no compunction taking up arms on Sunday. Hence, his decision to halt all progress on June 22, when speed was of the utmost importance and the fate of the Confederate capital hung in the balance, was baffling. Jackson chose an odd time to become observant of the Old Testament rules once again.

As detractors and admirers alike would agree, Jackson was prone to odd behaviors. At 38, Jackson was balding, bearded, and barrel chested. After West Point, Jackson had served in the Mexican War as an artillery officer and, like many officers in that war, had been brevetted for gallantry. Jackson had resigned from the army to become an instructor at the Virginia Military Institute, where he did not impress the cadets as a professor. Jackson was a quiet man, taciturn in his talk, and far from socially graceful. He was a devoted Calvinist Presbyterian and even hired his preferred minister—Reverend Robert L. Dabney—as his chief of staff, regardless of how unqualified Dabney may have been for the military job.[14] Jackson eschewed trappings of rank, dressed shabbily, and wore only a cadet's cap pulled far down over his eyes. He ate a simple diet, was prone to suck on lemons, and had bizarre physical routines that he believed improved his health. His eccentricity amused many of his junior officers and his soldiers. But Jackson was also a strict disciplinarian and a stern unrelenting taskmaster who had little compassion for those whose constitution was not made of the same iron as his own. Despite his flaws, victory had bred confidence in his soldiers, who took pride in serving Jackson and called themselves his "foot cavalry" for his tendency to march them more miles than soldiers were usually expected to march in a day. However, on June 22, no one marched a single mile, and Jackson's force remained strung out for more than 20 miles, when every hour counted. Even just a few miles on the 22nd could have significantly altered the narrative of the Seven Days' battles.[15]

Maintaining secrecy, Jackson indicated to his host at Fredericks Hall that he would breakfast with her in the morning, though he never intended to. Instead, he departed at 1:00 a.m. with one aide and two guides and began a 50-mile trek to meet Lee at his headquarters at the Dabbs house northeast of Richmond. After 15 hours in the saddle, Jackson arrived on the afternoon of June 23 to take part in the discussions for Lee's grand offensive. Jackson, having had little sleep the day prior, arrived weary and covered in dust from the dirt roads. When he arrived, Lee was busy and Jackson chose to rest against a fence post in the yard. A few minutes later, D. H. Hill came riding up and was surprised to see the familiar figure of his brother-in-law (they had married sisters). After exchanging pleasantries for just a few minutes, Jackson and Hill together walked into the Dabbs house to a back room that served as Lee's office. A little while later, James Longstreet and A. P. Hill arrived and Lee began to outline his plan. Magruder and Huger were not invited to this meeting because of their static roles in the offensive.[16]

By calling together his division commanders taking part in the offensive, Lee was trying to avoid repeating Johnston's mistake at Seven Pines. Lee wanted to ensure that everyone understood what was expected of each of them. He later reinforced this by writing out the orders and sending a copy to each commander. Over a map on the table, Lee explained his plan. McClellan's position at Beaver Dam Creek was too strong to take by direct assault. Therefore, Jackson would march southeast from Ashland on two roads to Hundley's Corners and then to the Mechanicsville Turnpike, coming in behind the flank of the Union forces and compelling them to retreat back toward their base. Jackson would then march east toward Cold Harbor in order to keep them running or cut them off. A. P. Hill was to deploy at the Meadow Bridge nearest the village of Mechanicsville, awaiting word of Jackson's arrival. This word would come via General Lawrence O'Bryan Branch, whose brigade Lee ordered to Half Sink, about eight miles above Mechanicsville. When Jackson approached, he was to communicate with Branch, who would then inform Hill and move his brigade south toward Mechanicsville. When Branch appeared above Mechanicsville on the right flank of the Union outpost there, those Yankee forces would retreat, uncovering Meadow Bridge and allowing Hill's division to cross unmolested. Hill would then move forward, driving whatever Union forces remained away from Mechanicsville, uncovering the bridges south of the village. On these bridges, Longstreet and D. H. Hill would cross their divisions. As A. P. Hill made a demonstration in front of the Beaver Dam line, Jackson's presence on the flank should become apparent, prompting the Union forces to retreat to safer ground. At this point, Jackson was to head down the roads to Cold Harbor and D. H. Hill was to cross A. P. Hill's rear and get on Jackson's right flank, pursuing the retreating Union forces. A. P. Hill would continue his pursuit on D. H. Hill's right flank, while Longstreet's division, the last to cross the river, would fill the gap between A. P. Hill and the river, also pursuing the Federal forces.

An army on the move is much more vulnerable to destruction than one waiting behind prepared defenses. Lee expected that the withdrawal of McClellan's right wing would force McClellan to come out of his defensive lines to the south and cross the river in order to protect his lines of supply. Once McClellan was on the move, Lee could adjust his plan accordingly, but he would be dictating the pace, and he had strong hopes of destroying a portion of McClellan's army. At the very least, he could force him to retreat back down the peninsula with heavy casualties. Either way, Richmond would be rescued.

To pull this off, Lee would leave Magruder's three-division force and Huger's single division in front of McClellan near the Seven Pines battlefield, with orders to hold at all costs. Magruder believed with some justification that he had been given the post of honor—he was the man responsible for holding the enemy at bay while Lee moved the majority of his forces away. Magruder would have to hold off a force nearly three times the size of his own. It caused him no small degree of anxiety. Magruder would sleep very little over the next few days, and his anxiety and stress resulted in a bad case of indigestion that would cause him to be irritable for much of the week.[17]

The exact number of troops that Lee had in his army varies depending on which source one consults, but it is generally agreed that he had approximately 85,000–90,000 troops with him, once Jackson arrived. Magruder and Huger would hold the Southern line with about 27,000 troops between them. Longstreet, both Hills, and the bulk of Stuart's cavalry would be moved north of the river to join Jackson's approaching 18,000 men, giving Lee between 55,000 and 60,000 troops to launch his left hook at McClellan's right flank.

At first glance, Lee's plan seemed like a good one, but closer scrutiny reveals some major flaws. Lee fundamentally misunderstood where McClellan's troops were located. He believed that the majority of McClellan's army, probably three corps, remained north of the Chickahominy, as they had been four weeks earlier when Johnston launched his attack at Seven Pines. Lee did not discover that, after the Seven Pines battle, McClellan had moved Franklin's and Sumner's corps south of the river, leaving only General Fitz-John Porter's V Corps and General George

McCall's recently arrived division from McDowell's corps north of the river. Therefore, nearly 80 percent of the Union army was south of the river facing Magruder's and Huger's thin line. Had he known the disposition of the Union army, even a military gambler like Lee may have been forced to rethink his plan. With 80,000 troops, an aggressive McClellan could have easily broken through the Confederate line and marched into Richmond before Lee could have crossed back over the river to stop him. Trading McClellan's supply base for the Confederate capital would not have been a successful swap for Lee or the Confederacy.

Second, Lee was trying to coordinate a complex choreographed movement of four separate forces (five if you count Branch's brigade) over miles of ground in the face of the enemy, which depended on precise timing. This is a difficult maneuver for veteran armies who had served together in many battles, where communication breakdowns or the fog of war disrupt the best plans. But Lee's army was serving together in its first battle as a combined force under a new commander. The generals did not implicitly understand each other as they would with time. A. P. Hill was carrying a division into battle for the first time, and he had never fought jointly with any of the other commanders. Longstreet and D. H. Hill had fought together at Seven Pines, but that did not necessarily inspire confidence. While Hill had fought well, Longstreet had grossly mismanaged the battle. None of these commanders had ever fought in concert with Jackson's army. None had ever taken orders in battle from Lee and did not know what to expect from his combat leadership. Would he leave them to make their own decisions? Would he micromanage? Would he expect regular reports? Would he alter the plan spontaneously? This was a complicated plan for a group of first timers.

Third, Jackson's arrival would set in motion the other parts of the plan and his presence would only be known through the liaison brigade of Branch. That brigade's commander had to make sure that he communicated with Hill and kept him informed of Jackson's arrival or any problems that Jackson encountered that may delay the plan. It was such an important role that it was not too much to expect a courier to be sent every hour to report on progress. Therefore, the commander chosen for that position needed to be someone skilled in military matters who knew his business well. Strangely, given all the veteran and professional brigade commanders in Hill's division, the nonprofessional Branch was chosen for this duty post. Branch, a 41-year-old Princeton graduate who had been an editor, lawyer, and U.S. congressman, owed his position to his political connections, not to any military experience that he brought with him. Why Branch was chosen for this particular duty has never been explained, though perhaps Lee and Hill thought: "How hard can it be to tell us when Jackson arrives?" However, when Branch sent no word, it forced those commanders to speculate on the silence and develop their own revised plans.

Finally, everything hinged on Jackson's arrival, so Lee should have made certain that Stonewall could meet the timetable required. Lee needed daylight to drive the Union army back toward their supply base; so, it was imperative that Jackson be in position in the morning hours. Yet, instead of taking the lead and setting a precise time to demonstrate that he was in control of his first offensive as army commander, Lee inexplicably did something that he, tellingly, would never do again—he left the room and let his subordinate commanders decide when the attack should begin. After discussing the plan for a few minutes, it was decided that since Jackson had the farthest march, he should set the attack time. Jackson quickly said June 25, indicating his men would be ready in just over 36 hours. Longstreet, long after the war, claimed that he urged Jackson to give himself one more day and that Jackson conceded. Therefore, June 26 was set as the day of the attack. This meant that by the time Jackson rode the long trek back to his army, he would have only 48 hours to move his men nearly 50 miles to be in position for the attack. That was a tall order for even Jackson's famous foot cavalry on the best roads in good weather. It proved too much for Jackson's army in the muddy roads of the Virginia piedmont. He would not be able to execute his part of the plan, and his was the most important part. When Lee returned to the room, he was informed of the attack date, did not challenge it, and dismissed the generals. Lee then sent out written orders to try to make doubly sure there was no confusion among the commanders. He should have taken the time to write better orders, for the ones he dispatched were ambiguous and left too much to the interpretation of the various parties involved. These interpretations would lead to Lee's best laid plans going astray on June 26.[18]

Jackson left the meeting and set off on the long ride back to his lines, losing a second consecutive night of sleep. At this juncture, we should be upfront, even at the risk of giving away a major plot line—Jackson's performance in the Seven Days was less than spectacular, to be charitable. Many have sought to explain why he performed so poorly in this campaign when he had performed so well in the previous months. Sleep deprivation has frequently been cited as the culprit and there is no doubt that it must have been one of the factors. However, Jackson gets singled out for suffering inordinately from fatigue, whereas others, who also were exhausted, rarely have the benefit of having their military sins absolved the same way. Exhaustion certainly played havoc with Jackson's mental state, as it would with anyone. Statements that Jackson needed "more sleep than most" seem consciously calculated to magnify his torpor and induce pity. The fact is that Jackson last had a full night's sleep on June 21. He spent the nights of June 22–23 and 23–24 in the saddle, without any sleep in between. On the night of June 24, either too excited about the impending campaign or, as some have suggested, too exhausted to snooze, Jackson did not sleep. He also caught very little sleep on the 25th as he moved into position, though he was well behind schedule. A more rational choice of June 27 as the attack day likely would have fixed all these problems, but Jackson originally (at least according to Longstreet) suggested June 25. If so, this was probably an indication of Jackson's fatigue already leading to bad decisions.

Despite this, blaming every one of Jackson's poor decisions or failures throughout the campaign on exhaustion is excessively exculpatory. No historian has gone further than Clifford Dowdey, who developed an elaborate thesis of "stress fatigue" being the reason that the Jackson of the Seven Days was not the Jackson of legend.[19] Such theories imply that Jackson would never make (and had never made) bad decisions if he was well rested. This is simply not true. Jackson had made several mistakes before the start of his Valley campaign, none more potentially disastrous than his ill-conceived attack on superior Union forces at Kernstown on March 23. An honest assessment of Jackson's performance in the Seven Days' battles must take more into account than just fatigue. Jackson had never worked directly with Lee; he had exercised independent command and now would be a subordinate; and he was entering country with which he was unfamiliar. As will become clear in the following pages, each of these factors played just as large a role as fatigue in Jackson's overall unsatisfactory performance.

Every commander—and many enlisted men, for that matter—had problems affecting their physical and mental states during the campaign. D. H. Hill had ulcers (dyspepsia in the term of the day) and A. P. Hill had a burning sensation in his loins that was caused not by his zeal for battle, but by the venereal disease he had contracted as a cadet (though not from another cadet) nearly 20 years earlier.[20] Magruder had terrible indigestion and slept little. Lee got very little sleep and was ill and exhausted by July 1. Lee had also learned on June 9 that his infant grandson—"Rooney" Lee's only son—had died.[21] Stuart did not sleep for four days straight, but accomplished his ride on horseback around the army in fine form. On the Union side, McClellan was ill and did not sleep much and Porter performed admirably without much sleep. Additionally, thousands of enlisted men on both sides struggled with camp diseases and had witnessed their brothers, fathers, sons, or best friends killed or mutilated in combat nearly every day of the week, only to suck it up and fight again the next day. Fatigue is endemic in war and combat, and Jackson would be tired in future battles, but perform well enough. So, we must not unnecessarily give Jackson a crutch that we are unwilling to give other commanders.

When the tired Jackson returned to his army, he discovered that he had left a mess of things when he had departed the previous night, long before any weariness had a chance to cloud his judgment. Jackson should have insured that his army continued making progress toward Richmond as rapidly as possible in his absence. He had many capable division commanders to whom he could have given that important responsibility. However, Jackson chose to entrust this duty to his personal friend and pastor, Robert L. Dabney, whom Jackson had appointed as his chief of staff. Jackson had convinced Dabney to join his army even though he lacked any military aptitude, nor would he develop any such skills through his association with Jackson. Jackson's officers thought Dabney was abysmal as a chief of staff, and those who suffered through his sermons—especially his three-hour marathon on predestination on Sunday, June 22—probably questioned his value as a minister, too.[22] Nevertheless, Jackson unthinkingly gave Dabney the task of keeping the troops moving while their leader was away. It is difficult to imagine that the fiery General Richard Ewell would have failed to keep the columns moving, but Dabney was hopelessly ill-prepared to force his will on the marching columns, and the progress slowed to a snail's pace.[23]

Jackson returned to find the men had a long way to go to get to where they needed to be for their part in the grand play. Lee expected Jackson to start at 3:00 A.M. on June 26 from a point five miles east of Ashland. Jackson had to consolidate his army and resume the march over the poor roads of the rain-soaked piedmont. By midnight, Jackson was still several miles short of his destination. He decided to begin marching at 2:30 A.M. on June 26, in order to make up some of the lost ground. He must have been aware that he would never be able to achieve Lee's expected morning flank attack. Yet, Lee's orders did not specify when Jackson should arrive, and Jackson may have misunderstood the importance of a morning arrival. There would be plenty of other misunderstandings before the day was over.[24]

* * *

While Lee was making his preparations, the Union commander was staying true to form—preparing for his siege and asking for reinforcements. The first part of McClellan's plan was severely disrupted by the weather.

Between May 20 and June 10, it rained no fewer than 14 days, and many of those were deluges that ruined bridges, roads, tents, and men's good moods. McClellan's June letters, whether official or private, are filled with constant references to the debilitating rains that must have had him expecting at any minute to see a bearded man leading two animals of every kind into a boat 300 cubits long. It was the rainiest late spring that the Chickahominy region had experienced in decades.

Though the rain delayed Little Mac's timetable, it did not alter his plan, nor did it prevent him from deducing his opponent's likely strategy. McClellan predicted as early as June 4 that his enemy would "probably attempt" to strike his flank north of the Chickahominy in order to threaten his supply base.[25] Despite that prescient realization, McClellan nevertheless weakened that flank by keeping Sumner's and Franklin's corps south of the river after Seven Pines. Perhaps he hoped that reinforcements in the form of McDowell's corps would soon fill that void, so he kept up his constant, redundant request for more troops. He demanded McDowell's corps and even requested that General Henry Halleck, who had just captured Corinth, Mississippi, send part of his army to the east to join the Army of the Potomac. Lincoln and Stanton acquiesced in sending one division of McDowell's corps—the troops under 60-year-old veteran General George McCall—to McClellan by sea. They departed on June 7 and arrived at White House landing on June 11. McClellan sent them forward north of the river to join Porter's corps.

Sandwiched between the calls for reinforcements, McClellan continued to elaborate how the siege would take place. He constantly promised the final battle would begin as soon as "the ground [was] fit for artillery to move."[26] As late as June 9, McClellan believed that he was preparing to attack an army commanded by his old friend, Gustavus W. Smith. He soon learned that Lee commanded the army, but that did not worry him. What did worry him, though, was the size of the army that Lee supposedly commanded. With each passing day, McClellan's belief in the number of enemy troops increased. He became convinced that not only was Lee there in large numbers, but also that much of the western Confederate army under General Pierre G.T. Beauregard had been sent to join Lee. On June 10, he wrote to Stanton that Beauregard had arrived ahead of his troops, and on June 25, he wrote that Beauregard's troops had arrived the previous day, increasing Lee's army to an astounding 200,000 soldiers![27] In actual fact, after performing poorly in Mississippi, Beauregard had pleaded illness and taken a leave of absence, which prompted Davis to replace him. Beauregard was in disgrace in Davis's eyes and he certainly was not coming to Richmond with thousands of soldiers.

McClellan was wrong about Beauregard, but he was right about Jackson, who had been unable to keep his movement a secret after all. McClellan was convinced that Jackson was heading his way and even accurately predicted that Jackson would attack the Chickahominy flank. That flank became a major concern for McClellan on June 15, when Stuart's cavalry troops finished their ride around the Union army. This action seemed to awaken McClellan to the fact that his supplies and communications may not only be the target of a Confederate assault, but also be too difficult to defend and maintain. McClellan started making arrangements to establish an alternate base on the James River, just in case he faced an overwhelming attack north of the Chickahominy. And he would consider any attack to be with overwhelming force.[28]

McClellan would later claim that he had only kept his supply line at White House because he was forced to maintain a link to McDowell's approaching corps. Therefore, he suggested it was really Lincoln's fault for denying him that corps for so long and exposing him to the devastating attack that Lee would eventually launch. This was a postbattle remembrance that passed the blame on to McClellan's enemies in the administration, but there is not a grain of truth in it. The fact is that McClellan had deliberately headed to the West Point station and White House landing on the York River Railroad as soon as he began his advance. Even after the Confederates abandoned Norfolk, scuttled the *Merrimac*, and ceded the James River to the Union navy, McClellan still decided not to utilize that river even though he had not progressed far enough to create difficulties in transferring his troops. The telling point is that, at that juncture, McClellan was not taking the Richmond and York River Railroad route because he needed to meet up with McDowell; he was operating under the assumption that he would not be getting McDowell's corps (and he was pretty mad about it). This route had always been McClellan's objective from the very first drafts of the plan. When Urbanna was his original landing point, he intended to force march his troops to the West Point station right away. It had always been the key factor in his approach to Richmond.

The reason was tied to the way McClellan had always intended to conquer Richmond—not with a dramatic and grand battle but with a slow and strangulating siege. McClellan's siege train consisted of more than 100 guns of varying calibers, but the real heavy hitters that would blast open the doors of Richmond were much too heavy to be moved overland by horses. They could only be moved by railroad or floated down the rivers. The meandering path of the James River did not provide an adequate approach to the city. The York River Railroad, however, approached the city from the east and provided an excellent avenue for the big guns.

It seems surprising that given how important the river and White House landing was for McClellan's campaign he would not have more adequately protected this flank. But it suggests that until Stuart's ride from June 12–15 McClellan had never seriously considered being attacked again. He was following his plan of advance, assuming that the enemy would react to his moves and never take the initiative again. Perhaps the Confederate failure at Seven Pines had led McClellan to doubt that they would try another attack. But this begs the question—if McClellan really believed he was outnumbered nearly two to one, then why would he not expect an attack in overwhelming force every day? Instead, even though he claimed that Lee had nearly 200,000 men opposing him, McClellan pressed on with his own offensive plans. Any scholar who studies this campaign is struck by this incongruity: McClellan believed he was massively outnumbered, but never seemed to expect an attack from his foe.

Indeed, even when McClellan discovered that Jackson was heading his way and suspected that the Valley commander was going to attack with heavy force against his supply line, McClellan did nothing to shore up that zone and continued his preparations for advance. Clifford Dowdy called this "acutely developed perseveration," suggesting that perhaps McClellan was so blinded by his own actions that he could not adapt or react to a change in the plans that he was making. Another possibility is that perhaps McClellan did not truly believe that Jackson was strong enough to turn him because deep down he knew he really had the numerical advantage over the Confederates.[29]

Whether McClellan believed Jackson was a serious threat or not, he ordered a limited forward movement south of the Chickahominy on June 25, in order to gain the ground necessary to allow his siege guns to come forward and do their work. McClellan had unloaded his first siege guns on June 21, indicating that he finally believed the time was near when he could open up his barrage on the Confederate forces guarding the capital. McClellan wrote to Lincoln on June 18 that he only waited for "a favorable condition of earth and sky." He wrote to his wife, Ellen, on June 22 that he had brought up the heavy guns to "give secesh a preliminary pounding tomorrow."[30]

McClellan had stopped writing of a grand Napoleonic-style battle. He wrote to his wife saying that he expected "the operations would resolve themselves into a series of partial attacks, rather than a general battle."[31] Wednesday, June 25, was going to be the day of the first partial attack. McClellan was scheming to capture the high ground of Old Tavern, on the Nine Mile Road, one and a half miles from the Union lines. This would grant him the high ground necessary to command the enemy's defenses with his own heavy siege weapons. He would first capture the ground to the south, so that he could eventually assault Old Tavern from front and flank. The woodlands south of Old Tavern were known as Oak Grove, where Union and Confederate pickets had been annoying each other since the Seven Pines battle. It was to this ground that Union forces would advance on June 25.

At 8:30 A.M. on that surprisingly mild Wednesday morning, two brigades of General Joseph Hooker's division, under the command of Generals Daniel Sickles and Cuvier Grover, advanced from the Union lines near the Seven Pines battlefield due west through the thick forests and swampy streams toward the Confederate lines. Their left flank to the south was buttressed by General John C. Robinson's brigade of General Phil Kearny's division. These Yankees encountered General Ambrose "Rans" Wright's Georgia brigade who drew reinforcements to their line from General Robert Ransom's newly arrived North Carolina brigade. Stiff rebel resistance and the inexperience of some of Sickles's regiments led part of his line to retreat in the face of the Confederate fire. On Hooker's report, corps commander Heintzelman ordered reinforcements to move forward. After several delays, McClellan ordered the advance to begin again at 1:00 P.M. The fighting carried on until dusk, though sporadic firing continued through much of the night on the front line. At the end of the day, Little Mac had only advanced his army about 600 yards and had lost more than 600 men doing it, while the Confederates had lost fewer than 450 men.[32] The Union commander decided that he had gained enough ground to allow for the flank attack on Old Tavern, which he stated in a letter would occur on the 26th or the 27th. Once his army had gained Old Tavern, McClellan declared, "the game is up for Secesh."[33]

The sounds of the firing brought Lee to the front lines on the afternoon of the 25th. He was in a bit of a sweat and not just because of the rising heat. Lee feared that McClellan had discovered Jackson's approach and correctly deduced that Lee had weakened his army south of the river. Observing the field, Lee guessed that this was not the harbinger of a major assault and decided to continue with his gamble, writing to the president that evening: "I have decided to make no change in the plan."[34]

If Lee had known what information was in McClellan's hands that evening, he would have been alternately dismayed and amused. The fact is that McClellan did know of Jackson's advance, but it was coupled with other bogus intelligence. McClellan received a dispatch from Fitz-John Porter at 5:30 P.M. on June 25 stating that a slave had just come into his lines claiming to have seen elements of Beauregard's army in the capital city. The source further claimed that there were now 200,000 Confederate troops and that Jackson was going to attack McClellan's rear. In fact, the day before, a deserter (who may or may not have been deliberately planted as a ruse) had already told McClellan's intelligence chief that Jackson was on the march and scheduled to attack McClellan's flank on June 28. That news by itself was bad enough, but the addition of the erroneous news of Beauregard was too much. All these stories from suspect sources combined, as Stephen Sears has written, to turn "fantasy to reality in General McClellan's mind . . . and he lost all composure."[35]

McClellan certainly adopted a bipolar attitude in his communications to the War Department. At 6:15 P.M., he sent a telegram advising Stanton of his enormous difficulties, saying that "I shall have to contend against vastly superior odds"—the 200,000 he estimated—and "I shall probably be attacked tomorrow."[36] He even tried to shuffle off the blame for any potential defeat, declaring, "the responsibility cannot be thrown on my shoulders—it must rest where it belongs." He concluded with a pout: "I feel that it is no use in my again asking for reinforcements."[37] After examining Porter's defenses, however, he wrote a more insouciant note at 10:40 P.M. proclaiming, "If I had another good Division I could laugh at Jackson."[38] Little Mac even wrote to his wife on the afternoon of June 26 that "the enemy is falling into a trap. I shall let the enemy cut off our communications in order to ensure success."[39] As McClellan went to bed late that night for the two to three hours of sleep that he would get, he was convinced that Jackson would attack the next day, but was unsure whether Jackson's assault would derail his plans.

For his part, Jackson was not displaying his accustomed swiftness, and it was becoming doubtful that he would be able to live up to his part in Lee's plan. Lee had instructed Jackson to move his army along the Ashcake Road to a point a mile west of the Virginia Central Railroad, as it ran south into Richmond. The rendezvous point was a place called Slash Church on the Ashcake Road. From there, it was only 10 miles to Beaver Dam Creek, where Jackson would arrive on the flank of Porter's force, beginning the day's action. To insure that Jackson's force would arrive early in the morning, Lee instructed Jackson to begin his flank march at 3:00 A.M. on June 26. This would have put Jackson's troops in the right spot no later than 9:00 A.M.

Jackson encountered many difficulties and made many poor decisions during this important march. In addition to not marching at all on Sunday, June 22, and leaving the army in charge of unskilled hands in his absence on Monday, June 23, a drenching rain and inefficient use of resources meant that Jackson's army was still strung out more than 20 miles on the Virginia Central Railroad on the morning of June 24. When Jackson rejoined the army early that morning, he found that his vanguard was parked at Beaver Dam Station (not to be confused with the creek of the same name that was nearly 35 miles away), only 10 miles ahead of where he had left it more than 24 hours earlier. Jackson spent the day trying to overcome this delay by pushing his army forward. After all, he had to be at Slash Church, 24 miles by road from Beaver Dam Station, by the night of the next day. Of course, his rear units would have to travel nearly 20 miles just to reach Beaver Dam Station, but almost all that journey could be by railroad car, at least. By the time darkness fell on June 24, Jackson had accomplished much: his lead unit was only 10 miles short of Slash Church and his rearmost unit was only 19 miles away.

Jackson spent most of June 25 uniting his forces. He undoubtedly did not believe this would be difficult, as in the past he had marched his Valley army much farther in more stressful circumstances. But this was a larger army than Jackson was used to directing, with an extra division and brigade consisting of 10,000 more men. Jackson was in front of the column and unable to personally apply his boot to the backside of those brigades in General Charles Winder's trailing division. Apparently, no other officers wore boots that day, or more likely, did not know the plan, and hence lacked the urgency necessary to move the army into its proper position. The end result of such a tepid response to the day's march was that Winder's division only marched 14 miles. Jackson's army bivouacked for the night 5 miles short of Slash church, which was 12 miles from Porter's line. From Jackson's starting point, his army would have to march between 17 and 19 miles to turn Porter out of his position.[40]

That night, Jackson sent a courier to Lee to say that mud and high water had prevented him from reaching any farther than Ashland, five miles short of his destination. He stated that he would move at 2:30 A.M. the next morning to compensate for some of the delay. Lee must have recalculated to recognize that the greater distance would not allow Jackson to appear any earlier than 10:00 A.M. Had Lee known what was happening in Jackson's camp, however, he would have been disappointed. While the rest of Lee's army that would participate in the day's offensive began stirring at around 3:00 A.M., Jackson insisted that his men eat first and as a result did not begin moving until nearly 5:00 A.M. Already, Lee's plan was badly out of sync, because Jackson's army would not be able to arrive before 1:00 P.M. at its fastest pace, and it would not set that pace on this day.[41]

Union cavalry patrols felled trees across Jackson's path, slowing his movement. Jackson also chose to advance with a deployed skirmish line, a necessity when advancing in unfamiliar territory where the enemy may be lurking behind every bend but one that further retarded his pace. He did not reach Slash Church until 9:00 A.M. The columns behind the skirmishers marched in the rising heat and humidity, through the dust kicked up on the road by thousands of shuffling feet and suffocated by dense woods on every side that seemed to block any breeze. Jackson probed cautiously forward, periodically shelling woods ahead of him to drive out suspected ambushers and skirmishing with small cavalry pickets. Those officers who had served with Jackson in the Valley felt the commander was moving more nonchalantly than normal, without the sense of urgency that they expected.

This delay indicates once again that despite Lee's best efforts to make sure that everyone understood the plan, something was still lost in the translation. Jackson's timid pace indicated that he did not know where he would come upon the enemy, even though Lee had clearly said it would be at Beaver Dam Creek, and that he did not comprehend the crucial time factor in Lee's plan. The plan would only work if Jackson arrived with enough daylight to force the Union to retreat and suffer losses in the pursuit. Jackson would spend all day marching to his position and not arrive at Hundley's Corner until 5:00 P.M. Once he arrived, his confusion over the orders caused him to sit and do nothing to help his comrades two miles away, whose firing he could clearly hear. Lee had been determined to avoid a futile frontal assault at Beaver Dam Creek. However, he would be doing the very thing he intended to avoid, thanks to Jackson's late arrival and his own fears of allowing McClellan to seize the initiative.[42]

* * *

Thursday, June 26, dawned hot and sticky in the Chickahominy morass. As McClellan was finally lying down to sleep a couple of fitful hours, Lee received Jackson's note from the night before stating that he had only made it to Ashland and would set off at 2:30 A.M. Meanwhile, A. P. Hill had marched his division down densely wooded lanes and past scattered farms to the Meadow Bridge vicinity. There, he waited in the same stagnant heat that plagues the area today. Hill was waiting for the word to come from Branch that Jackson was near. Jackson had contacted Branch at Half Sink at 10 A.M. to say that he was running behind schedule, but it is not clear that Branch ever forwarded that message to his division commander. Hill was left waiting at the bridge as the sun rose higher, perplexed as to what may have gone wrong.

At 38, Ambrose Powell Hill was a promising fighter, whom Lee had promoted to division commander. Hill had been a West Point graduate, though his graduation had been delayed by illness. The illness, a venereal

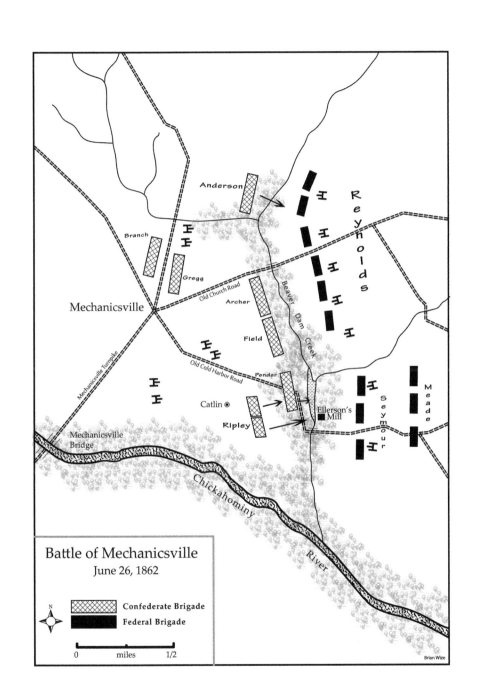

Battle of Mechanicsville
June 26, 1862

Confederate Brigade
Federal Brigade

0   miles   1/2

N

Brian Wize

Anderson

Branch

Gregg

Mechanicsville

Old Church Road

Archer

Field

Beaver Dam Creek

Reynolds

Old Cold Harbor Road

Pender

Mechanicsville Turnpike

Catlin

Ripley

Ellerson's Mill

Seymour

Meade

Mechanicsville Bridge

Chickahominy River

disease contracted by a "youthful indiscretion," had helped ruin his chances to marry Ellen Marcy, who later wed McClellan. The flare-ups from his illness would incapacitate Hill frequently during the war. On this day, however, it was not the familiar illness that had Hill out of sorts; it was the silence coming from Branch.

Unlike Jackson, Hill clearly understood Lee's plan. He also knew that the risk to Richmond grew greater with every passing second. Also, unlike Jackson, Hill knew that McClellan had launched a limited attack south of the river the day before and he wondered if this was a harbinger of a much larger attack to come. Only a heavy attack on McClellan's flank could prevent Hill's former rival suitor from breaking through Magruder's and Huger's thin line of defenses. Hill's frustration grew with every rising Fahrenheit degree and minute that passed. Noon came with no word from Jackson and no lunch for Hill's soldiers because they expected to be fighting any minute. As his troops dozed in the sultry heat, Hill chafed. He reasoned that surely Lee would want the plan to go forward today, and that he would prefer some action, any action, be taken rather than see an entire day pass quietly, allowing McClellan to resume the initiative. He also reasoned that whatever had caused Jackson to be late, he *must* be near and should arrive at any minute. Finally, at 3:00 P.M., realizing there was only about five hours of daylight remaining, Hill decided to read his new commander's mind. Without informing Lee or asking his permission, Hill forced a crossing over the lightly defended Meadow Bridge and set the day's battle in motion. He drove across the bridge and pushed toward Mechanicsville with little difficulty. The Yankees retreated rapidly because Porter had ordered them to fall back to the main line when the Confederates began their attack. Porter knew the strength of his position as well as Lee and had no intention of fighting anywhere else except behind his formidable line.

Lee was sitting astride his horse on the bluffs overlooking the Chickahominy River when he heard the firing coming from Meadow Bridge. As he trained his binoculars toward Mechanicsville, he saw blue-clad soldiers retreating. He turned to Longstreet, who had joined him on the bluffs and said calmly: "Those are A. P. Hill's men. You may cross over."[43] Longstreet rode off immediately and ordered the crossing. D. H. Hill's division was in front, since once he crossed the river he would have the furthest to go to get between Jackson and A. P. Hill. Hill's division was delayed for a short time as engineers repaired the damaged bridge. Shortly after 4:00 P.M., Hill's leading brigade of General Roswell Ripley's Georgians and North Carolinians was marching across the bridge to get behind A. P. Hill. Soon after the bridge was completed, Lee crossed the bridge and galloped to

Mechanicsville to confer with A. P. Hill and act as quarterback of the offense. He rode to Hill in the village crossroads shortly before 5:00 P.M. and probably learned that Hill had crossed without hearing from Jackson.

Many historians have heaped abuse on Hill for acting recklessly, and one would imagine that Lee was displeased by the rash act of his subordinate, advancing in defiance of Lee's carefully crafted plan. However, Lee may not have been surprised or upset (at least not with A. P. Hill) at all. Lee never reprimanded Hill for bringing on the battle, and as Brian K. Burton points out, Lee had come to the same conclusion that the army needed to cross the river with or without Jackson. Two independent sources from the battle, who were near Lee at 3:00 P.M. that afternoon, confirm that Lee had made up his mind to cross the river with his army before darkness fell. The most articulate was Major Joseph Brent, an aide to the anxious Magruder. Lee told Brent that he had not heard from Jackson, but had decided that he could not wait on the delinquent general any longer and claimed that he had sent orders to Hill to cross the Meadow Bridge. Though Hill likely crossed before Lee's new orders had reached him—testified by the fact that Hill did not refer to Lee's order in his report of the battle—it reveals why Lee was not upset by the maneuver.[44]

Lee was clearly upset, however, by the presence of President Davis and his acolytes on the battlefield. Soon after Lee crossed the Mechanicsville Bridge around 4:00 P.M., President Davis and several followers also crossed the bridge to observe the action for themselves. Lee noticed them well within range of enemy artillery and hurried over to have a brief and unfriendly chat with the president. "Who are all this army of people, and what are they doing here?" Lee curtly asked Davis. Davis, understanding that he was being rebuked by Lee for being too close to the action, hesitantly responded, "It is not my army, General," to which Lee tersely snapped, "It certainly is not my army, Mr. President, and this is no place for it." Davis was surprised by Lee's icy tone, but conceded. He said, "Well, General, if I withdraw, perhaps they will follow." With that, Davis and his entourage rode back toward the bridge, but simply found another place to view the battle once they were out of Lee's sight.[45]

When A. P. Hill had cleared Mechanicsville, he saw the impressive defensive line at Beaver Dam Creek and did not intend to assault it. He knew his one division could never carry it. He ordered artillery to unlimber and open on the Union position. Soon, his artillery and five infantry brigades came under an accurate and damaging fire from the more numerous Union cannons. Hill decided that he could not just leave his brigades in the open ground near Mechanicsville where there was little cover. Instead of withdrawing out of artillery range, Hill decided to move his brigades toward the enemy's position. He was not trying to attack the Federal lines directly, but only trying to tie them down so that Jackson could arrive in their flank and rear and force them to retreat. He also felt that the tree cover nearer the creek would shelter his men from the artillery blasts better than remaining on the open plains near Mechanicsville. Though no one had heard anything from Jackson since the wee hours of the morning, Hill made a giant leap of faith that Jackson would appear at any minute and spare his units the mauling they may suffer otherwise.

In fact, unbeknownst to anyone, Jackson had arrived at Hundley's Corners soon after Hill's brigades became engaged in the battle. Jackson, according to eyewitnesses on his staff, appeared confused and worried. He apparently expected Hill to be nearby on his right flank. He could also clearly hear the fighting, but did not know what it meant and he did not send an aide or courier to find out. Lee had spoken in the June 23 meeting of Jackson coming down to the Mechanicsville Turnpike to turn Porter's flank, which would have required Jackson to continue marching to the sound of the firing to pick up that road. But Lee's ambiguous written orders had only ordered Jackson to follow the Pole Green Church Road. That road ended at Hundley's Corners, about two miles north of the Mechanicsville Pike. Jackson did not seek out the roads nearby that would connect with the Mechanicsville Pike. Here was another example of Lee's orders being open to multiple interpretations. Lee intended for Jackson's army to drive to the Mechanicsville Pike on June 26 in order to force Porter to retreat, but Jackson believed he had fulfilled the letter and spirit of Lee's orders when he arrived at Hundley's Corners. By 6:00 P.M., with the sounds of battle raging nearby, Jackson ordered his men into bivouac for the night to rest, recover, and eat. He would not seek out the fighting or the enemy with so little daylight remaining. Jackson knew something had gone wrong because Hill was not there to link up with him, but Jackson was not aware that he was the culpable party. At any time, Jackson could have sent one of Stuart's troopers, who were guarding Jackson's left flank, as a messenger to Hill or Lee, but never did.[46]

While Jackson was packing it in for the evening, A. P. Hill was committing his division to battle. He sent General Charles W. Field's brigade off first across the fields for about a mile to the slight cover of a line of trees at the edge of the creek. They were trying to get close enough that Union artillery could not risk hitting their own troops. The 34-year-old Kentuckian brought his men within musket range of Union lines, but musket fire was more tolerable than artillery fire because they could reply in kind. Marching slightly behind and to the left of Field was General

James J. Archer's brigade. These two brigades engaged in front of the creek, but they had no intention of crossing the creek to get into Union lines. It would have been hopeless.

Other than sitting uncomfortably in the sun all day awaiting what may develop, there was not a lot to give the Union troops concern as they sat in their rifle pits east of the creek. They had a clear field of fire, helped by the cutting of trees on the opposite slope, a creek about 20 yards wide, and a swamp about 80 yards wide that would slow down even the fastest sprinter. They had constructed pits to provide protection and an abatis, a military obstacle composed of sharpened logs and branches, in front of them. To cap it off, they had batteries of artillery further up the slope behind them firing safely above their heads on a cleared range for several hundred yards. It would take an attack by superhuman legions to break their line.

On the Confederate far left, General Joseph Anderson, a 49-year-old West Point graduate and former superintendent of Richmond's Tredegar Iron Works, moved his brigade to try to capture the Union cannon from the flank and reduce the pressure on everyone. Confusion over the topography of the ground and poor maps (which would plague Lee's army throughout the campaign) resulted in Anderson's men not coming in far enough on the northern flank of the Yankees. Nevertheless, he pushed farther forward than any other brigade and actually crossed the creek briefly. There was some short-lived hand-to-hand fighting at the Yankee breastworks before Anderson's troops fell back and exchanged shots with their opponent until nightfall. The Union artillery was simply too strong to allow any success along this line. Anderson, Archer, and Field engaged in a five-hour firefight across the creek with brigades from General George McCall's division. The Confederate brigades suffered many losses trying to advance over the difficult ground to the creek itself. One Union artilleryman said the Federal fire on the rebels "left them sweltering in their own blood."[47]

While Hill's other brigades crossed the fields and engaged the enemy, General William Dorsey Pender, a promising 28-year-old North Carolinian in his first command, led his troops down the Cold Harbor Road toward the creek. About 100 yards from the creek, the road turns sharply south and parallels the creek for a quarter mile or more before turning east again and crossing the creek just south of Ellerson's Mill. Pender thought he saw an opportunity to turn Porter's left flank, which did not appear to be anchored on the Chickahominy. While traversing this road under artillery fire and confused by the inadequate maps, two of Pender's regiments veered off course and got tangled with the soldiers in Field's brigade, while two regiments continued south of the road. These latter two attacked General Truman Seymour's brigade of Pennsylvania soldiers, supported by 14 pieces of artillery. They got within 100 yards of the Union position before being forced to retreat with heavy losses. The 38th North Carolina regiment lost more than one-third of its force in this failed attack. One of Pender's aides, stunned to still be alive, wrote that night: "I never saw such a storm of shot and shells before . . . Fragments of shells literally hailed around me."[48]

However, Pender's failed assault indicated to Lee that perhaps an attack in force closer to the river might turn the position. At the very least, it would relieve the pressure on Pender's troops. Ripley's brigade of D. H. Hill's division had crossed the Mechanicsville Bridge and had advanced half a mile toward the village. Lee, seeing a slim opportunity to pry Porter out of his position on his left instead of his right, ordered Ripley's brigade to the Confederate right near the river in order to lead such an attack. Ripley's brigade suddenly became very popular, and the resulting developments would illustrate the growing pains of the new command structure.

The first person to confer with Ripley was A. P. Hill, who asked the balding, mustachioed 39-year-old West Point graduate to cooperate with Pender to drive away the battery near Ellerson's Mill, which Ripley agreed to do. All this was done without consulting either D. H. Hill, Ripley's division commander, or Lee. Ripley recalled in his report: "While the troops were in motion I received orders to assault the enemy from General Lee and also from Major General D. H. Hill."[49] Lee most likely intended a wider flanking movement, but D. H. Hill altered Ripley's route. D. H. Hill had conferred with Pender, who unwisely suggested another attack where his regiments had been repulsed. Thus, D. H. Hill ordered Ripley to send two regiments to the right of Pender and two more to attack the battery on Pender's left center. Ripley promptly obeyed and sent the 44th Georgia and the 1st North Carolina to attack just south of where the Cold Harbor Road crossed the creek at Ellerson's Mill. Thus, Ripley's orders came from A. P. Hill, D. H. Hill, and Lee, and all had a different idea of how Ripley should be used. Just for good measure, President Davis also sent an order to Ripley, without Lee's knowledge. Within the proper chain of command, a brigade commander was supposed to receive his orders from his division commander, though a direct order from the army's commanding general could supplant this. Ripley had the honor of receiving orders from his division commander, army commander, and the nation's commander-in-chief, all in a matter of minutes.

Ripley's final disposition would lead to severe casualties for the right flank of the 1st North Carolina and the wholesale slaughter of the 44th Georgia, who were experiencing their first battle. It would be a bloody baptism for these boys from the central Georgia piedmont who had only enlisted three months earlier. The Georgia regiment, with the North Carolinians following, reached the top of a rise on the Catlin farm a little less than 1,000 yards from the creek. When they saw what lay ahead, it must have been a sobering moment for even the most eager rookie soldier. They could see the cannons first, then the rifle pits, and of course the difficult terrain. They would have to cross some rugged ground only to find "a mill race, with scarped banks, and in some places waist-deep water" in front of the enemy.[50] Confederate artillery commander, E. Porter Alexander, later wrote, "A more hopeless charge was never entered upon."[51] Nevertheless, the 44th Georgia let out their first rebel yell and raced down the hill "through a perfect hailstorm of every kind of death dealing missile that the brain of man could invent," as one lieutenant remembered. The regiment's colonel had been in a hospital with a severe fever for nearly three weeks and was "scarcely able to walk," but insisted on being helped onto his horse to lead the regiment. He was mortally wounded by three shots in the charge to the creek. The regiment amazingly managed to get all the way to the millrace, within 50 yards of the enemy line, but was unable to go any further. One soldier wrote to his mother that the men "fought in water waist deep all the time." While the 44th Georgia succeeded in getting to the creek, where they were pinned down and slaughtered by musketry, the 1st North Carolina stopped halfway down the hill, unable to go farther but unwilling to retreat. These failed charges ended the day's fighting. When darkness fell and both units were able to fall back safely, the 1st North Carolina had suffered 142 casualties, whereas the 44th Georgia had 335 killed and wounded men out of 514 engaged in the creek and on the slopes leading to it. Three weeks after the fight, one humbled Georgia lieutenant wrote home: "Ma . . . my pen would fail to depict the scene as I saw it."[52]

If the charge had been a hellish nightmare, the battle's aftermath had its own haunting quality. A soldier in Pender's brigade wrote, "Nothing could be heard in the black darkness of that night save the ghastly moans of the wounded and dying."[53] Years after the war, D. H. Hill remembered sardonically, "We were lavish of blood in those days, and it was thought to be a great thing to charge a battery of artillery or an earth-work lined with infantry."[54] Lee's first battle had been a disastrous mixture of confused orders and poor execution. His army had assaulted a fortified line that Lee expressly desired to avoid. Out of 10,000 men engaged, Lee's army lost approximately 1,500 soldiers, a third of whom fell during the final charge at Ellerson's Mill. The Federals had lost only 361 soldiers out of 14,000 on hand for the fight.[55]

That night, Lee met his division commanders in a house in Mechanicsville. Lee could not help but be upset at the day's events. In fact, after the war, he would admit that he was "disappointed" at not finding Jackson that first day.[56] The simple fact was that Jackson did not arrive at the time or the location Lee expected him. Most historians who criticize Jackson blame it on his exhaustion rather than his misreading Lee's orders. A. P. Hill also takes a beating from historians for initiating the battle without consulting Lee. Hill's act is inexcusable if he acted on his own authority, but the rash act can be considered less disastrous simply because Lee had concluded at 3:00 P.M. to have Hill do the very thing he did anyway. Hill cannot be faulted for his demonstrations and attacks against Porter's line, because Lee was present and sanctioned those decisions and could have given contrary orders if he wished. Pender launched an ill-conceived attack against a strong Union force, and Lee decided to follow up one bad idea with another by ordering Ripley's brigade to try to do what Pender's could not. D. H. Hill rerouted Ripley's brigade from what Lee had in mind, but the fact is that Ripley's soldiers had no chance of breaking the Union line short of an airborne assault to the enemy's rear.

For all the hand-wringing and finger-pointing at the subordinates who failed Lee, it was the army's commander himself who ultimately was responsible for the day's failure. Lee's greatest flaw was a failure to utilize his staff to ascertain exactly what was going on. He never ordered A. P. Hill to send a courier to find Jackson. He never sought to gather any information as to why the plan was behind schedule. To be fair, Hill, Branch, and Jackson also failed to communicate with each other effectively or coordinate their activities. But Lee was the one responsible for finding out why his plan was failing. Ultimately, the Southern commander was learning on the job. It was tough job training, to be sure.

The night descended on a melancholic Confederate force and a euphoric McClellan. In mid-afternoon, right about the time that A. P. Hill began crossing Meadow Bridge, McClellan had arrived at Porter's Headquarters to check on things. From there, he watched the day's fighting and saw the fruits of Porter's skillful defensive alignment. McClellan's initial thoughts were that he had turned back Jackson's flanking force. At 9:00 P.M., McClellan sent a triumphant telegram to Secretary of War Stanton extolling the day's success and bragging: "I almost begin to think that we are invincible."[57] But the Young Napoleon's jubilation did not last the night. Lee could not know it, but his disastrous opening battle had actually planted the seeds for Confederate victory. During the darkness, after the initial elation had subsided, McClellan's fears gripped him again and compelled him to abandon his grand campaign to capture Richmond. He would spend the rest of the week trying to save his army from the Confederate hordes that existed only in McClellan's mind.

3

⸻∞⸻

Gaines Mill, June 27

The precise moment when McClellan abandoned his quest to capture Richmond came around 1:00 A.M. on June 27, when he ordered Porter to fall back to a new defensive position at Boatswain's Swamp, nearly four miles east of Beaver Dam Creek. Earlier in the evening, McClellan had sent upbeat telegrams to both his wife and Secretary Stanton, but after midnight he completely changed his tune. Scouts had reported to the general late that night that Jackson had not been the victim of the day's fighting, but was instead on his right flank, rendering Porter's current line indefensible. He would have to be pulled back to keep from being cut off. At that moment, McClellan had a decision to make: should he try to protect and maintain his supply line at White House—keeping alive the campaign to besiege Richmond—or should he change his base to the James River, abandoning the White House line and any hope of taking Richmond by using his beloved siege guns, which required the railroad line for their transport? Of course, a third option was available: McClellan could hold Jackson and his accomplices north of the Chickahominy River while launching an attack toward the city south of the river. Porter and other generals recommended this course of action to McClellan. Porter, seeing Lee's attack for the desperate gamble it must be, encouraged McClellan to send just a few more units north of the river to help him block the Confederates, and then attack with every bit of strength he had south of the river to capture Richmond. But that course of action required a bolder and more flexible-minded general than McClellan.

When McClellan left the V Corps headquarters that night, he had already decided to change his base, though he did not explicitly say as much to Porter. Instead, he impressed upon Porter "the absolute necessity of holding the ground, until arrangements over the river can be completed."[1] Porter later recalled that he thought McClellan was telling him he was going to attack Richmond even if the V Corps must be sacrificed to allow it. Believing he was being asked to act as Leonidas leading the Spartans at Thermopylae so that McClellan could launch the potential war-winning attack, Porter confidently assured McClellan: "I shall hold it to the last extremity."[2]

The reality, however, was that McClellan never contemplated the assault others urged on him. He persisted in his claim that he faced an overwhelming force and began planning to save his army. When he returned to the south side of the river, he informed his staff that the army was retreating, though he did not share that decision with his field generals. He ordered Porter to fall back to Boatswain's Swamp, in order to guard the four bridges crossing the Chickahominy and connecting his army. He knew it was too late to move all of Porter's corps across the river that night and it would be impossible to cross the river in the face of the expected Confederate attacks the next day. So, McClellan desired Porter to hold off the Confederate attacks for one more day and then retreat to the south side at night. McClellan would not be sending units north of the river to defend his supply line. He would abandon it and the hopes of pounding Richmond to rubble with his heavy guns. He ordered all the supplies that could be moved from White House to be loaded onto boats and transported to Harrison's Landing on the James River. The siege guns, of which only a few had been unloaded, were ordered back on the boats and removed as well. McClellan would not be retreating back down the peninsula from which he came, as Lee expected, but instead would take the shortest route cross country due south to camp at the James River, under the protection of the heavy guns of the navy's gunboats.

The beginning of the campaign was characterized by completely dichotomous interpretations by the opposing commanders. Lee had correctly read his opponent as being defensive and cautious. McClellan had completely misread Lee's audacity. Contrary to McClellan's earlier prediction, Lee had "venture[d] upon a bold movement on a large scale," and McClellan refused to do likewise, even though any offensive initiative on his part may have taken Richmond and perhaps ended the war. But that required a belief in reasonable and rational estimates of enemy strength. It is ironic that Lee's first battle, which had been a confused and colossal failure on par with Johnston's Seven Pines debacle, was all it took to drive

McClellan into a full-scale retreat. So much for McClellan preferring Lee to Johnston.[3]

* * *

The position to which Porter retreated was a formidable one. About four miles east of Beaver Dam Creek was another boggy stream, referred to in the local parlance as Boatswain's Swamp. It was a sluggish watercourse that offered a barrier to cross from the west or north. Behind the creek, the land rose in elevation to a plateau between 40 and 80 yards high and approximately a mile and a half wide. The plateau then fell off to the south to the Chickahominy River. On top of the plateau were three houses: on the northwest was the Watt house, one mile due east was the McGehee house, and completing the inverted triangle was the Adams house about equidistant from and south of them. Porter established his headquarters at the Watt House. The modest frame structure was the home of the 77-year-old widow Sarah Watt, her granddaughter, and a maid, and sat on a farm of several hundred acres with 28 slaves. When Porter claimed the house as his headquarters, the family was compelled to leave, with the elderly Sarah Watt having to be carried to a wagon by her slaves. She died in April 1863, never returning to see her house, which had been perforated by bullets and soaked with the blood of the wounded that were treated there.[4]

Locals referred to the plateau as Turkey Hill, and that's how it was listed on Confederate maps, but bizarrely (and reflecting the poor scouting) none of the Confederate maps showed Boatswain's Swamp with its close underbrush and tree-lined stream. Instead, Confederate maps, including the one used by Lee, only showed Powhite Creek (pronounced "pow-hite," not "po-white"), about half a mile west of Boatswain's. The farm of Dr. William Gaines was at the midpoint of Powhite Creek a mile and a half north of the Chickahominy, while his brick mill lay a mile further north. It was across his land that Lee expected to encounter McClellan's army, and since he was the largest landholder in the area, the Confederates still named the ensuing battle Gaines Mill, even though the actual fighting would take place over a mile southeast of it.

Porter established his defenses facing west and north. He placed the division of General George Morell (who had finished first in his West Point class of 1833) behind the swamp facing west and the division of General George Sykes (known as "Tardy George" in the old army because of his lack of aggressive instincts) facing north. Both were a few hundred yards in front of and wrapped around the Watt House, as Stephen Sears noted, "in the shape of an archer's bow a mile and three quarters long," with Sykes division extending to nearly a mile east of the Watt House.[5] They were arrayed in two lines, one near the swamp and another halfway up the slope, while artillery formed a third line at the crest of the plateau. Since McCall's division had done much of the fighting the day before, Porter had placed it in reserve on the crest of the plateau. Due to a shortage of axes, his men improvised a hasty bricolage of breastworks using fence rails, logs, and knapsacks. He had 17 batteries of artillery, totaling 96 guns, available to repel any attack, while General William Franklin's VI corps south of the river had three batteries of long-range guns able to disrupt any attack from the west. Porter could field nine brigades and a little more than 27,000 men to hold off whatever Lee threw against him. Unlike the day before, this time Lee was going to get nearly all of his 55,000 troops into the fight.[6]

The terrain was a mixture of open slopes and a thin belt of woods around the stream. In places, the woods were open enough that the sun would have shone on some Yankee troops, depending on their placement in the line. Because of the heavy rains in June, those soldiers who took the time to notice would have seen several mud channels where the rain had run off in winnows down the slopes to the swamp, which was a little higher than the sluggish stream barely two feet wide in normal weather. On the plateau, there was a scorching sun relieved only occasionally by a waft of wind, while down in the stagnant bottom one was lucky to get even a breath of a breeze. The open woods near the swamp were awash in the damp smell of deciduous leaves and tree stumps rotting on the forest floor. The high-pitched whine of gnats entering one's ear canal was ever present. The arrival of 27,000 Union troops would have scattered most of the wildlife, but not the insects that were unconcerned about the momentous nature of the events about to occur. As the soldiers waited in their positions, they were pestered by the flying and crawling bugs getting stuck in the sweat on their necks and arms. Anyone who walks the battlefield trail on a hot, muggy summer day can experience each of these blessings of nature.

Porter expected some reinforcements, and in fact some were on their way in the form of a division of Franklin's corps under the command of General Henry Slocum, a West Point graduate who had resigned to become a lawyer in his home state of New York before rejoining the army after the war began. However, as the head of Slocum's column reached the bridge to cross the Chickahominy, McClellan ordered them to stop and return to their previous position. Although McClellan knew an attack was coming north of the river, he was suddenly afraid of an impending attack south of the river as well. Beginning soon after daylight, reports started coming in to McClellan's headquarters from all four corps south of the river that the Confederates seemed to be preparing for an attack. In fact, McClellan had already convinced himself that this was likely and the morning warnings only confirmed his fears. Aerial reconnaissance, which should have dispelled these fears, only added to them. At 9:20 A.M., Thaddeus Lowe went aloft in his balloon and looked through the dense forest cover into Confederate lines below. In addition to being surprised to see a rival Confederate balloon up in the air, Lowe completely misread what he saw on the ground. He magnified the threat in a note to McClellan: "By appearances I should judge that the enemy might make an attack on our left at any moment."[7]

The fact is that all the Union commanders were hoodwinked by the energetic and theatrical Magruder. Magruder was very nervous and had not slept at all that night, fearing that at any moment McClellan would wake up to the fact that only a thin line of gray-clad soldiers blocked his path to Richmond. Lee's lack of success on June 26 and subsequent order to Magruder to "hold at all costs" had only increased Prince John's anxiety. Magruder loudly and ostentatiously shifted troops back and forth and created a commotion of shouted orders and drum beats to try to keep the enemy off-guard as long as possible. He succeeded beyond his wildest hopes. Thanks to Magruder's deception, McClellan spent the day paralyzed, waiting to see what Lee would do to him.

Lee had a very clear idea of what he wanted to do to McClellan's army, but it first required making up for all the mistakes of the previous day. The first thing he did, and something he should have done the afternoon before, was to send an aide to find the missing Jackson and bring his Valley forces to join the rest of Lee's army. Shortly after dawn, the Confederates noticed the Union forces had abandoned their line and immediately set in motion to follow them. Lee's offensive was a day behind schedule, but nevertheless could still be successful if all went according to his plan today.[8]

All would not go according to plan, quite simply because Lee's plan was wrong. Lee grossly misconstrued what McClellan intended to do. Lee believed that McClellan was going to fall back on his supply line and protect it against all hazards. When looking at his map, Lee determined that the best defensive position available was at Powhite Creek, three and a half miles east of Beaver Dam Creek, where the Gaines farm and mill stood. He rather unimaginatively expected McClellan to fight the exact same defensive plan as he had on June 26, lining his troops and artillery behind the creek facing west. As a result, he intended to do what Jackson's late arrival the day before had prevented—get around the Union army's right flank and come in behind the line, forcing Porter to retreat again. As he retreated, Longstreet and A.P. Hill would push him onto the waiting brigades and batteries of Jackson and D.H. Hill. Lee was sending Jackson and Hill to Old Cold Harbor, which he expected to be well beyond the Yankee flank. But Lee had not counted on McClellan's abandoning his base and his campaign so quickly. And he did not count on the very capable Porter hunkering down on high ground behind a swamp Lee did not even know existed. Hence, Lee was putting into operation a plan that was obsolete the moment he conceived it. He would have to revise his strategy in real time during the day.

The pursuing Confederates skirmished with some Union rearguard elements in the early daylight, but without much delay they began the pursuit in earnest along four roads that led eastward. D.H. Hill's division set out early from Mechanicsville northeast along the Old Church Road. He would follow the road about four miles before turning south at Bethesda Church and following a winding road another three miles to Old Cold Harbor, a tiny hamlet named after an inn for travelers. Along the way, he would cross in front of Jackson's army, which was headed south to Walnut Grove Church where it would turn east onto Old Cold Harbor Road and five miles later join D.H. Hill there. A.P. Hill's division marched over the gloomy battlefield of the day before and crossed over the bridge at Ellerson's Mill and followed Old Cold Harbor Road to the Walnut Church crossroads. Longstreet's division crossed the bridge after Hill's and turned off on to the River Road to the south, which ran parallel to the Chickahominy.

As A.P. Hill's troops marched to the Walnut Church intersection, where they were to turn right onto Telegraph Road heading southeast, they were greeted with artillery fire coming from their left, which wounded two men. It came from Jackson, who was finally making his presence known to the rest of the army by accidentally shooting his allies. Shortly after 10:00 A.M., Hill rode into the church yard and encountered Jackson arriving near the head of his column. Hill had only spoken with Jackson for a few minutes when Lee rode up. Hill greeted Lee, saluted, excused himself, and rode off down the Telegraph Road with his troops. Lee and Jackson dismounted and walked and talked in the shade of some cedar trees near the church. While Lee sat on a stump, Jackson stood in front of him with his dirty cadet cap in his hand. Lee went over the day's plan with his dilatory lieutenant. None of their staffs overheard what was said, but undoubtedly Lee was trying to make sure that Jackson knew exactly what was expected of him on this day, so as to avoid a repeat of Thursday's confusion. Jackson was to march his division to Old Cold Harbor, passing well beyond Gaines Mill. At 11:00 A.M., they concluded their conference and went their separate ways—Jackson northeast on his indirect route to Old Cold Harbor and Lee down the Telegraph Road to Selwyn, the home of local planter William Hogan, which he intended to use as his headquarters. After conferring there with A. P. Hill and Longstreet shortly before noon, Lee expected the battle to commence in less than an hour at Powhite Creek.[9]

In fact, shortly after noon, the first Confederate troops did encounter the main Union defensive line, but it was not A. P. Hill's troops and it was not where Lee envisioned. D. H. Hill had made good time marching his men to Old Cold Harbor. As he advanced two brigades south of that crossroads, maneuvering to get into the rear of Porter's troops, he encountered a line of Union troops facing north ready to receive him. These were the troops of Sykes's division and there was a personal interest to this meeting for both men, as Hill and "Tardy George" had been roommates at West Point in the 1840s. Hill brought up a battery of artillery to try to disperse the troops blocking his path, but that single battery ended up receiving far more punishment from enemy cannon than it meted out. Hill realized he was facing significant resistance that was not supposed to be there. Already there were problems with Lee's plan. Hill decided to fall back to Old Cold Harbor, deploy his forces, and wait for Jackson to arrive. It would, once again, turn out to be a lengthy wait.[10]

Lee was unaware of these developments because, thanks to some atmospheric acoustical anomaly, the sound of the cannons decimating D. H. Hill's battery never reached Selwyn, less than four miles away, and also because Hill never sent a messenger to Lee with the news that he was not beyond the enemy's flank. Instead, the first indication that Lee received that the Federal troops were not where he expected them to be came when the troops of A. P. Hill's lead brigade under General Maxcy Gregg encountered only slight opposition at Gaines Mill on Powhite Creek. When Gregg, a Mexican War veteran and South Carolina lawyer, forced a crossing of the bridge at the mill, the enemy skirmishers fell back and disappeared into the woods further east. As Gregg continued another three-fourths of a mile to New Cold Harbor, he faced his brigade south, where he saw evidence of Union troops. As he moved his troops quickly down the slope toward the heretofore unknown Boatswain's Swamp, his brigade came under heavy fire that broke their momentum and caused them to fall back. As Union artillery shells exploded among them from the plateau east of the Watt House beyond the mystery stream, Gregg rallied his men and reported to Lee that he had found the missing Union line. In fact, Gregg had wandered into the center of Porter's line, hitting the left of Sykes's division, east of the Watt House and nearly a mile west of where D. H. Hill had met the right portion of Sykes's line about an hour earlier.

From the Watt House, Porter had seen the Confederates advance against his center and right, and with his binoculars could see many more of A. P. Hill's troops arriving on the field. Turning his glasses to the left, he could see the dust clouds of Longstreet's men marching to the front. Realizing that the battle was about to get as hot as the day's temperature, he sent a message to McClellan at about 2:00 P.M. requesting Slocum's division, which had been denied to him earlier. McClellan granted the request, and within the hour Slocum's division was again on the march for Alexander's bridge. Of course, Porter was just asking for reinforcements necessary to fulfill his mission. Porter was rolling up his sleeves and preparing to hold the ground "to the last extremity" as he promised, while McClellan attacked south of the river.[11]

Rather than launching the crushing blow, McClellan was at the telegraph office of his headquarters at the Trent House in a completely defensive frame of mind. All the scattered reports from his generals and balloonists had convinced him that he would soon be attacked everywhere at once. He would never visit any of the lines to see the tactical situation for himself, but instead would cocoon himself at his headquarters hoping for the best and expecting the worst.

Lee was taking a very different tack from McClellan. When it became apparent that Porter was not at Powhite Creek, Lee left Selwyn and joined A. P. Hill's division as it groped for the enemy. When Gregg encountered Porter's line, Lee was at New Cold Harbor with A. P. Hill. Lee recognized that this new position was a very strong one, and he calculated that McClellan had decided to commit to one big battle at this location. He believed that McClellan had moved a majority of his army north of the Chickahominy to this position, so that Lee was facing the bulk of the Army of the Potomac. Lee decided to commit all of his nearly 55,000 troops to breaking this line and destroying the Union invaders. Once D. H. Hill and Jackson made their presence felt at Cold Harbor, he believed that McClellan would have to shift eastward to protect his supply lines making his defensive line vulnerable to a breakthrough.[12]

Of course, Lee was mistaken. This was not the bulk of McClellan's army, it was just one reinforced corps determined to hold its ground. If McClellan really had as many troops in the position as Lee thought, say 60,000 or so, then Lee's decision to attack seems foolhardy at best. Lee was going to have a difficult enough time breaking through Porter's line of fewer than 30,000 troops. If Porter had twice that number, as Lee assumed, the Seven

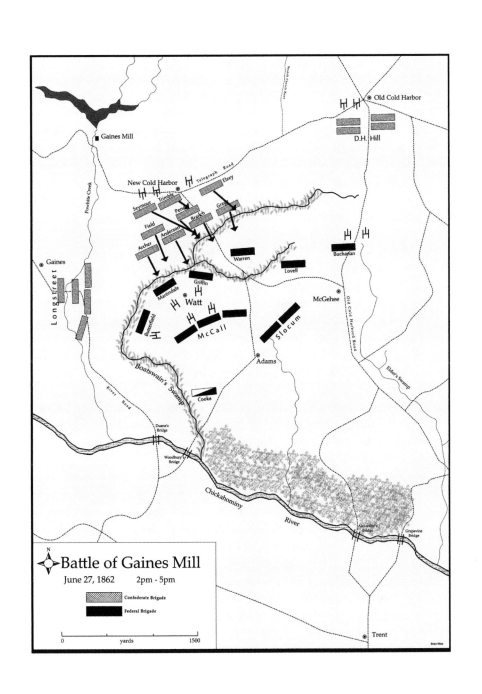

Gaines Mill

Old Cold Harbor

D.H. Hill

New Cold Harbor

Telegraph Road

Elzey

Seymour

Trimble

Pender

Branch

Gregg

Field

Anderson

Archer

Warren

Buchanan

Gaines

Lovell

Martindale

Griffin

Watt

McGehee

Longstreet

Butterfield

McCall

Slocum

Boatswain's Swamp

Adams

River Road

Cooke

Elder's Swamp

Old Cold Harbor Road

Duane's Bridge

Woodbury's Bridge

Chickahominy

River

Alexander's Bridge

Grapevine Bridge

Powhite Creek

Meadow Church Road

N

Battle of Gaines Mill

June 27, 1862   2pm - 5pm

Confederate Brigade

Federal Brigade

0   yards   1500

Trent

Brian Wise

Days' battles likely would have been the Three Days' battles, as much of Lee's army would have been butchered in the morass of Boatswain's Swamp. Luckily for the Army of Northern Virginia, Lee's interpretation of the tactical situation in front of him was flawed.

If Lee wanted to have the greatest possible chance of breaking the enemy line, he needed to utilize the principles of mass and concentration. Mighty barrages of artillery from several batteries simultaneously would be able to neutralize Union artillery and potentially blow holes in defensive lines, while a coordinated mass assault of his six infantry divisions all along the line would have the greatest effect. Neither of those things happened. The Confederates failed to mass their artillery; instead, they chose to send them into action one battery at a time as they came onto the field. Just like the day before, the batteries would be greatly outgunned and rendered largely ineffective while suffering heavy casualties. Similarly, a series of mistakes, poor communication, and the general fog of war would lead the Confederate infantry brigades to attack in a piecemeal fashion, with no sense of coordination until there was very little daylight left.

The attacks were not coordinated because Jackson was late again. Expecting Jackson and D. H. Hill to offer support at the sound of the fighting, Lee sent A. P. Hill into Boatswain Swamp to drive the forces from their position while there was still ample daylight left to accomplish his plan. Though there is some confusion among the commanders about the time of the assault, Hill was most likely correct when he said he ordered his men to attack at 2:30 P.M. Hill's men attacked in echelon as his brigades arrived on the field from east to west, which seems counterintuitive to Lee's plan to drive them east; but Gregg's brigade was farthest east when he encountered the line.

Now, we need to point out before we begin describing the battle that the timing of these disjointed attacks is hard to pinpoint precisely. Historians do not always agree on where specific units were located or when they entered the fight.[13] However, they all agree that Gregg's brigade was the first to venture back into the fray, grasping a toehold across Boatswain's Swamp, but was unable to push any further because of the intense fire. The fighting was so severe that the 1st South Carolina Rifles of Gregg's brigade suffered 315 casualties, the largest loss of the day for any one regiment. Hill's brigades were attacking in the strong center of Porter's position, curving around the Watt House. Gregg's attack was about three-fourths of a mile northeast of the Watt House. Overall, Hill's six brigades fought on more than a mile-long stretch of the swamp and, with only a few brief exceptions, failed to penetrate any part of the Union line. To quote E. Porter Alexander: "Every body else seemed to stand still &

let A. P. Hill's division . . . wreck itself in splendid, but vain & bloody, isolated assaults."[14]

Attacking to the right of and nearly simultaneously with Gregg was Branch's brigade. However, Branch sent his regiments in disjointedly—the 7th and 37th North Carolina regiments went in first, next to Gregg, receiving heavy fire. As they were forced to retreat, Branch then sent in his remaining three regiments, but they fared no better. As a testimony to the fierceness of the fight, the battle flag of the 7th North Carolina was riddled with 32 bullet holes and witnessed the death of four men, including the regiment's colonel, who carried it. As another regimental commander wrote of Branch's staggered attack and the enemy's stout defense: "Nothing but the thickness of the woods saved us from total destruction."[15]

To Branch's right came Joseph Anderson's brigade, without any artillery support. Anderson, along with two regiments of Field's brigade, launched three different charges that failed to get across the stream. To Anderson's right was James Archer's brigade. Archer had some artillery support as a battery opened behind his men, who lay in an apple orchard. The order to attack came after the attacks of Gregg, Branch, and Anderson had already passed their peak. Archer's men charged 500 yards through open fields down the slope to the stream, encountering a storm of lead. Showing remarkable courage the brigade managed to get within about 20 yards of the Union line before finally breaking and retreating, with one Alabama regiment leaving its colors behind to be captured by the enemy.[16]

Two of Hill's brigades were in support and not in the first line. Pender's brigade was behind Branch's brigade. As Branch's men retreated and took cover, Pender launched his attack (which was likely just a few minutes after Anderson began his attack). Pender's brigade benefited from the smoke and confusion of Branch's failed attack, and two regiments—the 16th and 22nd North Carolina—actually broke through Union lines ever so briefly before Union reinforcements drove them back, stopping the forward momentum of the brigade. They rallied in the swamp, but were unable to advance again in the face of renewed defensive fire. Pender's brigade was retreating as Archer's was advancing, and almost at the same time, between the two, Field's brigade, which had been at the rear of Anderson, launched its attack. Field fared no better than had Anderson or Archer, attacking three compact lines of Union defense just north of the Watt House. Field's retreat ended the first Confederate attack at Gaines Mill. It had lasted nearly two hours and had been conducted by A. P. Hill alone, which had not been Lee's intention. No coordinated attack occurred because Jackson did not arrive at the right place at the right time.

Jackson arrived nearly 90 minutes behind schedule because of a detour on his way to Cold Harbor. His guide, not being given any specific directions, was leading Jackson by the shortest route to Cold Harbor, but when firing was heard near Gaines Mill (as Gregg was forcing a crossing at the lightly defended Powhite Creek), Jackson told the guide that he was supposed to go well around that place. The guide said he would have if Jackson had said as much at the beginning of the march. Jackson was trying to get to the flank and not risk a fight in the wrong place, so he countermarched his units. Had he been in place earlier, the weight of his army may have allowed for a breakthrough. It certainly would have tied down the reinforcements that drove back Gregg and Pender's attack.

It became apparent quickly that Jackson was not on the flank of the Union and that no Yankees would be forced his way. Porter had committed to fighting and obviously, given the alignment of his forces, would only retreat south, not eastward. Lee finally recognized this and decided to keep the pressure on and break the Union army on the plateau that Porter was defending. If Lee could take the position in daylight, the Yankees would have a difficult time retreating across the river in the face of an attack, nor would a flight east help. Lee felt the success of the entire campaign hinged on driving McClellan's army off the hill, regardless of how many troops he had to overcome to do it.

A. P. Hill's attacks convinced Lee that McClellan was committed to fighting here. So, Lee sent messengers to both Longstreet and Jackson to bring their men into the fight. Longstreet was on the west side of Powhite Creek, waiting until he had orders to attack, but hoping he would not have to be used unless for pursuit. He was in the same position as A. P. Hill had been the day before at Beaver Dam Creek—looking across a boggy stream at a strong defensive line laced with artillery. A frontal assault by him would be a very difficult proposition, for as Longstreet later wrote, he was "in the position from which the enemy wished us to attack him."[17]

Word arrived from Lee in the late afternoon (Longstreet thought it was 5:00 P.M., though it was undoubtedly earlier) to create a diversion in his front. Longstreet immediately sent four of his six brigades across the Powhite Creek to the woods on the other side, from where they were to harass the Union forces. Between the two lines was a quarter mile of open fields before Boatswain's Swamp, which was particularly boggy in this section of the line. Some of Longstreet's brigades approached to within 100 yards of the Union line before stopping, hitting the ground, and exchanging fire with the enemy. In this contest of harassing fire, however, the Union troops delivered the stronger punch. The troops were New

York, Pennsylvania, and Michigan men of General Daniel Butterfield's brigade in Morell's division, and they had no fear of Longstreet's feint.

Not much time had passed before Longstreet received another note from Lee urging him to do something more. Longstreet determined to commit his entire division to an assault. He moved Richard Anderson's and James Kemper's brigades over Powhite Creek to support the brigades that had already crossed over. As Longstreet was preparing his assault, he saw part of Jackson's command to the north launching an attack over the route previously taken by A. P. Hill's troops. Longstreet decided to join that attack. This finally led to the day's first and reasonably concentrated mass attack all along the line. It was nearly 7:00 P.M. and daylight was fading fast.

The troops Longstreet saw were the brigades of Generals Evander M. Law and John Bell Hood from William H. Whiting's division, and their trek to the battlefield was a complicated story. Lee had sent an urgent message to Jackson—probably at the same time he had asked Longstreet for a diversion—calling for troops. The timing of these messages is difficult to determine exactly. Jackson probably arrived at Old Cold Harbor crossroads at 3:00 P.M. to rendezvous with D. H. Hill's division. Jackson was ahead of his last two divisions, which were strung out on the road behind him, and he had lost touch with Ewell's leading division. When Jackson arrived, he was perplexed by the situation. His orders—explained clearly and perhaps rather sternly to him by Lee only four hours earlier—had stated that Porter should be retreating across Jackson's front once he gave up the Powhite Creek line. However, Stonewall discovered Porter to be facing him with strong artillery support. Jackson could also hear the intense firing occurring less than a mile to the west, as A. P. Hill's brigades took on the center of the Union position. The Union troops obviously were not being driven, yet Jackson continued with his previous orders, as if the situation had not changed at all. He had received no new orders from Lee. He ordered D. H. Hill further to the east to be in a better position to attack an enemy that was never going to retreat across his front, and he sent a messenger back to hurry forward Whiting's and Winder's divisions to Cold Harbor, where he would arrange the brigades in line, building a bridge between the two Generals Hill. He then sent his chief engineer to report to Lee.

Unknown to Jackson was that Lee, wondering where Jackson was during his marching debacle, had sent his aide, Colonel Walter Taylor, to locate Jackson's men. Lee wanted to inform Jackson that the plan had changed and instead of attacking the flank, Lee needed Jackson's men to pitch in to break Porter's line. Jackson had ordered Ewell's men to take

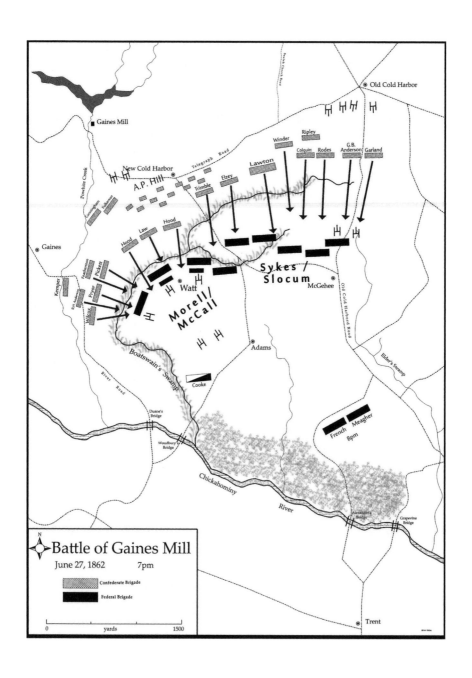

Battle of Gaines Mill

June 27, 1862   7pm

Old Cold Harbor

Gaines Mill

New Cold Harbor

Winder
Ripley
Colquitt
Rodes
G.B. Anderson
Garland

Lawton

Elzey

Trimble

A.P. H

Powhite Creek

Cunningham

Vickers

Hood
Law
Hood

Gaines

Kemper

Featherston

Pryor

Pickett

Wilcox

Rit Ander

Watt

Morell/
McCall

Sykes /
Slocum

McGehee

Old Cold Harbord Road

Adams

Elder's Swamp

Boatswain's Swamp

Cooke

River Road

Duane's
Bridge

French
Meagher
8pm

Woodbury
Bridge

Chickahominy

River

Alexander's
Bridge

Grapevine
Bridge

Confederate Brigade

Federal Brigade

0   yards   1500

Trent

Telegraph Road

Beulah Church Road, which went three-fourths of a mile up the Old Cold Harbor Road to intersect the Telegraph Road, roughly halfway between New and Old Cold Harbor. He intended to place Ewell in line to D. H. Hill's right, and probably felt this road would be more quick and efficient than following behind Hill's division on Old Cold Harbor Road. As Ewell was moving forward, he met Taylor who told Ewell to march a little faster and a little farther west to A. P. Hill's assistance.

At approximately 3:30 P.M., an hour or so into Hill's fight and about the time that Pender's men were falling back, Lee met Ewell on the Telegraph Road behind A. P. Hill's line. Lee instructed Ewell on where to put his three brigades into the fight, over almost exactly the same ground that Hill's division had trod. Lee also sent Ewell's staff officer, Major Campbell Brown, to locate the rest of Jackson's forces and bring them forward. Under Lee's personal direction, Ewell sent General Arnold Elzey's brigade into the woods east of the road from New Cold Harbor to the McGehee house and the brigades of General Isaac Trimble and General Richard Taylor (under command of Colonel Isaac Seymour because Taylor was ill) to the west of the road. Ewell's brigades ended up attacking one at a time and disconnected from each other. The nature of the terrain and the confusion of marching past huddled remnants of Hill's survivors undoubtedly played a role.

Apparently, Seymour's brigade attacked first, whereas a part of Trimble's and Elzey's brigades attacked later in a disconnected fashion, with some of their regiments getting lost in the woods and not even taking part in the eventual charge. In Seymour's brigade was the 1st Louisiana Special Battalion led by Major Roberdeau Wheat, a noted military adventurer who had served in several filibuster campaigns and fought with Giuseppe Garibaldi in Italy. They marched into the teeth of a Union line that had just been buttressed by reinforcements. Porter had ordered regiments from McCall's reserve division into the threatened zones; these troops had just arrived at the line when Seymour's troops neared the stream. A devastating fire killed Seymour, mortally wounded the indomitable Wheat, and even sent a bullet into Ewell's boot. The Louisianans wavered and retreated, giving the Union forces an excellent target into the flank of the part of Trimble's brigade that was advancing. It took heroic efforts by the regimental officers, the omnipresent Ewell, and even a private who mounted a riderless horse and rode up and down the line exhorting his comrades to rally and hold, to prevent a rout. Elzey's brigade, who had attacked Sykes's division, had not been able to do any more than Gregg had earlier over the same ground. Ewell's attack reached a stalemate around

5:00 P.M. His surviving troops remained intermingled with A. P. Hill's brigades from their earlier failed assault.[18]

Porter had been watching the fighting intently and was generally pleased with the results. When a messenger arrived from McClellan and asked how it was going, Porter gestured to the field and said, "See for yourself. We're holding our own, but it's getting hotter and hotter."[19] A few minutes after 4:00 P.M., as Ewell's attack was just getting started, Porter sent a telegram to his commander at the Trent House stating that all was well. The arrival of Slocum's 8,500-man division had eased his concern. But an hour later, after Ewell's attack had receded, Porter sent a less reassuring message to McClellan. He could see Longstreet's five brigades marshaling to the west and more troops arriving across his center, where Jackson's divisions were adding their weight to the fight. He already knew that D. H. Hill's division was on his right flank, though that sector was quiet at the moment. He began fearing the worst. His men had marched all morning and fought all afternoon. Many had exhausted the 60 rounds of ammunition they carried on their person and had rifle barrels too hot to load any longer. Porter also realized by this time that he was not holding on for McClellan's grand attack to the south, because there was no such attack. So, Porter sent an earnest call for reinforcements lest McClellan sacrifice the entire V Corps for no greater gain.

McClellan seemed genuinely surprised by Porter's 5:00 P.M. distress call. So concerned had he been all day with the impending attack south of the river that he had not investigated ways to assist Porter. If Porter really faced the 80,000 troops that he and McClellan both believed were opposing him, then it was expecting an awful lot to think that Porter's reinforced 35,000 men could hold on indefinitely. But McClellan, encouraged by Porter's cheerful 4:00 P.M. message, had written to the general: "If the enemy are retiring and you are a chasseur, pitch in." This was ludicrous if the odds were as bad as he feared. Throughout the day, McClellan had withdrawn into a shell of indecision, waiting to discover the outcome of the fight across the river before he made any further decisions for the army. He did not make any serious effort to gather further reinforcements for Porter, only bringing two brigades to headquarters by the evening when it would be too late to help Porter.[20]

* * *

While McClellan fretted and Porter held on by his fingernails, Lee was trying to get all of his units into the battle in order to break through the Union line before darkness put an end to this opportunity. After Ewell plunged into the fight, Jackson had sent for his remaining divisions to have them move down the Beulah Church Road and move in echelon from east to west (from D.H. to A.P. Hill) and engage the enemy. Jackson oddly chose to send his quartermaster, Major John Harmon, instead of a regular courier to convey these orders. When Harmon encountered General Whiting, whose division was first on the road, he bungled the orders so badly that Whiting chose to stay put until someone came with intelligible orders. Fortunately, he did not have long to wait. As Dabney saw Harmon ride off, he was convinced that Harmon would probably muddle the orders, so he waited only a few minutes before he personally rode to Whiting on his own initiative. When Whiting said he had not been able to understand the message that Harmon delivered, Dabney— demonstrating that perhaps he was not entirely useless as Jackson's chief of staff—filled him in on Jackson's true orders, and Whiting set his division in motion at once.

Whiting marched to the west in the direction of Gaines Mill. Whiting could not decide where to put his men in, for it looked as if the entire mile-long front needed help. Sometime after 5:00 P.M., Whiting met Lee on the Telegraph Road, and Lee told him where he wanted him to go: to the right of A.P. Hill's troops, toward the left center of the Union line. As Whiting put his brigades in line—Hood on the left and Law on the right—he ended up bridging much of the gap to Longstreet's force. Longstreet and Whiting would, coincidentally, attack at almost the same time.

After showing Whiting where he wanted him, Lee rode east behind the lines, surveying the situation. There was not much time left before darkness. Somewhere near the Beulah Church Road intersection with the Telegraph Road, Lee met Jackson and greeted him with a mild rebuke: "Ah, General, I am very glad to see you. I had hoped to be with you before." Jackson mumbled some reply and Lee did not continue his reprimand for Jackson's tardiness; there was too much to do. "That fire is very heavy," he said. "Do you think your men can stand it?" Stonewall replied with bravado and liveliness: "They can stand almost anything! They can stand that." After discussing some troop dispositions and the urgency of a strong attack, the two men separated, Lee to go back to New Cold Harbor and Jackson to Old Cold Harbor. The meeting with Lee apparently lit a fire under the lethargic Jackson. Several aides commented on how Jackson seemed more animated and energetic than he had all day. He sent orders to his commanders over on the east side to press the attack. Jackson sent one aide with the stern message: "Tell them this thing had hung in the balance too long; sweep the field with the bayonet." For all this grand talk, however, Jackson's role in the final attack was basically superfluous. He did not personally place any of his divisions (Lee had placed Ewell's and

Whiting's himself), and his order to sweep the field was sent only after the attack had already started. Perhaps his greatest contribution to the fight was a negative one, restraining D. H. Hill from entering the fight earlier, when he could have relieved some of the pressure on A. P. Hill's attack. Once again, it was not Jackson's finest performance.[21]

Nevertheless, the day was setting up for the climactic assault. Longstreet and Whiting were on the right while A. P. Hill's and Ewell's men were in the center. D. H. Hill was on the far left, preparing to attack. Filing in between D. H. Hill and Ewell was Jackson's last division, under the command of Winder. On the march from Beulah Church Road, Winder got separated from Whiting. In the confusion, two of Winder's brigades followed Whiting (and ended up as a reserve force behind Whiting and Longstreet) while Winder led his own and Lawton's large brigade to the left near where Ewell had gone in. Ewell even helped position Lawton's men for the final attack as they arrived on the field.

As late evening approached, Lee had scrabbled together his army in a confused, makeshift manner, but finally had a strong order of battle. D. H. Hill had started his advance shortly after 5:00 P.M., but had made little headway thus far. Longstreet had begun his diversion around the same time, before he ordered a full assault at 7:00 P.M., D. H. Hill's and Longstreet's efforts had tied down many enemy troops, making the center susceptible to strong thrusts. A. P. Hill's six brigades and one of Ewell's brigades (Seymour's) were too badly beaten up to participate, but from D. H. Hill to Longstreet, Lee had approximately 32,000 troops in a nearly continuous line more than two miles long, ready to bring pressure on the Union line all at once. The charge would not be flawless. It jerked into motion and had ebbs and flows, entanglements, and confusion, but it finally had the semblance of the mass, concentration, and coordination that Lee had been seeking all afternoon. Lee believed that nothing less than the outcome of the battle for Richmond hung in the balance. It was going to be a very tense twilight for the Confederate commander.

* * *

On the south side of Boatswain's Swamp, the situation was every bit as tense for Porter. Although he had roughly an equal number of men to oppose Lee's final attack (Sears even suggests that Porter had 34,000 men), many of them had been under rifle and artillery fire for nearly five hours. Despite Porter's call for help at 5:00 P.M., no more reinforcements had arrived since Slocum's division crossed Alexander's Bridge earlier in the day. Porter had inserted nearly every available man into the firing line to plug gaps or relieve exhausted troops. If there was a breakthrough anywhere on the line, it could be catastrophic, for it was unlikely to be contained quickly, if at all. Adding to the difficulty, Porter had inserted McCall's and Slocum's regiments individually throughout the line, wherever aid was needed at that moment. As a result, the division and brigade commanders would not be able to organize or exert control of their units during a breakthrough. It would be every regimental commander for himself. Porter had not had the luxury of pulling whole brigades out of line and replacing them, because the Confederate pressure had been too great throughout the day.[22]

From his right, Porter could count on Sykes's division of regulars, in the brigades of Colonel Robert C. Buchanan, Major Charles S. Lovell, and Colonel Gouverneur K. Warren, with supplemental help from Colonel Joseph J. Bartlett's brigade of Slocum's division. These men would face the attack by D. H. Hill's five brigades, along with Winder's brigade, Lawton's brigade, and two brigades of Ewell's division, which had mustered for a second attack. To Sykes's left was Morell's division of General Charles Griffin's, General John Martindale's, and General Daniel Butterfield's brigades, who were supplemented with units from McCall's and Slocum's divisions. They fronted the Watt House plateau in a crescent three-quarters of a mile long and would face the onslaught of seven brigades from Whiting's and Longstreet's divisions. While Butterfield's section on the far left had been relatively quiet, Martindale and Griffin had already faced A. P. Hill's multiple tenacious assaults and had been under long-range fire continuously ever since. Whiting's division would test their ability to endure and hold on. As 7:00 P.M. approached and the yelling and firing grew into a continuous roar, everyone knew that this was the final stand of the day. The possible survival of the Army of the Potomac depended on it.

Those looking to find the precise moment that the charge began will be disappointed. No officer blew a whistle that sent 32,000 screaming rebels forward. What came to be the final charge was really just the continuation of the constant attacks throughout the day. As Ewell's attack flamed out after 5:00 P.M. and Whiting and Winder were struggling through the woods to get into position, D. H. Hill launched a fairly limited and slow-developing attack on the far left, with one brigade east of the road past the McGehee house. His pace was slow, as he tried to eradicate a battery on his left flank that had been tearing holes in his line all day. He fought over this position for quite some time, with the rest of his division only advancing slowly and getting tangled up and hopelessly confused in the thick woods near the head of the swamp. Some of his brigades wound up behind others and Ripley's brigade never got into the fight at all. Although

Hill did not advance very far in more than an hour of fighting, he did tie down much of Sykes's division.

At the same time that D. H. Hill was gingerly beginning his advance, Longstreet, at the other end of the line, was beginning his diversion in which four of his brigades approached within 100 yards of the Union line and exchanged shots. After nearly an hour of this, Longstreet received an order from Lee to do more. He brought over a fifth brigade in order to launch an attack. At this time, he met Whiting and coordinated their assault, which began around 7:00 p.m., after Longstreet had engaged the soldiers of Butterfield's brigade for nearly two hours.[23] Between these two flanks, Winder's and Lawton's brigades had entered the line on D. H. Hill's right and in the same location that Ewell had attacked two hours earlier. Winder and Lawton probably began their attack around 6:00 p.m., after D. H. Hill but before Whiting. Two of Ewell's brigades, under Elzey and Trimble, joined forces with Winder and Lawton's fresh brigades, providing support for their attack. These combined assaults pressed Sykes's division to the breaking point.

D. H. Hill's division pressed the U.S. regulars under Sykes back very slowly. They fell back to the McGehee house where the fighting ebbed back and forth, as Confederates would drive off Sykes's men before being driven back themselves by determined counterattacks. In this fierce fighting, the 20th North Carolina regiment of General Samuel Garland's brigade suffered 272 casualties—40 percent of its force—in its first ever combat action. The fighting was so intense that it seemed that anyone upright could not live. One New York soldier recalled, "The air at this time was too full of lead for standing room."[24]

As the fighting raged around the McGehee house, Lawton's brigade entered the fight about 400 yards to the west of Hill. Lawton, an 1839 West Point graduate who had resigned from the army to practice law and politics in Georgia, led the largest brigade (3,600 men) in Lee's army into its first combat on this day. They hit the woods behind Ewell's line as that general was still trying to rally his division from its failed attack. When Ewell saw Lawton's brigade forming into line, he couldn't contain his excitement and shouted, "Hurrah for Georgia!," and helped maneuver the green brigade into line. Lawton's troops charged and managed to push back the Union line with the sheer weight of their numbers. After a struggle of nearly an hour, they crossed the stream and pushed onto the plateau on the Union side. The Union line fell back and reformed. Lawton paused to regroup his own men who, he said, were "disunited by the smoke, dust, and confusion of the battlefield."[25] He also could not tell friend from foe in the dimming light, and was being shot at by both sides. Winder's brigade came into position between Lawton's enthusiastic troops and D. H. Hill's hard-slogging soldiers, who had been fighting for mere yards for nearly two hours. As Winder pushed forward to come up with Lawton across the stream, Elzey's and Trimble's remaining soldiers joined him, sensing the moment of victory may be at hand. It was probably around this time that Jackson's message to "sweep the field with the bayonet" reached his commanders.

As Lawton's men were pushing across the stream and pausing to regroup, Longstreet and Whiting launched their coordinated attack. Longstreet's men crossed the 400 yards of open field to get to the swamp. One soldier in General Cadmus Wilcox's Alabama brigade declared that they came under "such a perfect storm of lead right in our faces that the whole brigade literally *staggered* backwards several paces as though pushed by a tornado."[26] Longstreet's brigades stumbled down to the swamp, but continued pushing forward despite the severe toll it was taking. Longstreet's five brigades would lose more than 2,000 men on this day, the vast majority occurring during this dusk charge.

While Longstreet's men charged toward the Union position of Butterfield's relatively fresh troops, Whiting's two-brigade division attacked over well-trodden ground against Union soldiers who were weary from fighting off A. P. Hill's brigades earlier in the day. Shortly before the advance began, while artillery shells fell all around them, Lee rode across the lines to General Hood and explained the situation and the enemy's position. "This must be done," Lee said emphatically and then asked, "Can you break this line?" Hood replied simply, "I will try."[27] Whiting then ordered Law and Hood to advance their brigades rapidly toward the Union position without pausing to fire. He knew that the mass of men had to close the distance quickly if they were to have a chance. Law wrote later that "had these orders not been strictly obeyed, the assault would have been a failure. No troops could have stood long under the withering storm of lead and iron that beat into their faces." They still suffered nearly 1,000 casualties during the double-quick rush.[28]

As the attack began, Hood saw a gap forming between Law's brigade and Longstreet's line, so he personally led two regiments—his old 4th Texas and the 18th Georgia—behind Law's brigade to come up on his right flank and bridge this gap. On foot, Hood led the men into this valley of death at the quickstep, shouting, "Steady, steady, I don't want you to run," as the Yankee fire began to take down comrades on every side.[29] Not a soldier returned fire, and they moved forward at a trot. Law later recalled, "Men fell like leaves in an autumn wind, the Federal artillery tore gaps in the ranks at every stage."[30] Once they got within 100 yards of the stream, Hood shouted for the charge. Hood's men raised the rebel yell and crashed into the Union's first line at about the same time that Longstreet's men splashed through the stream, also yelling at the top of their lungs. These seven brigades of screaming men "sounded like forty thousand wildcats," one of Longstreet's men remembered.[31]

After hours of constant fighting, the Confederates finally broke through the Union position. The men of Martindale's brigade, unable to stem the tide of humanity, broke first and raced up the hill when the Confederates got within 10 paces of their line. Though he had been a New York district attorney, none of Martindale's oratorical efforts or arguments could persuade his men to halt. As they retreated, they carried the second line with them. Hood's men now loosed the volley they had been saving, causing enormous damage to the retreating foe. Longstreet's men, especially those under Cadmus Wilcox, broke through Butterfield's lines at almost exactly the same moment. In fact, after the war, Hood would admit to Wilcox that his men had probably reached the Union artillery on the crest before Hood's men, suggesting that Wilcox's breakthrough may have occurred moments before Hood's.[32]

In actuality, it is impossible to know which troops broke the Union line first, though that did not deter the rivals from claiming credit. D.H. Hill was able to finally force the depleted Union troops of Sykes's division to retreat from the McGehee house position. He later admitted, "I have always believed this the first break in the Federal line."[33] Many thought one of Longstreet's brigades had punctured the Union line first, while the men of Lawton's brigade had reason to believe that their initial push across the stream had led to the unraveling of the line. But the simple truth is that the Union line broke nearly simultaneously across the two-mile front. Porter was unable to seal the crack in any one place, because there were too many local crises erupting at once and he had no reserves remaining.

Once the Union retreat began, it did not manifest itself the same way all over the field. Some units fell back grudgingly and in good order, while others panicked and fled in haste across the plateau's fields toward the river. Sykes's division conducted a fighting retreat that kept their pursuers in check until it was too dark to pursue further. However, other units fled so quickly that their neighbors were cut off. Two regiments of General George Taylor's brigade of Slocum's division were completely surrounded and captured (nearly 1,000 men), and large pockets of men all along the line, particularly on the Union left at the site of Hood's breakthrough, suffered a similar fate.[34]

Once they sent the infantry retreating, Confederate troops went after the artillery that had peppered them with shells all afternoon. Sitting at the top of the rise, the Union artillery switched to canister as the Confederate infantry came within point-blank range. In some places, the artillery could not fire because the Confederate and Union soldiers were too intermingled. In others, cannons got off shots, but could not hold back an infantry assault without support from its own infantry, and despite the oaths, curses, and pleadings of several officers, few Yankee infantry were willing to remain on the field to cover the withdrawal of the artillery. Confederates picked off many of the cannoneers and their horses to inhibit the artillery's retreat. Across the length of the Union line, 10 of these frontline artillery pieces were abandoned. Porter also had several batteries of reserve artillery south and east of the Watt House. These became the next targets of the Confederates in the chaos of retreat and the rapidly fading light.

As the disjointed rebel line approached this last stand of Porter's artillery, an unusual event happened. General Philip St. George Cooke, Porter's cavalry commander, decided to take matters into his own hands. He had been stationed on the far left, guarding the flank where Boatswain's Swamp met the Chickahominy River. A few minutes after 8:00 P.M., when he saw the Rebels nearing the reserve artillery, Cooke galloped his force toward the artillery well south of the Watt House—in Confederate hands by this time—and launched an unauthorized cavalry attack on the approaching Southern troops. About 250 cavalrymen drew their sabers and in a quixotic attack, reminiscent of the British cavalry's hopeless Charge of the Light Brigade in the Crimean War, rode into their own valley of death, charging past their own artillery to the Confederate infantry a couple of hundred yards beyond. They charged Longstreet's troops, who quickly formed into line, fired a volley, and unhorsed about six dozen troopers. The remaining horsemen wheeled about and retreated back through their artillery, creating so much confusion that it hampered efforts of the cannoneers to limber up the guns and retreat. In the ensuing chaos, nine more cannon had to be abandoned by Porter's men. One infantry corporal in Wilcox's brigade wrote of the ill-fated cavalry charge: "[We] taught them a lesson that when infantry are fighting they should keep out of the way."[35] Trying to save face after his defeat, Porter wrote that this foolish cavalry charge was the sole reason for the defeat, which was preposterous. Other than costing the lives of more than 50 horsemen and as many horses, the charge did not materially alter the circumstances. Porter's corps was defeated and retreating in a flood back to the bridges across the Chickahominy River.

The outcome could have been much worse for Porter if the final Confederate charge had not come so late in the day. His greatest accomplishment was holding out just long enough for darkness to prevent a complete rout. By doing so, he left too little time for Lee to exploit the breakthrough. Of course, if Lee could have managed to concentrate his infantry and artillery to launch a coordinated assault even one or two hours earlier, he could have gained a much more significant victory. Porter was not getting any more substantial reinforcements. Only two brigades of Sumner's corps were sent by McClellan late in the day, and they did not arrive until nearly 8:00 P.M., and had to force their way through the retreating Union troops in order to provide support against any possible attacks.

To recap the Confederate attacks: A. P. Hill fought alone from 2:30 to around 4:30 P.M.; Ewell fought from 4:00 to a few minutes after 5:00 P.M.; D. H. Hill from 5:00 to 8:00 P.M.; Longstreet began his demonstration shortly after 5:00 P.M., but did not launch his full-scale assault until 7:00 P.M.; Whiting sent Hood and Law forward at 7:00 P.M. in conjunction with Longstreet; Lawton attacked sometime around 6:00 P.M., while Winder attacked sometime after 6:00 P.M. D. H. Hill pushed past the McGehee house at 7:30 P.M., just a few minutes after Lawton had paused on the Union side of the stream. Wilcox and Hood broke through the left of the Union line at 7:30 P.M. If Hood had breached the line at 6:30 instead of 7:30 P.M., much could have been gained in the remaining two hours of daylight. Stephen Sears even argues (unpersuasively) that the attack could have happened three or four hours earlier if not for Jackson's march mishaps.[36] Three brigades had not participated in the fight. General James Kemper's brigade was deliberately kept in reserve by Longstreet, and Colonel Samuel Fulkerson's and Lieutenant Colonel R. H. Cunningham's brigades of Winder's division had gotten lost in the woods and accidentally ended up in reserve behind Whiting's division. They could have been used to exploit the breakthrough. Two hours would have also allowed plenty of time for Lee to send artillery forward along the roads to the Watt and McGehee houses, from which they could have lobbed shells into the Union troops crowding the roads leading to the Alexander and Grapevine bridges, slaughtering many more Union soldiers as well as increasing the panic and demoralization. A dusk attack on the flanks of the two recently arrived brigades serving as Porter's rear guard could possibly have sealed what Lee most desired—the destruction of a substantial part of McClellan's army. This did not happen, of course, and Lee had to settle for his more limited and costly victory.

Ultimately, the Confederate victory honors went to Hood's brigade, specifically his 4th Texas regiment, for breaking through Porter's line. He became a Southern hero as a result and earned an outsized reputation as one of Lee's toughest fighters—a man who could seemingly do the impossible. But there was plenty of glory to spread around, just as there were plenty of casualties for all. Whiting would lose more than 1,000 men in the final charge; A. P. Hill lost more than 2,000 soldiers in his fruitless afternoon attacks; Longstreet would lose 2,000 men for his part; and D. H. Hill, Ewell, Winder, and Lawton would account for nearly 4,000 casualties between them. Though Lee had finally claimed his first victory, the cost in blood was inordinately expensive.[37]

Lee had initially misread his opponent's intentions, but he had adapted quickly once he realized where the enemy was. Though better than the day before, communications with his subordinates was still spotty. D. H. Hill did not report to Lee the situation on the left, even though he learned that Porter was drawn up to give battle as early as 1:00 P.M., well before Lee had A. P. Hill launch his attacks. Jackson was late again because he got delayed by a 90-minute march detour, which brought his divisions to the front much later than Lee had desired. Lee frequently took direct command of Jackson's troops without consulting that officer.

Jackson performed poorly again. The perceptive but critical E. Porter Alexander argued that "had Jackson attacked when he first arrived, or during A. P. Hill's attack, we would have had an easy victory."[38] Stonewall was probably not only flummoxed by his misguided march, but also seemed unsure of how to exercise judgment on the battlefield when he was under Lee's command. He arrived at the front at 3:00 P.M., but seemed unable to grasp what was happening and showed a dogged determination to stick to Lee's original orders, even when it became obvious that they no longer applied because there was no Union flank to attack. D. H. Hill thought Jackson should have sent his divisions farther to the east to try to flank Porter's position. Instead, each of Jackson's divisions came on the field and went into battle with very little, and often not any, direction from Jackson himself.[39]

It took Lee a long time to mass his troops, even after he realized how the situation had changed. He sent A. P. Hill's division into an attack because he assumed that Jackson and D. H. Hill would be in place and follow the lead, but he did not seek out Jackson until after A. P. Hill was fully committed. Given his confusion the day before, Lee could have sent his trusted aide, Walter Taylor, to make sure Jackson and D. H. Hill were in line and ready before beginning the first assaults. Yet, despite his difficulties, Lee's personal control of the battle managed to get a massed and loosely coordinated assault to occur in the late evening, just in time to drive the enemy from the field. Lee maintained a tighter leash on his division commanders, which was already an improvement from the debacle at Beaver Dam Creek 24 hours earlier.

Lee's Union counterpart does not get a similar passing grade for his day's actions. McClellan left everything to Porter, who did the best he could with what he had and fulfilled McClellan's desire that he hold out north of the river for one more day, even though it cost him nearly 7,000 casualties to do so. But McClellan never launched or even contemplated an attack south of the river as Porter had expected. Unlike Lee, who abandoned his headquarters at Selwyn after only half an hour in order to direct events from the field, McClellan never left his headquarters at the Trent House unless it was to answer the call of nature. Little Mac did not take charge at the front because he expected attacks everywhere; he never visited any of his lines. If he had, perhaps he would have seen through Magruder's ruse that fooled his lieutenants, though even that was doubtful. Magruder represented, in McClellan's mind, the vanguard of about 120,000 men. McClellan was committed to the defensive, but he was slow and stingy with reinforcements for Porter even though he suspected Porter was going to be attacked by overwhelming force. When word came that night that Porter was defeated and would have to cross the bridges under cover of darkness, McClellan took it hard and became despondent. He also became bitter, convinced that he was in this position because the government had not heeded his repeated calls for more troops.

Sometime between 9:00 and 11:00 P.M. that night, McClellan gathered his corps commanders together, except Keyes, whom he had already ordered to begin retreating through White Oak Swamp. McClellan acted as if he was considering leading a great assault across the Chickahominy where Porter had fought, but it was just that—an act. In fact, he had already committed to retreat (and had told his staff as much the night before), but McClellan tried to make himself look like the aggressive commander, purely as theater for his corps leaders. He painted the consequences of defeat in such dire terms that his corps commanders urged him not to risk it, but to save the army instead. In this way, McClellan cleverly was able to get his generals to recommend the plan that he had already conceived, only now they could claim ownership of it and would not feel constrained at his orders to retreat. McClellan, of course, though feigning a reluctance to concede, ultimately agreed with their decision and dismissed the generals.[40]

Not all of McClellan's officers were satisfied with the decision to retreat. When III Corps commander Samuel Heintzelman informed his division commanders Phil Kearny and Joseph Hooker of the decision, they insisted on talking to McClellan to try to persuade him to launch an attack toward Richmond instead. The day-long feint of Magruder had finally convinced them that there was no substance behind Prince John's theatrics. Telling McClellan that the enemy lines were thin and "must be broken," the outspoken Kearny angrily denounced McClellan's decision: "An order to retreat is wrong! Wrong sir! I ask permission to attack Magruder at once." McClellan, tired and piqued at having a division commander question his judgment, tersely responded, "Denied!" When Kearny—who had lost his left arm in the Mexican War and was referred to by General Winfield Scott as "the bravest man I ever knew"—suggested an attack could be successful if led by just two divisions, McClellan stood firm and ordered the retreat to continue as ordered. At this point, the hard-fighting, straight-talking New Yorker verbally ripped his commander for all to hear. One of his generals recorded: "Phil unloosed a broadside. He pitched into McClellan with language so strong that all who heard it expected he would be placed under arrest." He was not and the retreat would continue. Not long after this exchange, at about 12:20 A.M., McClellan returned to his telegraph office to send perhaps the war's most notorious telegram to Stanton.[41]

McClellan was in an angry and maudlin mood. The strain of the day had so affected him that he was convinced that he had been attacked by superior forces on both sides of the river. He wrote a long, melancholic, and accusative telegram: "I have lost this battle because my force was too small. I again repeat that I am not responsible for this." He further lamented, "I feel too earnestly tonight—I have seen too many dead & wounded comrades to feel otherwise than that the Govt has not sustained this Army." He concluded with the startling lines: "If I save this Army now I tell you plainly that I owe no thanks to you or any other persons in Washington—you have done your best to sacrifice this Army." Lest we think that McClellan hit the "send" button before he carefully considered it, he wrote to his wife: "they will never forgive me for that . . . I knew it when I wrote it; but as I thought it was possible that it might be the last I ever wrote, it seemed better to have it exactly true." Indeed, the telegram's final sentence was rank insubordination, and perhaps the only reason that Lincoln did not relieve McClellan of command was because Lincoln never read it. The telegraph office clerk in the War Department was so stunned by the intemperate declaration that he cut it from the transcription before giving it to the secretary of war.[42]

After news of the defeat, Lincoln wrote to McClellan to "save your army at all events" and promised to send reinforcements. Shortly after that message was transmitted, Confederate cavalry cut the telegraph lines. For many hours, there was no news in Washington from the peninsula and the city was on edge. In Richmond, there was much excitement as word came of a great victory north of the river. Many anticipated that Lee was going to destroy McClellan's army. Lee was certainly hopeful of doing so. He had not accomplished as much as he had hoped on June 27, but it was a victory nevertheless, and it boosted the spirits of the army, the city, the country, and not inconsequentially of Lee himself.[43]

George B. McClellan (Library of Congress).

Robert E. Lee (Library of Congress).

Alfred R. Waud sketch of a Confederate attack at the battle of Gaines Mill, June 27 (Library of Congress).

Image based on a Waud sketch of the Union side of battlefield at Savage Station, June 29. An ordnance train is detonated in the distance by Union soldiers (Library of Congress).

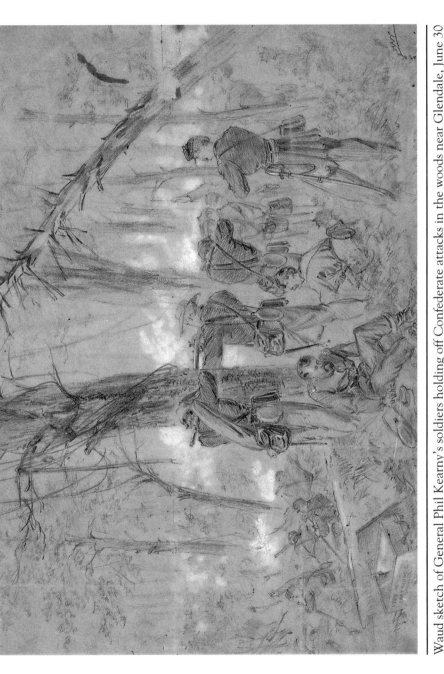

Waud sketch of General Phil Kearny's soldiers holding off Confederate attacks in the woods near Glendale, June 30 (Library of Congress).

Waud sketch of Union artillery firing on advancing Confederate lines at the battle of Malvern Hill, July 1 (Library of Congress).

Political cartoon during McClellan's 1864 presidential campaign ridiculing his performance at the battle of Malvern Hill. McClellan's opponents accused him of cowardice during the battle (Library of Congress).

4

⁓∞∞⁓

From the Chickahominy to the James, June 28–29

Though June 27 had been a long day, it was an even longer night for men on both sides. The tired Union troops under Porter spent the dark hours of the night crossing the Chickahominy River, knowing that to still be on the north side at dawn would mean destruction or capture. Still, some were just too exhausted to march and were captured the next morning. One of that number was General John F. Reynolds, a well-respected Pennsylvania officer and brigade commander in McCall's division, who fell asleep under a tree during the slow withdrawal and slept so soundly that he only awakened after daylight surrounded by Confederate troops, much to his mortification. When he was led through Richmond with other prisoners, he was confronted by a Southern acquaintance who jocularly taunted him: "General, this is in accordance with McClellan's prediction; you are in Richmond." In a dark mood, Reynolds retorted, "Yes, sir . . . and d—n me, if it is not precisely in the manner I anticipated."[1] For the surviving Yankee soldiers left behind—haunted by what they had seen and experienced, thirsty, hungry, caked with black powder, and soaked through with sweat, which was not relieved by the night's high humidity level—the morning's march was a dispiriting trudge over the narrow bridges. In the darkness, three separate artillery pieces missed their hold on the bridges and pitched over the side into the river below. There was no time to retrieve them, and the V Corps moved on, having officially lost 22 cannons on the day—19 to the Confederates and 3 to the Chickahominy.

Before the sun broke through the muggy mist on the morning of June 28, the V Corps commander had successfully extracted all of his units and destroyed the bridges, but there was still a much longer trek ahead for these troops. The James River was 15 miles away as the crow flies, but there was no road that led directly to it, and the men were not going to be able to harness the crows to carry them there. It would be a circuitous march for far more troops than Porter's roughly 29,000 men who emerged from the battle alive. McClellan was going to have to move 100,000 soldiers, more than 300 pieces of artillery (which included 26 heavy siege guns that had already been brought forward), nearly 4,000 wagons, tens of thousands of horses, and 2,500 cattle. It was going to be a torturous and slow journey for many reasons, one of them being that the cattle and horses, which were generally in the vanguard, chewed up the dirt roads with their hooves and left behind thousands of unwelcome and noxious "pies" in the road for the following soldiers to shuffle through. The ensuing rains would turn the roads into soupy, stinking streams of muddy manure. It is no wonder that rates of illness rose dramatically during the Seven Days' campaign.[2]

McClellan had sent engineers the previous day into White Oak Swamp to find the best path through that dense and tangled area. They had to rebuild the bridges they had destroyed weeks earlier to prevent any flank attack from the south. By 7:00 A.M. on June 28, the White Oak Swamp Bridge was rebuilt and the lead troops of General Keyes's IV Corps were crossing it soon after on their way south. A few hours later, a second bridge had been completed at Brackett's Ford, one and a half miles upstream (to the west), allowing more of Keyes's corps to cross and putting the supply train of cattle and wagons in motion. As Stephen Sears points out, for all his claims of the efficiency of the change of base, McClellan's retreat was actually surprisingly inefficient for a former engineer who prided himself on his organizational ability. McClellan did not have the routes scouted, resulting in the entire army crowding on the same road when multiple others were available (and some alternate routes were discovered quite by accident), and he did not organize the march effectively. As a result, the troops were constantly starting and stopping—a long, halting, wearying hike through the eastern Virginia swamps. Though crossing the Chickahominy River had bought him some time—it would be nearly 24 hours before Lee finally divined where McClellan was heading and began pursuing—Little Mac wasted nearly all of his advantage by mismanaging the march. This set up the specter of several more battles, in which the Federal army would have to hold off furious Confederate attacks before it reached the safe shelter of the gunboats on the James River.[3]

For the Confederates, the night of June 27 was somber and bittersweet. Though elated over their hard-earned victory, they were wiped out by the effort and haunted by the remains of that bloody fight. Not only were there nearly 2,400 dead bodies on the grounds, but also there were approximately 9,000 wounded of both armies scattered all over the swamps and fields. The groans, plaintive calls for help, and pitiful cries for mothers echoed throughout the dark landscape. A. N. Erskine of the 4th Texas wrote, "In going round the battlefield with a candle searching for friends I could hear on all sides the dreadful groans of the wounded and their heart piercing cries for water . . . May I never see any more such in life."[4] The living offered succor to the wounded, while thousands were carried to makeshift hospitals where the surgeons spent all night sawing off shattered limbs by lamplight. Dawn may have brought more light to see, but it did not stop the flood of bodies coming in.

With daylight, many participants ventured over the ground of the battlefield and marveled that anyone could have survived. The lines of bodies, gruesome final poses of the dead, and the ripped and mangled trees, shredded and stripped bare of bark, all bearing the scars of the lead that sliced through the air for nearly six hours, gave many soldiers pause to reflect on the mysterious workings of a divine being that allowed them to see another sunrise. When Stonewall Jackson rode over the ground that Hood's men had crossed and up the hill where they had broken the Union position, he was impressed. "The men who carried this position were soldiers indeed," he admiringly remarked.[5]

It was only on the morning of June 28 that Lee learned that he had not faced the majority of McClellan's army as he had presumed. When Jackson questioned a prisoner as to who the opponent was, he was surprised to learn it was only one corps plus one division; in fact, so surprised that he angrily dismissed the information at first as a lie.[6] Much of that day would be spent tending to the wounded and burying the dead. There were so many dead that not even the Confederate corpses (of which there were nearly 1,500) could expect a decent burial. Soldiers were buried in mass graves, hastily and without ceremony or even respect. It was a gruesome business that certainly tempered whatever joy the men had of the victory. They could only take comfort that they were the ones digging the trenches rather than the ones being thrown in them.

Although dismayed by the high cost of his victory, Lee could not spend much time fretting over the carnage of battle. He was doing his best to ensure that there would be another somber postbattle clean up, but hopefully next time the victims would primarily wear blue and the victory would be all the sweeter. Lee was forced to pause while he considered all of McClellan's possible options. Lee could not force the issue like he had the previous two days. It was impossible for him to cross the river and attack McClellan from the north with Union artillery guarding the crossings and the bridges destroyed. Now that McClellan's entire army was south of the river, Magruder and Huger could not attack and have any hope of success against nearly four to one odds. But Lee determined correctly that McClellan was in a completely defensive mode now and would not launch an attack against the undermanned Magruder and Huger.

Lee decided that McClellan was going to take one of three possible courses, all involving retreat. Little Mac could move east to protect his supply line and the railroad, thus retaining the possibility of eventually turning the tables and relaunching an offensive against Richmond. McClellan could also choose to retreat back the way he had come, down the peninsula toward Yorktown, Fort Monroe, and the York River, where his gunboats could assist him. There, he could regroup and potentially start the campaign over again if he wished. Last, McClellan could retreat south to the James River, where he could be supplied by water and have the protective umbrella of Union gunboats. Lee did not know which path McClellan would take, though his hunch that had driven his campaign so far was that McClellan would protect his supply line. Lee assumed that McClellan would want to maintain an offensive option once he weathered the Confederate storm and he needed the railroad to do so. But Lee was not going to move his entire army on that hunch because he had been wrong the day before. Instead, Lee sent Stuart's cavalry and Ewell's division east to White House landing to see what efforts McClellan was making to guard his base and the railroad. They were to seize both if the opportunity presented itself. Lee was forced to wait until he learned something definitive about McClellan's plans.[7]

By mid-afternoon on June 28, Lee had received word from Stuart that effectively eliminated the first option. Stuart had arrived at Dispatch Station on the railroad, about four miles southeast of the scene of the Gaines Mill fight, and found it unguarded. His troopers cut the telegraph lines (which caused panic in Washington, D.C.) and tore up some tracks. As Ewell's troops marched toward the river searching for the enemy, they witnessed McClellan's troops destroy the railroad bridge and Bottom's Bridge a mile further south, thus conclusively showing that McClellan was not going to fight for his railroad line. As Stuart's troopers rode to White House, they found an enormous pile of supplies furiously burning. Much to the dismay of "Rooney" Lee, the White House itself was also engulfed in flames, destroyed by a retreating Union soldier who did not share McClellan's compunction to protect rebel property. Stuart's troops salvaged much from the flames and gorged themselves on the delicacies they retrieved.

When word finally reached Lee that the two bridges had been destroyed and the White House base had been abandoned, he determined that McClellan was heading directly for the James River. That knowledge, however, did not reach Lee until early on June 29. In a case of bad timing, Lee sent a courier telling Stuart to scout the other possible crossings south of Bottom's Bridge, so that Lee would know definitively that McClellan was not retreating down the peninsula. If he was, Lee needed to keep his infantry north of the river in order to cut off the retreating foe. However, Lee's courier arrived only after Stuart had taken his cavalry east to White House landing. Had Stuart still been at Dispatch Station when the messenger arrived, he could have scouted the crossings and reported back to Lee in time for Lee to get his troops moving on the evening of June 28, perhaps as many as 12 hours earlier than they eventually started.[8]

When he awoke before daylight on Sunday, June 29, Lee had become convinced that McClellan was heading to the James. He sent a dispatch to Jefferson Davis stating, "His only course seemed to me was to make for the James River and thus open communications with his gunboats and fleet." He declared confidently that "the whole army has been put in motion upon this supposition."[9] Indeed it had, for by the time Lee sent the note to Davis, he had already issued orders for his divisions. He had accomplished the first task he had set on accomplishing—he had compelled McClellan to come out from behind his fortifications and abandon the siege of the city. Now, Lee wanted more. He was not satisfied with merely driving the Yankees away from the Confederate capital. He saw a golden opportunity to destroy or capture McClellan's army. Such a decisive result would possibly end the war. Lee and McClellan both believed as much.

Lee devised a rather intricate plan for June 29, which he hoped would set the stage for the coup de grace the following day. Magruder was in the best position to take the initiative on the 29th, and Lee would send him east directly down the Williamsburg Road and York River Railroad to attack McClellan's retreating army. Lee hoped that Magruder's attack would force McClellan to stop his retreat in order to fend off the threat. To assist Magruder, Lee ordered Jackson to rebuild the Grapevine Bridge, cross the Chickahominy, and approach the Union army from the north, putting him on Magruder's left flank. While these two were tying McClellan down, Lee would have others moving to cut off his retreat south of the swamp. Benjamin Huger (pronounced "oo'-zhay") was to march his division down the Charles City Road, which ran southeast and went to the crossroads village of Glendale, also known as Riddell's shop, below the exit from White Oak Swamp. The longest and hardest marching would belong to A. P. Hill and Longstreet. Lee had them march back to New Bridge and head south past the Williamsburg and Charles City Roads, until they came to Darbytown Road, which they would follow east until it merged with the Long Bridge Road. The Long Bridge Road also led to Glendale from the west (while Huger would approach it from the northwest). Lee knew that they had too far to go to be of combat value on the 29th, but he anticipated using them as his prime offensive punch on June 30. Lee kept Ewell's division on the north side of the Chickahominy, watching the roads over that river just to be sure McClellan didn't fool Lee and head that way instead.

It was a complex plan, requiring three separate elements—Magruder, Jackson, and Huger—to hit their marks properly in order to be successful. Additionally, Lee was operating on supposition, for he did not know exactly where McClellan's different corps were located, but guessed accurately that they were moving south through White Oak Swamp and past Glendale. He also knew McClellan had a 24-hour head start, so alacrity on the part of his own commanders was crucial.

In the early morning hours of June 29, Longstreet had sent two engineers across the river to investigate the Union position facing Magruder at Golding's Farm, the scene of two brief but bloody skirmishes the previous two days. Shortly after dawn, they reported that the works were empty, proving to Lee that the retreat had begun. At almost the same time Lee learned of the withdrawal, he received a note from Magruder announcing that general's intention of attacking the Golding's Farm position. In a moment of levity, Lee sent a jocular note back telling Magruder to be sure not to hurt Longstreet's two engineers when he attacked the empty works. Once he knew McClellan was on the move, Lee sent his marching orders to his division commanders and crossed the river to speak with Magruder directly.[10]

Despite Lee's witty note, Magruder had not been wrong about the Golding's Farm position. When he last scouted it in the early morning, the Union troops were still there. Only at about 3:00 A.M. did they begin quietly retreating. McClellan had set the retreat in motion the day before with the IV Corps of Keyes and the supply trains crossing south through the White Oak Swamp. Keyes's divisions took up a defensive position at Glendale facing west and guarding the bridge crossings. McClellan next ordered Porter's V Corps to move toward the swamp bridge. It would be a long march for many of the men of those three divisions. Morell's division, the survivors of Hood's and Longstreet's breakthrough, departed the Trent House for the nearly two-mile march south to Savage Station shortly after noon on June 28. From there, they continued another half mile south to Williamsburg Road. They followed that road southeast for nearly four miles until it merged with White Oak Road, which they followed south one mile until they crossed the swamp bridge. They made relatively good time, because they traveled ahead of the supply wagons, and reached Glendale before dark. The other divisions would not have as smooth a journey.

The army's wagon train departed Savage Station at 4:00 P.M., became strung out for miles, and encountered so many hindrances and obstacles that they did not reach their destination until late the next morning. The trip was so exhausting that teamsters driving the wagons fell asleep during the constant halts. Sykes's division began marching from the Trent House late that afternoon and found the going so slow that Sykes turned onto a secondary road to get off the Williamsburg Road. He tried to head for Brackett's Ford, but the guide could not find the right passage in the darkness, so Sykes halted his strung-out column at 2 A.M., about the time a tremendous thunderstorm struck, dropping a torrential rain of biblical proportions and only increasing the misery level of the soldiers who had fought such a professional retreat in the face of D. H. Hill's onslaught on Friday.

McCall's division was the last to begin leaving the Trent House grounds at around 8:00 P.M. He had to carry the artillery reserve with him and was following a route taken by two divisions and a supply train already. His own artillery train would eventually form a line seven miles long, stretching almost the entire way from Trent House to White Oak Swamp. It would be an incredibly dispiriting and tiring march, as McCall's men marched in fits and starts behind hundreds of cannons, wagons, and thousands of horses and cattle. The thunderstorm only guaranteed that those defenders of Gaines Mill would be marching through a malodorous mud mixture.

On the afternoon of June 28, General Israel Richardson's division of Sumner's II Corps, which was facing Magruder, sent its supply and baggage wagons to Savage Station. With them went all the wounded and sick that were in II Corps hospitals. They would increase the total number of wounded soldiers at the large field hospital there to more than 3,000. Some 500 wounded men had been loaded on a train that headed toward White House. However, after only going three miles it stopped and reversed course when it saw Confederates on the opposite bank and the bridge destroyed. Many of those wounded men would be in no condition to march on the retreat to the James. On the morning of the 29th, the Union soldiers destroyed mountains of supplies and their trains by setting the supplies on fire and crashing the trains at full speed into the river. They also abandoned nearly 2,500 wounded comrades at the Savage Station field hospital.[11]

On the night of June 28, McClellan ordered Sumner, Heintzelman, and Franklin to withdraw from their advanced positions to a new line of defenses west of Savage Station. This did not set well with everyone, and not just Kearny, who had already given McClellan a piece of his mind the night before. Private Robert Knox Sneden, a cartographer in Heintzelman's headquarters, who made his way to Savage Station during the night's rain, noted that "a general feeling of despondency prevailed which was enhanced by the rain storm and the knowledge that the morning would bring another battle and that we would probably retreat through White Oak Swamp whether we repulsed the enemy or not."[12] Sumner also disagreed with the retreat and refused to pull his men all the way back to Savage Station. On the morning of the 29th, he fell back only to Allen's farm, two miles in front of Savage Station. This was the beginning of a communication breakdown throughout the army. McClellan did not designate a single commander in charge, largely because he disliked the pompous Sumner who was the most senior general. At 9:00 A.M., Sumner engaged in a fight with elements of Magruder's advance for nearly two hours before falling back to where he was supposed to be.

Sumner had to be persuaded to fall back. While he was fighting, he had not communicated with Heintzelman on his left, who continued to move toward Savage Station. On his right, Franklin realized that a single division under General William F. "Baldy" Smith—a quick-tempered McClellan loyalist with a receding hairline who had graduated fourth in the West Point class one year ahead of his commander, taught at the academy for more than a decade, and suffered from periodic flare-ups of malaria, which he had contracted in Florida during the Third Seminole War—was left having to guard a wide gap between the river and Sumner, and was isolated if attacked. Even more disturbing, when Franklin searched for his other division under Slocum, he learned that it was already well on its way to White Oak Swamp. McClellan had ordered it away without bothering to inform its corps commander. Franklin sent a note to Sumner suggesting that he fall back to secure both flanks, but Sumner haughtily replied that he was in action and would not break it off. After consulting with Heintzelman and Smith, Franklin rode to Sumner's position to personally (and likely with feigned obsequiousness) urge Sumner to fall back to prevent Smith's division from being cut off. Sumner conceded and broke off the fight about 11:00 A.M. By 1:00 P.M., the line was unified.[13]

Heintzelman was the next general to decide to obey his own inner commander and not bother to enlighten his fellow generals. Heintzelman arrived at Savage Station and scouted the terrain. He observed that the area "was crowded with troops—more than I supposed could be brought into action judiciously."[14] Trusting that Sumner and Franklin could fend off whatever force might threaten them, Heintzelman decided to strike off for White Oak Swamp. He found a road heading south that appeared to be clear of troops and wagons, so he turned his corps south and in the early afternoon left the field. He did not inform Sumner or Franklin of his decision, and each expected him to hold the left flank. Because of the thick woods in the area south of Savage Station, no one could see his corps and naturally assumed that he was where he was supposed to be. They did not discover otherwise until it was almost too late, when in the late afternoon Confederate brigades began threatening that exposed left flank.[15]

* * *

Those brigades were from Magruder's command and their rather timid advance was the result of a long day of confusion, misunderstood orders, and mismanagement on the Confederate side of the lines. Magruder was one of the root causes of the confusion, and the origin of his managerial malady really began on Thursday, June 26, when he first feared that McClellan would realize his advantage and storm through his lines into Richmond. On both June 26 and 27, Magruder did his best to dupe the Yankees into believing not only that his force was much stronger than it actually was, but also that he had aggressive intentions. He played this role beautifully and was more successful than he could have ever expected to be. But Magruder's days and nights were very anxious ones. In his nervous condition, he could not sleep and the stress had created a severe case of indigestion, which made him irritable. On June 27, part of his force, under the impetuous and headstrong Georgian politician-turned-general, Robert Toombs, attacked a stronger Union force under "Baldy" Smith at Golding's Farm and was turned back with several hundred casualties. Though Magruder did not authorize the ill-conceived attack, it did serve the purpose of convincing McClellan that he was under strong attack on the south side of the river as well as at Gaines Mill.[16]

June 28 was not a relaxing day for Magruder, even though he was now in contact with the remainder of Lee's forces north of the river via the recently captured and repaired New Bridge. As Magruder saw it, now McClellan's entire army faced his little band, only increasing the danger to Richmond. Lee's steady messages ordering Magruder to "hold at all costs" did not reduce the rebellious acid in Magruder's stomach.

When Lee ordered Magruder on June 28 to push the enemy if he was moving, Magruder listened as Toombs once again in the late afternoon launched another ill-fated advance at Golding's Farm. Magruder stayed awake all night scouting and preparing for an attack to push the Yankees away from that farm the next morning. They obligingly withdrew before Magruder had a chance to attack. They were Smith's troops obeying orders to fall back the two miles to Savage Station, where Magruder's troops could see great plumes of black smoke rising over the mounds of burning supplies.

In the early daylight hours of Sunday morning, June 29, Lee crossed the river at New Bridge to personally explain Magruder's orders to him. Lee wanted to make sure that Magruder understood completely what was expected of him. Lee had no reason at all to complain of Prince John's performance, thus far. Other than being a little excitable, Magruder had done everything that Lee had asked of him and more. Lee must have been confident that Magruder would continue his good service, and perhaps this confidence blinded him to Magruder's agitation when they rode together the two miles along the Nine Mile Road from Old Tavern to Fair Oaks Station. Along the way, Lee outlined his plan to Magruder. When they reached Fair Oaks Station, Lee asked his subordinate if he understood the plan and Magruder said yes, but he clearly had not grasped everything Lee had said. Although Magruder knew that he had primary responsibility for pursuit, he was under the erroneous impression that Huger was going to be on the Williamsburg Road on his right flank, when in fact Huger was to march down the Charles City Road. He also believed that he was to act in concert with Jackson on his left, though that was not what Lee intended. Magruder was to be the initiator and Jackson would support as he crossed. As Lee rode off on this scorching Sunday to brief Huger on the day's plan, Magruder faced the enemy on his own again, and showed hesitation and confusion throughout most of the day.

As his troops moved cautiously forward, some leading elements encountered Sumner's corps drawn up at Allen's farm near Orchard Station two miles west of Savage Station. But Magruder did not push forward to fully engage the enemy, and Sumner withdrew on Franklin's special pleading at 11:00 a.m. Not only had Magruder not pushed forward as Lee desired, but the small skirmish, in which only two Georgia regiments were engaged losing fewer than 30 men, also convinced the easily frightened Magruder that he was greatly outnumbered—which he was—and about to be attacked by that large force—which he was not. He rushed his aide, Major Joseph Brent, to Lee to tell him that he was greatly outnumbered and to ask for assistance from Huger. Lee found this inconceivable. He could not imagine that McClellan would launch an offensive while retreating. The commander asked Brent, "Have you yourself seen and formed an opinion upon the number of the enemy?" When Brent said he had not, Lee pressed him: "But what do you think? Is the enemy in large force?" Lee was searching for a more rational interpretation than the excitable Magruder's, but Brent refused to venture an opinion. Lee relented and agreed to send two brigades to the Williamsburg Road, but only with a time limit. If they were not fighting by 2:00 P.M., they were to return to the Charles City Road, because Huger had to get down that road to Glendale before nightfall.[17]

Shortly before he sent Brent to Lee, Magruder had sent another messenger to Jackson to learn of his progress. Fully expecting Jackson to have crossed the river by now, Magruder was dismayed to learn that Jackson was behind schedule in rebuilding the bridge and would be delayed. Magruder decided to wait for Huger to arrive on his right and Jackson to take up position on his left—and he constantly warned his brigade commanders in that area not to accidentally fire on Jackson's troops. Though Magruder knew that Lee expected him to push the pursuit vigorously and promptly, he decided to disobey Lee's orders and modify them to his own preferences. As Peter Carmichael has argued, Magruder's orders were not dependent on assistance from Jackson or Huger nor were they discretionary. But Magruder still refused to carry them out as Lee intended.[18]

The problem was that Magruder fundamentally misunderstood what his role was supposed to be. The crucial element was *time*. Lee wanted Magruder to move out and engage the enemy quickly. He did not expect Magruder to break the Union line, he simply wanted Magruder to force the Union rearguard to stop their retreat and deal with the threat. Magruder's role was to tie down the Union forces and delay their retreat, even if that meant sacrificing many of his 14,000 men to do so. If Magruder had just kept a constant harassing engagement all across his front, then he would have accomplished Lee's goal, because a quick movement that morning would have forced Heintzelman to keep his corps near Savage Station to guard the southern flank. Lee was likely not aware that the majority of three corps were facing Magruder (and he expected Jackson to help tie down these troops by threatening their northern flank). Therefore, Magruder's potential casualty rate would have been higher than Lee anticipated, but it would possibly have had a positive effect on the overall campaign.

For Magruder, the early afternoon brought more bad news. While waiting for Jackson to cross the river, the hours slipped past and 2:00 P.M. came with no fighting. At that time, Huger informed Magruder that he was taking back his two brigades. Shortly after that news, Magruder received an especially unwelcome note from Jackson that stated mysteriously that he would be unable to cooperate with Magruder because "he has other important duty to perform."[19] Magruder knew that he had to carry out Lee's pursuit orders with no help from either flank.

What was the "other important duty" that Jackson had to perform? It was actually a product of further miscommunication and confusion of orders. Lee had briefed Jackson on his plan that morning before he set out to confer with Magruder. But later that morning, Lee had his chief of staff, Colonel R. H. Chilton, draw up an order to send to Jeb Stuart across the Chickahominy. Lee wanted to guard against the relatively remote possibility that McClellan would try to cross the river further south. Therefore, he ordered Stuart to monitor the crossings, "advising Genl Jackson who will resist their passage until reinforced." Stuart forwarded this dispatch to Jackson when he received it and it was in Jackson's hand shortly after 3:00 P.M. Jackson erroneously interpreted this to mean that he was no longer to pursue but instead to remain north of the river. This was a strange judgment to make since Lee never sent him a direct order to that effect, and Lee later admitted that Jackson's interpretation was a mistake. Lee was just drawing up a contingency plan, but he intended Jackson to contest McClellan's crossing from south of the river, after he had crossed it.[20]

Of course, Jackson was moving very slowly in crossing the river, something that the former engineer Lee believed would occur in short order during the morning. But Jackson was repeating his lethargic performance from the previous two days. E. Porter Alexander later claimed that Jackson's dedication to the Sabbath is what caused his delay, and there is likely at least some truth to this.[21] Jackson did not make the bridge repair an urgent matter that morning as he observed his religious devotionals. There were actually two bridges under repair—the Grapevine Bridge, which was a narrow bridge that was only fit for infantry, and the Alexander Bridge 400 yards upstream, which was sturdy enough for artillery as well. Jackson sent the ubiquitous and unqualified Dabney to lead the construction party of the larger bridge. In an army full of West Point graduates with training in engineering, Jackson chose Dabney, who had no training or practical engineering experience. It went poorly, in what Dabney called a "shilly-shally" affair. Jackson belatedly sent his engineer, Captain C. R. Mason, to fix the problem.[22]

During the course of this episode, Jackson must have still been confident that he would get across, since he sent Magruder the note shortly after noon saying he would be finished in a couple of hours. Jackson even put Winder's brigade and Whiting's division in motion to cross the bridges as soon as they were complete. But the Alexander Bridge repair took longer than anticipated (and it would not be finished until that night), and then at 3:00 P.M. Stuart's courier arrived with the dispatch that persuaded Jackson to stay where he was and inform Magruder that he would be unable to assist him.

Once again, the Jackson of the Valley Campaign seemed to be missing. *That* Jackson would have crossed his brigades on a rope bridge, if necessary, to get them into attack position on a retreating foe. This Jackson was content not to press the bridge construction and ultimately let pass a chance to attack a foe in flight. Like Magruder, Jackson must have also misunderstood Lee's plan and the urgency it required. Lee told Magruder that he expected Jackson to cross quickly and "push the pursuit vigorously."[23] Jackson never understood that to be his role or, presumably, he would have moved more quickly. In the afternoon, he rode over to the Trent House to inspect the land, but did not order his troops to cross until next morning.

Lee is not blameless either. He could have made sure the order was written more clearly by Chilton to avoid misunderstanding, or he could have written Jackson directly explaining the contingent nature of Stuart's order and repeating that he needed Jackson to cross the river soon. Lee also could have sent a staff member to find out what was preventing Jackson from crossing. After all, no firing could be heard along the front that afternoon until 5:00 P.M. When Magruder wrote Lee to ask what Jackson's duty was, Lee assured Magruder that Jackson had been ordered to pursue the Yankees. At this time, Lee could have tried to discover what had happened and straightened out the problem while there was still daylight remaining, but he did not. The fog of war once again settled over Lee's vision of the battlefield.

At 4:00 P.M., having lost the aid of Huger and now of Jackson, Magruder had not lost sight of the fact that Lee's orders to him were to pursue the Yankees in his front. Fed up with the frustrating sequence of events, Magruder ordered his troops to move forward and his generals to attack any Yankee force they met, no matter the odds. The odds were much more equal by 5:00 P.M. than they had been just a few hours earlier. Heintzelman had marched south with his corps around noon, but in the mid-afternoon, "Baldy" Smith, who had been holding down the right flank of the Savage Station position, decided that his defensive services were no longer needed since the Confederates did not appear to be attacking, and he began marching his division toward White Oak Swamp, following the path that Slocum's division had taken. Therefore, Sumner

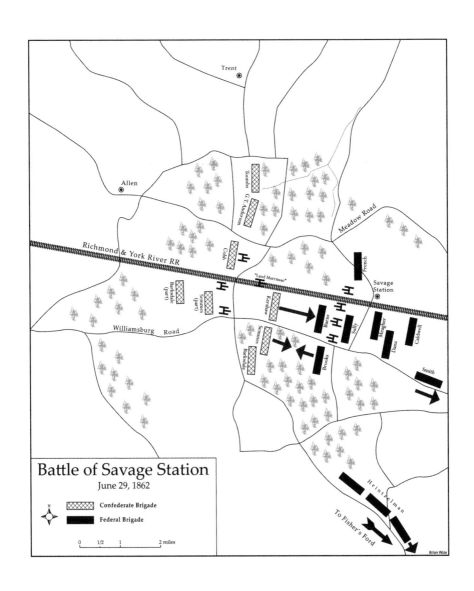

Trent

Allen

Toombs

G.T. Anderson

Meadow Road

Richmond & York River RR

Cobb

French

Savage Station

"Land Merrimac"

Barksdale (part)

Semmes (pt)

Kershaw

Burns

Sully

Meagher

Caldwell

Dana

Semmes

Williamsburg   Road

Barksdale

Brooks

Smith

Heintzelman

To Fisher's Ford

Battle of Savage Station
June 29, 1862

N

Confederate Brigade

Federal Brigade

| 0 | 1/2 | 1 | 2 miles |

Brian Wize

would face Magruder's 14,000 troops with his 16,000-man corps and practically no support. Even a late crossing by Jackson at this juncture could have treated Sumner's II Corps much the same way that Porter's V Corps had been treated the day before, inflicting severe casualties and capturing large numbers, but Jackson had already called it a day.

The first troops under Magruder to make contact with the Yankees were those in General Joseph Kershaw's South Carolina Brigade, the leading unit of General Lafayette McLaws's division. They had been fortuitously spotted by Generals Franklin and John Sedgwick, who were riding out in front of Savage Station. They were going to pay a visit to Heintzelman and initially mistook Kershaw's troops for Heitzelman's corps. Sedgwick, looking closer, stopped and shouted, "Why, those men are rebels!" Both officers galloped back to their lines. Franklin mused, "This ludicrous incident prevented what might have a disastrous surprise for our whole force."[24] It was only then that Sumner knew for the first time that Heintzelman had departed. He was not happy and refused to speak to Heintzelman when he saw him the next day.

As Kershaw's brigade emerged from the woods on the western side of a cleared field in front of Savage Station, it did so with the sun at its back. Private Sneden remembered this moment: "The heat was terrible . . . Not a breath of air was felt. The sun threw its red glare on the red soil and railroad track, making it difficult to see clearly."[25] Kershaw's left flank rested on the railroad and his right was north of the Williamsburg Road. On the left flank, he had some heavy artillery on the railroad for support. Lee had ordered the construction of a 32-pound naval gun mounted on a railroad car, dubbed the "Land Merrimac," in order to disrupt McClellan's use of the railroad to bring forward his siege guns.[26] The gun was impressive but ineffective, and this was its only major usage in the campaign. Kershaw's brigade engaged General William W. Burns's brigade of Sedgwick's division, which was posted in advance of the main line in an open field, and broke through it, wounding Burns. At that point, Private Sneden watched Kershaw's men valiantly charge "to within twenty feet of our artillery, when bushels of grape and canister from the cannon laid them low in rows."[27]

As the fight progressed, General Paul Semmes's brigade arrived on Kershaw's right, straddling the Williamsburg Road and extending the line well to the south of that avenue. Sumner, watching the progress, sent forward individual regiments from several different brigades that just happened to be nearest to him. Sumner even led one of the regiments personally to the front. To Semmes's right was General Richard Griffith's brigade, commanded in Griffith's absence by Colonel William Barksdale.

It had difficulty extending the Confederate right and engaging the enemy due to the disorienting and dense woods. In the confusion of the forest, several Confederate regiments who were going into combat for the first time fired on friendly units before they finally got straightened out and met the enemy. In the end, only half of Barksdale's men even found the enemy, before darkness put an end to the skirmish.

The disappearance of Heintzelman's corps left Sumner's southern flank in a vulnerable position and a stronger attack by Magruder may have made some significant gains. But Sumner recalled Smith's division and ordered it to fill the void south of the Williamsburg Road. Smith's closest brigade, under General William T.H. Brooks, turned about and raced to the threatened spot. On this sweltering Sunday, Brooks's men pitched into the thick woods, where part of Semmes's and Barksdale's brigades were advancing and met a Confederate fire that was every bit as scorching as the weather. Brooks's brigade suffered nearly 450 casualties and the 5th Vermont lost nearly half of its force in the fighting, but they held the line. Firing continued along this three-brigade front in a stalemate until 9 P.M., with neither side trying to push for a breakthrough. Magruder, having ridden to the front and scouted the enemy's position, decided it was useless to send in his remaining brigades; Sumner's line was too strong to be broken by such a small force. The fighting slowly died away in the darkness, leaving between 600 and 1,000 Union casualties and between 375 and 475 Confederates behind. Despite having three divisions, Magruder only got nine regiments, or barely more than 3,000 men, involved in the fight.[28]

The pursuit had ended for the day with results far short of what Lee had anticipated. Frustrated by the myriad delays and failures on the day, Lee could not hide his disappointment when he sent Magruder a strongly worded note that night. He wrote, "I regret much that you have made so little progress today in the pursuit of the enemy. In order to reap the fruits of our victory the pursuit should be most vigorous."[29] Most historians argue that Lee was unfair to Magruder, because he had been outnumbered and Jackson had not helped. But as Peter Carmichael argues, Lee was correct in being harsh on Magruder for essentially disobeying orders. Lee undoubtedly used Magruder as the target for his frustration with everyone, including Jackson who failed to cross the river and do his crucial part in the pursuit. But Lee may have singled Magruder out because he had actually expected much more from him. Lee had been satisfied with Magruder's performances on June 26 and 27 (far more than he was with Jackson's performances on either of those days).

The key to Lee's anger was in the concluding statement of his dispatch, and this applied to all of his commanders: "We must lose no more time or he will escape us entirely."[30] *Time*. That was the most crucial element in Lee's plan that Magruder and Jackson failed to grasp. Confederate success depended on the rapidity of movement. Lee did not necessarily expect Magruder to overwhelm the Union rearguard, but he did expect him to go in with guns blazing in order to tie down as many Federal units as possible for as long as possible. When Jackson appeared on their northern flank and threatened their right and rear, he could either capture a large number or at the very least force even more Union brigades to stop and face about to meet the threat he posed. Much of McClellan's army would then still be north of White Oak Swamp, and Huger, Longstreet, and A. P. Hill were marching their divisions to cut off the Yankee escape south of the swamp. But Magruder's late hour of movement allowed one entire corps (Heintzelman's) to retreat that otherwise would have remained. Even causing that one corps to remain behind and help clog the roads during the night march south through the swamp on June 29 might have allowed Jackson to catch Sumner's corps in the middle of crossing White Oak Swamp and tear it to shreds, rather than arriving two hours after the last Union unit crossed the bridge to safety.

As for Jackson, an urgent and determined effort to rebuild the bridges could have put either all or at least the vast majority of his army across the river in time to occupy Union troops in combat during the afternoon. At the very least, his infantry could have crossed by 5:00 P.M. and added its contribution to Magruder's evening attack, discomfiting Sumner and perhaps keeping Smith's division from retreating early. Even if Jackson's men had never fired a shot, just crossing his troops over on the evening of the 29th would have saved a few hours in marching time during the pursuit on June 30 and allowed him to engage Sumner's rearguard north of the White Oak Swamp Bridge that morning.

Ultimately, however, Lee must shoulder much of the blame. The fact that both his commanders so fundamentally misunderstood his plan indicates that he must not have explained it very clearly to either of them. He did not send explicit written orders to either general, as he had on June 26. Once again, Lee did not utilize his staff to investigate delays or prod his commanders into action. If Lee was so stunned that Magruder thought he was about to be attacked, then he could have personally ridden the two miles to Magruder to see for himself or sent a staff officer with a peremptory order telling Magruder to push on regardless of consequences, but he did not. While one could argue that Lee could not be everywhere at once, he did not have to be. By his own account, Magruder was the most important element of the plan, so looking over Magruder's shoulder to make sure he did what was expected would be demonstrating good generalship. Similarly, when Lee learned late in the day that Jackson was not going to cross the river, he could have sent an officer to order that general to cross the river regardless of difficulties and press the pursuit. Instead, Lee trusted that things would work out until it was too late, and then all he could do was to rebuke Magruder for not being the general he thought he was. In fact, it was Lee who was not being the general that he thought he was on this day.

Some historians have argued that Magruder's delays actually saved Lee's army from a substantial loss. Brian Burton argues that "a vigorous pursuit may have decimated his command."[31] It is true that if Magruder had moved early he would have faced Sumner and Heintzelman and the latter could have inflicted serious damage on Magruder's flank. But Magruder could just as easily have backed off the throttle and used his deceptive ruses of limited assaults to fool the enemy into thinking he would attack with a larger force than he really had. He had already successfully done so numerous times. Magruder likely would have suffered heavier casualties, but he would have also kept Heintzelman on the battlefield. It shows that Lee misunderstood what he faced. He likely did not assume that the better part of three corps remained. Also, if Jackson had crossed in a timely manner, he could have induced a form of panic in Sumner, Franklin, or Heintzelman, and no one commander was in charge of the field to make an executive decision.

Although Magruder engaged the enemy to little profit and Jackson dawdled at the Chickahominy—only D. H. Hill's division would cross at 3:00 A.M. the next morning—all the other Confederates were marching. The divisions of Longstreet and A. P. Hill spent a long and largely uneventful day crossing the river at New Bridge and marching south behind the lines. The leading elements reached the Atlee house on the Darbytown Road about seven miles from Glendale. Their greatest enemies had been the stifling heat, sapping humidity, and suffocating dust kicked up by the shoes of nearly 20,000 soldiers and artillery horses along the same road.

Huger's division was strung out along the Charles City Road, largely because Lee had ordered him to send two brigades to support Magruder until 2 P.M. Thus, Robert Ransom's and "Rans" Wright's brigades got a very late start and were going to have a difficult time getting to Glendale before dark. They caught up to the rest of Huger's division fairly quickly, however, because in the mid-afternoon, Huger had encountered unexpected Union troops near Jordan's Ford, about four miles short of their destination at Glendale. The troops that Huger's lead brigade encountered at the intersection of the Jordan's Ford Road were those of Heintzelman's missing corps. Once Heintzelman had ordered the retreat, General Phil

Kearny decided to avoid the immense traffic jam at White Oak Swamp Road by crossing at Jordan's Ford, about three miles west. He had scouted the route that morning and, of course, saw no Confederate troops at that time. It was only a three-mile march for Kearny to reach Jordan's Ford, and he sent David Birney's brigade to the ford. As Birney's troops crossed the ford, they met skirmishers from General William Mahone's brigade. Mahone had encountered cavalry scouts on the road, and so had formed his brigade facing north to contest the crossing. Birney's troops met Mahone soon after his deployment and realized their route was blocked. Kearny rode forward to see for himself and decided to backtrack and send his division toward Brackett's Ford, a mile and a half to the east. After a confusing march in which regiments got mixed up, one of his brigades crossed at Fisher's Ford, between Jordan's and Brackett's, but the rest of his division crossed the swamp at Brackett's Ford by 10 P.M. that night and camped on the Charles City Road.[32]

Huger, however, believed Kearny was still near Jordan's Ford and feared that further progress down the Charles City Road would allow Kearny to attack his rear. Huger ordered Mahone's, Lewis Armistead's, and Ransom's brigades to stop on the Charles City Road at the Jordan's Ford Road intersection, well short of their destination. Further concerned that Kearny might get behind him using the New Road, which ran parallel to the Charles City Road, but on the north side of the swamp, Huger sent Wright's brigade back to where the New Road intersected the Charles City Road. Wright would actually march east down the New Road the next day, making much faster progress than the rest of Huger's division.

While the Confederates finally settled down for the night in scattered locations, many Union soldiers saw no rest that night. For them, it was another night of marching over unfamiliar roads in the sultry darkness. Though already south of the swamp, Keyes's corps marched all night to reach Haxall's Landing on the James River. His progress was aided by accidentally discovering another road east of the Willis Church Road (which was also confusingly referred to as the Quaker Road). Slocum's division of Franklin's corps and McCall's division under Porter's command guarded the Glendale crossroads, while Porter's other two divisions under Morell and Sykes made their way down the Willis Church Road to Malvern Hill almost three miles south of Glendale.

This left only the troops at Savage Station, who McClellan ordered to retreat down the White Oak Swamp Road that night. However, Sumner demonstrated some characteristic bullheadedness when he received the order. Claiming he would never leave a victorious field, he forbade Franklin from retreating with Smith's division. When Franklin showed him McClellan's direct order, Sumner proclaimed that "General McClellan did not know the circumstances when he wrote that note." When further explicit orders arrived from McClellan that night, Sumner reluctantly relented and the retreat began, with Franklin in the lead, followed by Sedgwick's division, and then Richardson's division. These men had not had time to eat anything all day and now had to march many miles to cross the swamp. To make matters worse, a violent thunderstorm drenched them throughout much of the night. Misery was not a strong enough word to describe the experience. Private Sneden referred to it as "very confusing and demoralizing." Three thousand wagons mingled with infantry, cavalry, and artillery on the stretch of road in a pouring rain. Another soldier summed up the interminable and exhausting night: "March and wait and march and wait and then countermarch. May you never experience how tired we were."[33]

Smith's division crossed the swamp at dawn, with the last of the other two divisions crossing shortly before 10 A.M. Captain George Hazzard's battery was the last to cross. He had slept on the Savage Station battlefield and awakened at dawn to the sound of Confederate bugles. He quietly and hastily limbered up his guns and set out down the Williamsburg Road to the White Oak Road. They arrived at the swamp only moments before the bridge was destroyed. It had been an exhausting night, but if Lee had his way, Monday, June 30, was going to be every bit as exhausting as any day of the week thus far.

5

⁓

Glendale, June 30

The long night march had managed to get all of McClellan's units south of White Oak Swamp, but they were tossed into a scattered pattern around Glendale that prevented any sort of organized leadership on the part of individual corps commanders. Two divisions of Porter's corps were at Malvern Hill, but his third division under McCall was west of the Willis Church Road guarding that avenue of retreat. Heintzelman's corps had been the next to cross the swamp after abandoning Savage Station prematurely, but he had been unable to keep his corps together. Because Kearny had been delayed by his run-in with Confederate troops at Jordan's Ford, Hooker's division had crossed first and had eventually moved down the Willis Church Road to a point near the Willis Methodist Church. That put them on the left of McCall's division, also facing west. Kearny's division eventually stopped and dug in on the Charles City Road, to the right of McCall's division. Thus, Heintzelman's two divisions were separated by three-fourths of a mile and could not act in union. McClellan had ordered Heintzelman's divisions into their disparate positions during a 10:30 A.M. meeting with his generals, but he apparently forgot that McCall's division (which he had also placed) was between them.

Franklin's corps faced a similar split as Heintzelman's. Slocum's division had been sent down the Charles City Road to the intersection with the Brackett's Ford Road. He was to defend against any approach from the west or from the ford to the north. He was on Kearny's right. Meanwhile, Franklin's other division under "Baldy" Smith was nearly two miles east, on the right of the White Oak Road, protecting against any Confederate approach from the White Oak Swamp Bridge. Franklin personally was with Smith's division, leaving Slocum in independent command. On Smith's left was the division of the 46-year-old Vermonter, Israel B. "Fighting Dick" Richardson, of Sumner's Corps. His had been the last troops to cross the bridge that morning. Sumner was with his other division under John Sedgwick, along the Willis Church Road to the left and rear of McCall's division. As the men took their positions around the battlefield, the never-ending line of wagon trains continued passing down the Willis Church Road, giving them all clear understanding of what was causing their own delays in retreat.

The units were not deliberately arranged, so the line was not continuous. Some units were in advance of others and few knew exactly who was on either side of them. While everyone knew there would be some tough fighting on this blistering hot day—remembered as the hottest of the entire campaign by many soldiers—they did not know who exactly they would be fighting alongside.[1] Though, in theory, these three corps could be managed effectively if there was one guiding hand, in practice it proved to be a case of every general for himself. Division commanders would fight their own battles, with only occasional cooperation with those around them.

This confused situation occurred because of an irresponsible absence of leadership by the army's commander. With his entire army stretched out over several miles between White Oak Swamp and the James River, McClellan was well aware that June 30 was a pivotal day. He believed that Lee would stop at nothing to try to make this last day of June the last day of the Union army. Little Mac knew he had to hold off attacks for at least one more day before his army would be secure at the James River. Knowing all that was at stake, one would assume the army's commander would want to be present, to make sure that his line held under his direct authority. However, McClellan did not want to be anywhere near the scene of his potential disaster. His personal course of action on this Monday is difficult to explain for those who wish to think favorably of the commander.

After personally scouting the Union position, McClellan rode off with his staff to Haxall's Landing on the James River south of Malvern Hill at 10:00 A.M., where he effectively cut himself off from the army at Glendale. Indeed, sometime after 3:00 P.M., McClellan even boarded the *Galena*, steamed upstream to shell some Confederates, and had "a good dinner with some good wine" with the ship's captain.[2] All this while his army fought for its life in the fields and woods surrounding Glendale. This had become such a common occurrence that Private Robert Sneden remarked

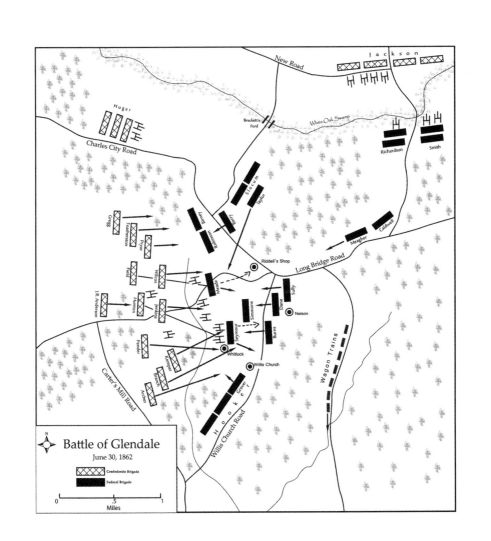

Battle of Glendale
June 30, 1862

Confederate Brigade
Federal Brigade

0   .5   1
Miles

N

Jackson

New Road

Huger

Brackett's
Ford

White Oak Swamp

Charles City Road

Richardson

Smith

Slocum

Taylor

Gregg

Featherston

Robinson

Kirby

Pryor

Meagher

Caldwell

Long Bridge Road

Riddell's Shop

Field

Wilcox

Meade

Sully

J.R. Anderson

Mahone

Nelson

Simmons

Sedgwick

Burns

Pender

Kemper

Seymour

Whitlock

Willis Church

Branch

Archer

Hooker

Grover

Willis Church Road

Carter's Mill Road

Wagon Trains

on it: "Why he left was an enigma. He generally places the troops on the eve of a battle, then goes off to the rear some miles away, leaving his generals to fight it out as best they can without his further assistance." The unsympathetic Sneden noted, "In the event of a victory, he alone gets the credit."[3] Not only did McClellan refuse to personally be in charge of the battle, but he also deliberately refused to appoint a commander of the field in his stead because the senior corps commander was Sumner, whom Little Mac despised. So, for professional and personal reasons, McClellan left the army essentially leaderless. As one soldier acerbically wrote after the war: "Curiously enough, there was almost always something for McClellan to do more important than to fight his own battles."[4]

Historians who have tried to explain McClellan's bizarre actions throughout the campaign have difficulty justifying his behavior on June 30. In even the most positive light, McClellan's actions were irresponsible, and in the least positive light, they were indications of cowardice. His biographer, Stephen Sears, leans toward the latter, declaring that McClellan "had lost the courage to command." He argued that each day of the campaign had disheartened McClellan a little more, so that by June 30 "the demoralization was complete; exercising command in battle was now quite beyond him, and to avoid it he deliberately fled the battlefield."[5] He left his soldiers on their own baking in the heat. For many troops that day, even combat would provide some stimulus to take their minds off the oppressive weather. One Minnesota soldier in Sedgwick's reserve division wrote in his diary: "Each man seemed to think that he could not live 15 minutes from the burning sun that was shining and not a sign of any wind."[6]

As the Yankees tried to deal with what Mother Nature threw at them, they all waited anxiously to see what the Confederates would toss into the mix. Lee was busy trying to organize the pursuit and eventual attack on this steamy Monday morning. However, he would also make some strange managerial decisions on this crucial day. He expected that Glendale was going to be the scene of battle. He knew that the Army of the Potomac was strung out and he was confident that if he could hit McClellan's line at Glendale with enough power he could break it, and perhaps capture or destroy a significant part of the Union army—the elusive goal he had been seeking for days now. He had units converging on the crossroads from three directions and a concerted attack could bring about decisive results. He was not the only officer to think so. Colonel E. Porter Alexander reminisced after the war that there were only a few occasions during the war where a major military victory may have ended the war with Confederate independence. He declared, "This chance of June 30th '62 impresses me as the best of all." He further mused that "never, before, or after, did the fates put such a prize within our reach."[7]

To exploit this opportunity, Lee put six separate units in motion. It all started at 3:30 A.M., when Jackson, unable to sleep because of the storm, rode up to Magruder's headquarters and informed that bedraggled general that he had just put the Valley army in motion to cross the Chickahominy River. Magruder had spent the night, thus far, preparing for a possible Union counterattack, and Jackson's news relieved him enough that he decided to go to bed for the first time in two days. Lee came to Magruder's headquarters at dawn to order him to turn his troops around and move down the Darbytown Road where he would be a reserve force for Longstreet and Hill. Lee had decided that Jackson would take up direct pursuit of the Union force through the White Oak Swamp. This was likely not so much a further rebuke of Magruder, but acknowledgment of the fact that he had a shorter route to get behind Longstreet and Hill. Lee was determined that if things went well, he would call on Magruder's force to seal off the Union wing.

After leaving Magruder, Lee rode down the Williamsburg Road to Savage Station where he met with Jackson.[8] The two generals stood in the road, with Jackson talking in an excited and frenetic manner. He drew something on the ground with his boot. At the end, Jackson stamped on the diagram and exclaimed, in the only words anyone could clearly hear, "We've got him!"[9] Afterwards, the two generals mounted and parted ways, but one assumes they were in agreement as to what was to be done. Jackson would pursue the Union troops through the swamp along the route the Yankees were still using at that moment. No one knows exactly what Lee expected Jackson to do once he reached the stream, but it is clear that he considered an aggressive Jackson to be an integral part of any successful battle on this day. One must conclude that Lee certainly expected Jackson to do more than he ultimately did. In a week of poor performances by Jackson, June 30 is generally considered, by both his own befuddled officers and his scholarly defenders, to be his nadir.

While Jackson moved against the rear of McClellan's retreating army, Lee had four units designated to attack the Union flank. General Theophilus Holmes's 7,000-man division had recently crossed over the James River from the south side. Holmes, a nearly deaf 57-year-old North Carolinian who had graduated 44th (out of 46) in the same West Point class as Lee, marched along the River Road toward Malvern Hill. Though he was on a path to intercept the head of the retreating column, Lee did not give him such orders. His men were not veterans and would have been too small a force to accomplish much against a corps. But Lee did intend for them to harass the Union wagon train crossing Malvern Hill, and perhaps prevent troops from coming to the aid of those at Glendale.

It was at Glendale that Lee aimed his three remaining divisions to pierce the Union line. He had Huger's 12,000-man division and the combined 20,000 men of Longstreet and A. P. Hill heading in that direction, with the promise of Magruder's remaining 13,500 men lending their weight in a supporting assault if necessary. Lee could approach Glendale from several angles because the Charles City Road and the Long Bridge Road intersected at the place. Huger had stopped the night before at Brightwell's farm, near the Jordan's Ford Road, leaving him only three miles to go to Glendale. Longstreet was still on the Darbytown Road at Atlee's farm, about seven miles away from Glendale, by way of the Long Bridge Road. Therefore, Lee expected Huger to open the battle from the Charles City Road, at about the same time that Jackson would threaten the Union rear. While the Union forces were engaged with these forces to their north and northwest, Longstreet and Hill would add their offensive punch by striking from the west along the Long Bridge Road. It was a solid plan, but as had been the case all week long, very little went the way Lee had envisioned.

Huger began his march at daylight, with William Mahone's brigade in the lead. It was a slow and tentative march, because the brigade was constantly worried about its left flank in the direction of the swamp. When Mahone came to Fisher's Ford Road, he deployed his men into line of battle facing north, just in case. They had not gone much further when they encountered Union pickets and, more substantially, obstructions in the form of trees felled across the road. While no problem for infantry, the impediments would prevent artillery from passing. Mahone scouted the road and estimated that the obstruction continued for nearly a mile. Rather than move the obstructions out of the way, by dragging them or cutting up the trees and moving them, Mahone, a thin, wiry, heavy-bearded railroad construction engineer before the war, convinced Huger, an old ordnance officer, that the best solution to the problem was to hack their own road out of the woods rather than clear the one they were on. This was a bizarre suggestion, but Huger agreed to it, and it led to the even more bizarre "battle of the axes"[10] (as it has been dubbed by some scholarly wags), where Confederates hacked a road out of the woods for a mile while Union axmen simultaneously laid further obstructions along the road. Needless to say, progress slowed to a snail's pace. Many regiments never even moved before the march stalled. Huger sent a note to Lee saying he would be a little delayed because of obstructions, but he did not relate the full extent of his solution. Lee had expected Huger to be the signal of the day's attack; instead, Huger would not get a single infantry soldier into the fight that entire day. At this point, every historian of this campaign has their obligatory deriding of the 56-year-old South Carolinian's abilities, and the criticisms all have merit.

While Huger was failing in his pivotal role in Lee's plan for that day, Jackson was not performing any better. Though he had crossed the river early in the morning and met with Lee shortly after daybreak, he did not make very rapid progress in his five-mile march from Savage Station to the bridge over the White Oak Swamp. Much of this was because he allowed his troops to help themselves to the enormous amount of material left behind by the retreating Union troops. Union efforts at burning all their supplies had not been completely successful, and the Confederate soldiers loaded up on everything—from coffee beans to clothing to ammunition. The reverend Dabney claimed, "For weeks afterward, the agents of the army were busy gathering in the spoils."[11] Jackson was impressed by the extent and quality of the large hospital at Savage Station, and he interrogated some of the Union prisoners before continuing on his route.

The first of Jackson's units reached the slope leading down to the swamp shortly before noon. Jackson's chief of artillery, Stapleton Crutchfield, arrived first and inspected the field. He saw the road going down a slope to the destroyed bridge over the swamp. On the far side of the stream, the ground rose to a crest about 300–400 yards away. Crutchfield could see some Union infantry and artillery on the hills east of the road, but his view of the west side was blocked by dense woods. Nevertheless, he began locating a good position for his artillery on his own hill north of the swamp. At noon, Jackson arrived, approved of Crutchfield's actions, and waited until all 31 pieces had been loaded and wheeled into place before he allowed them to open fire.

At approximately 2:00 p.m., Jackson announced his presence with an artillery barrage that startled and scattered the Union troops dozing in the sun. One Yankee lieutenant recalled that he was awakened "by the thunder of artillery, the shrieks of shells, and the horrid burning of their fragments. Hell seemed to have opened upon us."[12] "Baldy" Smith was taking a bath in a local resident's home when the shrieking shells began falling all around him. While Smith hastily and unceremoniously dressed, Franklin sent back word to Sumner at Glendale that he needed reinforcements, because he was certain that such a barrage was the prelude to a large ground attack. Sumner sent two brigades of Sedgwick's division to Franklin, but the attack never came.

Under the cover of the bombardment, Jackson decided to cross the stream and reconnoiter the enemy's position. He ordered Colonel Thomas

Munford to take his 2nd Virginia Cavalry regiment across the swamp to scout the enemy position. When Munford said he doubted the horses could cross the deep stream, Jackson ordered him to "try it." Jackson followed, joined by D. H. Hill. The generals stayed on the south side for only a couple of minutes before heavy fire from previously hidden infantry and artillery on the west side of the road forced them to beat a hasty retreat. Munford also had to get out of there, but could no longer cross the deep swamp without suffering heavy casualties. He steered his regiment off to the east to search for another route to cross. Less than half a mile downstream, he found a little-used crossing, a "cowpath" as he called it. The crossing was undefended and he sent back word to Jackson that any infantry that crossed there could appear on the enemy's right flank undetected, but Jackson did not respond to Munford's report. Munford later confessed that he never understood why Jackson did not take advantage of this opportunity: "I know that I thought, all the time, that he could have crossed his infantry where we recrossed. I had seen his infantry cross far worse places, and I expected that he would attempt it."[13] It would not be the only opportunity Jackson would let pass that day.

Jackson must have been duly impressed with the strength of the Union position during his brief and harrowing reconnaissance, so impressed perhaps that he immediately decided he would not risk a crossing of the creek. But he never said as much to his officers or staff, and in fact sent mixed messages throughout the afternoon. One has to believe that Lee's conversation with Jackson that morning did not conclude with an order to park his army north of the swamp and just annoy the Federals with artillery. Lee undoubtedly expected Jackson to pitch into the Union forces in some way to complement the other flank attacks. But Jackson chose to sit tight, and a few days later justified to his staff, who were still debating Jackson's course of action that day: "If General Lee had wanted me he could have sent for me."[14]

One of Jackson's brigadiers, Wade Hampton, was an enterprising sort that afternoon. Hampton, a wealthy South Carolina officer who had been seriously wounded at Seven Pines but had returned by force of will and been named commander of one of Whiting's brigades, earnestly sought a way to get at the enemy. Though he had not been privy to Jackson's orders, he assumed they had not marched all this way simply to be stymied at the swamp. While Jackson and Munford were crossing and recrossing the swamp, Hampton began scouting for a shallow section of the creek to cross. About a quarter mile east of the bridge, and closer than Munford's cowpath, he found a narrow, shallow portion of the stream and crossed over. When he emerged on the other side and advanced a little ways, he found that he was to the rear of Smith's defensive line, which was drawn up and focused to the northwest facing the White Oak Bridge. Hampton recrossed and personally reported to Jackson. Jackson seemed very interested and asked if the crossing could be used for all arms. Hampton said that he could bridge the creek easily for infantry but not artillery, and Jackson unhesitatingly ordered Hampton to do so. Hampton took a small squad of men with him and cut down enough trees out of earshot and dragged them to the swamp. Finally, after a couple hours of hard work in the breathless heat, Hampton had erected a crude bridge across the stream. When he crossed the swamp to scout again, he found not only were the Yankees unaware, but also that he could get to within 150 yards of them without being discovered.

The enterprising general rode back to Jackson and found him sitting on a pine log with his eyes closed and his cap drawn low. Hampton reported that the bridge was complete and the Union flank still open. He offered to lead his brigade across the bridge. Jackson seemed in a daze, and in the inimitable words of Shelby Foote, "sat there on the log, silent, collapsed like a jointed doll whose spinal string had snapped." Then he rose and walked away without saying a word.[15] Hampton did not know what to make of this reaction, and after awkwardly standing by the log Jackson had vacated and undoubtedly getting no help from Jackson's staff who were just as confused by their chief's behavior, he returned to his brigade to await orders that never came. Soon after his departure from Hampton, Jackson lay down and went to sleep under a tree. One of General Whiting's aides commented wryly: "It looked to me as if on our side we were waiting for Jackson to wake up."[16]

There was one more possible avenue for Jackson to break the stalemate and contribute something useful to the battle. Shortly before Hampton finished his bridge, General Wright's brigade of Huger's division reached Jackson's position. Wright had marched the length of the New Road to White Oak Swamp and found the north side clear of Yankees. He reported to Jackson soon after that general had returned from his recon across the stream and likely after Hampton had already been ordered to build his bridge. Jackson ordered Wright to see if he could find another suitable crossing upstream in the direction from which he came. However, Jackson apparently did not order Wright to report back what he found. Wright found Brackett's Ford and pushed across a skirmish line, until he saw Slocum's division facing west down the Charles City Road. Wright withdrew and decided not to force the action here. Nor did he report to Jackson that Brackett's Ford, only a mile and a half away, could be crossed by infantry at the very least. Instead, he marched further west and recrossed the swamp at Fisher's Ford and rejoined Huger's stalled division.[17]

When Longstreet sent an aide to Jackson for help later in the afternoon, Jackson told him that he could do nothing. He had no plan to provide assistance to Longstreet's attack. As it was, Jackson fell asleep soundly while the artillery continued to fire, and could not easily be awakened. He even fell asleep eating his supper that evening. He roused himself awake long enough to say to his staff, "Now, gentlemen, let us at once to bed, and rise with the dawn, and see if tomorrow we cannot *do something!*"[18] The latter part of this statement suggests that even Jackson, in his torpor, recognized that his performance had been lacking.

Jackson's inaction on this day perplexed many of his officers and has befuddled historians. General Whiting was upset that Jackson did nothing. Longstreet wrote after the war that "Jackson should have done more for me than he did."[19] D. H. Hill suggested that Jackson was saving his men, who had fought hard over the last month. A courier said that "the truth of the matter is that he and his men had been completely worn out by what they had gone through."[20] Historians have largely accepted this last suggestion as the underlying cause of Jackson's poor performance. Clifford Dowdey offers the most elaborate defense of Jackson by identifying and explicating a stress fatigue symptom. Though he accepts Jackson's failure at White Oak as "unredeemable," he blames it all on clinical exhaustion. Stephen Sears agrees, saying, "What happened to Stonewall Jackson that Monday afternoon is obvious enough—with striking suddenness he reached the end of his physical endurance." Brian Burton accepts that fatigue, lack of sleep, and lack of food combined "to affect him on this, perhaps the worst of all possible days." Douglas Southall Freeman, musing as if he was a friend and personal physician of Old Jack, concludes that the general was brought down by "loss of sleep, on which his physique was especially dependent."[21]

However much some acknowledge that Jackson was fatigued and wish to grant him some peculiar susceptibility to that malady over every other commander in either army, there are other factors that were at play. Jackson's division commander and brother-in-law, D. H. Hill, who knew Jackson as well as any fellow officer, dismissed physical exhaustion as a determining factor and suggested instead that Jackson performed better as an independent commander than he did when subordinate to another's command. "Jackson's genius never shone when he was under the command of another" was how D. H. Hill put it. While one of Jackson's defenders dismissed this as "ridiculous" because it was not shown in his "character," whatever that means, the charge has merit.[22] Hill was not suggesting that Jackson deliberately performed poorly because he chafed under Lee's command. But there is no disguising that Jackson did perform much less dynamically in his first campaign under Lee's direction than he did when exercising independent command in the Valley. He was getting used to Lee's orders, with their ambiguity and discretion for commanders to implement the tactics as they deemed best. In some cases, he misunderstood the urgency of the orders; in others he took his orders too literally, believing he could not deviate from them. Some orders had been written, some verbal, some directly from Lee to him, and some indirectly through others (as was the case with the order to Stuart that Jackson thought authorized him to stay north of the Chickahominy River on June 29). Though Jackson greatly respected Lee, he did not yet implicitly understand his commander's orders and expectations. That would come in time and Jackson would perform well, even sensationally, in future battles with Lee. But that intuitive relationship was not established here in the week outside Richmond.

When Jackson spoke with Lee that morning and received his orders for the day, he knew he was to push on to White Oak Swamp. However, from that point, he could not decide what to do. Would Lee have wanted him to force a crossing and risk heavy casualties? Would Lee be satisfied with artillery harassment? At the very least, he seemed to be waiting to take any initiative until he received a more definite order from Lee. At Gaines Mill, Lee gave him further orders that altered his original ones and even commanded some of his men. Was Jackson perhaps expecting a similar follow-up order? It was Jackson's responsibility to inform Lee of the difficulties he faced and the possible avenues open to him and ask for further orders. Jackson would do so in future battles, but he had not developed that rapport with Lee yet.

It is impossible to know exactly why Jackson remained inactive when there were several opportunities to take action. At the very least, he was supposed to tie down Union troops and prevent them from reinforcing their western flank. But he did not do that, as four brigades (nearly 10,000 men) left his front and ended up fighting Longstreet and Hill. General William Franklin, who faced Jackson across White Oak Swamp, was as perplexed as anyone as to Jackson's inactivity. He was especially surprised Jackson did not discover or use Brackett's Ford to get on their flank. "It is likely that we should have been defeated," Franklin speculated, "had General Jackson done what his great reputation seems to make it imperative that he should have done."[23] Jackson's performance in the Valley had created such an outsized reputation among Confederate soldiers, civilians, and even fellow officers that any performance in the Seven Days that was less than spectacular would have been deemed a disappointment. As it was, however, Jackson's performance was less than even mediocre.

* * *

Huger finally arrived at Brackett's Ford Road, probably between 2:30 and 3:00 P.M., after Jackson's artillery had opened on Franklin's position. From his edge of the clearing, Huger could see a ridge half a mile away across the creek, lined with the artillery and infantry supports of Slocum's division straddling the Charles City Road. Huger decided to bring up artillery to shell the enemy's position, but he inexplicably only brought forward two guns, though several batteries were nearby and available. Once they began firing, the result was predictable—several Union batteries opened on the two guns, making for a very dangerous environment around them. Huger could have sent his infantry forward to challenge the Union line, but he deemed the position too strong. Without Wright's brigade, which was working its way back on the New Road, Huger did not have a significant numerical advantage over Slocum's 6,500 men. Huger considered sending troops off to his right to try to flank Slocum's position, but he never acted on that impulse until it was too dark to accomplish anything.

Not long after Huger arrived in this position, he must have heard the firing that was off to his right, for Longstreet's men had begun their attack by 4:00 P.M. It would not have taken long before Huger could tell by the volume of fire that a major action was occurring only a mile off to his right. Even this did not spur Huger into either sending his brigades into the fight or sending a courier to Lee to seek further orders. While Longstreet's and eventually A. P. Hill's men grappled with the better part of four Union divisions to the south, Huger fretted and hesitated about what to do with the one division facing him. The chances of Huger overwhelming his opponent were slim, but his orders were very specifically to attack. His attack would have put a further strain on the Union line and prevented Slocum from sending one brigade to bolster the Union line at Glendale, as he did late in the day. Lee was clearly disappointed in Huger's efforts and rebuked Huger in his final report for "not coming up" and supporting Longstreet and Hill's attack. As Burton deduces, the way that Lee phrased his passage meant that "Lee clearly thought Huger *could* have come up but did not."[24] Despite the opportunity and sounds of a violent contest a short distance away, Huger never got a single soldier into combat. The few casualties he incurred that day were from heat-related maladies and enemy artillery fire.

Although Huger and Jackson were performing significantly below Lee's expectations (though he did not know it yet), Longstreet and Hill were

giving him no reason to be displeased. Joining Longstreet after his morning meetings with Magruder and Jackson, Lee was in generally positive
spirits and excited by the possibilities of that Monday's battle. Longstreet
and Hill stepped off promptly from Atlee's farm in the early daylight hours,
marching down the Darbytown Road for four miles until it intersected the
Long Bridge Road. They turned east and marched two miles until about
11:00 A.M., when they halted one mile short of Glendale after meeting
enemy pickets. In the early afternoon, President Davis rode up to the
front of Longstreet's column where he met Lee and decided to needle him
in the same language Lee had used at Mechanicsville four days earlier.
"Why General," Davis asked Lee, "what are you doing here? You are in
too dangerous a position for the commander of the army." Lee replied,
"I am trying to find out something about the movements and plans of those
people." Then he turned the rebuke back on Davis, "But you must excuse
me, Mr. President, for asking what you are doing here, and for suggesting
that this is no proper place for the commander-in-chief of all our armies."
Davis responded, "Oh, I am on the same mission as you are." Longstreet
joined them and described what ensued as a "pleasant conversation, anticipating fruitful results from the fight."[25] Everyone was in high spirits, as
Yankee artillery shells started to land in the area around the horsemen.
As the shells fell too close for comfort, General A. P. Hill rode up and
diplomatically ordered both Lee and Davis to the rear, and they obeyed.[26]

Those shells were in response to what Longstreet and Lee thought was
the signal to begin the attack. Just before Davis joined them, firing had
been heard off to the north. Lee and Longstreet both assumed these were
the signal guns fired by Huger, and Longstreet ordered his batteries to
reply. There is some disagreement among scholars as to who had actually
fired those cannons. Dowdey claimed that they were Huger's guns and
they were fired at 2:30 P.M. Sears and Burton each say the artillery fire was
from Jackson's opening barrage at about 2:00 P.M. Yet, Longstreet claimed
he heard the firing at "about half past 2 o'clock," which would be more
in line with Huger's timetable. Longstreet suggested in his postwar memoir that he was aware of Jackson's artillery duel with Franklin, but was
still waiting for Huger's signal much closer than Jackson's. Regardless of
who was firing the cannons, sometime during the 2:00 P.M. hour, Lee and
Longstreet heard firing and assumed it was the signal of Huger's general
attack. Lee did not order Longstreet to send his troops in yet, preferring to
wait until it was clear that Huger had developed the attack.[27]

Around 3:00 P.M., Colonel Tom Rosser, who had been scouting down
the River Road well in front of Holmes's advancing force on the Confederate right, reported to Lee that McClellan's troops were crossing over

Malvern Hill to the James River. Concerned that Little Mac's army was getting away, Lee decided to ride to the River Road to see for himself. When Lee got to the road, he saw what Rosser had seen—many troops arranged in a defensive line at Malvern Hill and wagon trains crossing over the hill on their way to the safety of the James. Lee met with Holmes and ordered him to bring up his division and open fire on the Malvern Hill position with artillery. Lee hoped that at the very least he could disrupt the supply trains on their route to safety. Holmes dutifully brought his rifled guns forward—no more than six—and began shelling the strong Union position. No sooner had he opened fire than artillery from Malvern Hill and from gunboats in the river (including the *Galena* with McClellan on board) began firing in return, destroying or scattering Holmes's artillery and forcing his rather green infantry into a panicked retreat. The panic was so bad that even President Davis, who had followed Lee toward the River Road, felt compelled to try to rally the troops before giving it up as a lost cause. He duly commented that their flight "plainly showed that no moral power could stop them within range of those shells." As his troops fell back around his headquarters, the nearly deaf Holmes emerged from the house, cupped a hand to his ear, and in comic understatement declared, "I thought I heard firing."[28]

Unlike Huger and Jackson, there was little that Holmes could have done to engage the enemy. Geography and mathematics were stacked against him. Holmes had fewer than 6,500 men of all arms. He faced Colonel Gouverneur K. Warren's brigade on the crest of Malvern Hill, who, given its position, may have been able to hold him off alone. But, just for good measure, he was backed up by the rest of Sykes's and all of Morell's divisions of Porter's V Corps, with even more troops within easy supporting distance, not to mention all of Porter's reserve artillery. Nearly 24,000 men and a dozen batteries awaited Holmes on superior defensive terrain. Holmes called any idea of an attack "perfect madness" and he was right.[29]

Yet, Lee's scouting of the enemy position led him to a different conclusion. Lee apparently decided that if Holmes was supported by Magruder's 13,500 men, then their combined forces may be able to push back the defenders and challenge McClellan's escaping columns. Lee could not know the depth of the defender's ranks, but he gambled that an attack on Malvern Hill might place an additional strain on McClellan's lines and gain the breakthrough that he sought. Lee ordered Magruder's division, which was making good time marching southeast down the Darbytown Road toward Longstreet's division, to turn west and head to the River Road where he could deploy beside Holmes. Lee diverted Magruder away because he could arrive in time for an evening attack at Malvern Hill. Lee must have been convinced that there was already adequate force to deal with the Union opponents at Glendale without Magruder's troops. Of course, he could not know that Huger and Jackson would not bring any of their combined five divisions into the fight. Thus, he felt the added punch that Magruder could bring would be more useful at Malvern Hill than Glendale. It is unclear when exactly Lee made this decision, for his conference with Holmes did not include any orders to prepare for an attack when Magruder arrived. Perhaps Lee made his decision after talking to Holmes and thinking the situation over further and forming a new plan in his mind. Around 3:30 P.M., Lee sent the order to have Magruder support Holmes.

Magruder's experience on the afternoon would be a bewildering sequence of orders, marches, and countermarches. Before the day ended, Magruder would receive no fewer than seven orders, some from Longstreet, some from Lee's aide, R. H. Chilton, and presumably all under the direction of Lee. Magruder energetically tried to carry out his constantly evolving orders, perhaps seeking to redeem himself in Lee's eyes from the day before. Magruder rode to meet Chilton, who personally showed Magruder where Lee wanted his troops to deploy. Magruder ended up covering a lot of ground that evening, riding from one brigade to another and seeing to it that they were in the right position and correcting mistakes. Though some historians, especially Douglas Southall Freeman, criticize Magruder for his performance, one could argue that he was the only general on the day who obeyed Lee's orders promptly and to the letter. Perhaps he micromanaged a bit, but he was conscientiously trying to do his duty, even when that duty kept changing.

First, Magruder received orders to go to Holmes, then he was ordered to leave his artillery behind to expedite his movement, then he was shown where to put his troops in line. As he was doing that, around 6:30 P.M., he received an order from Longstreet to bring half his men to the Glendale fight. Magruder promptly put them in motion, and then as dark descended over the hills east of Richmond, he received an order from Chilton to bring his whole force to Glendale. With hardly any rest, he marched his units down the Long Bridge Road to Glendale, where Lee gave him his final order well after dark to relieve Longstreet's men on the front line. Magruder completed this task at about 3:00 A.M., when he fairly collapsed into sleep. Magruder's day had been as fruitless as it was exhausting. His men had marched and countermarched roughly 20 miles over a 20-hour period on the hottest day of the campaign. He could have been of best service to the Confederate cause that Monday if he had never been diverted to Holmes, but continued along the Long Bridge Road to join the fighting at Glendale. He would have been able to support A. P. Hill's attack, and perhaps may even have helped Lee realize his dream of crossing Willis Church Road and cutting the Union forces in half, but it was not to be. Though Lee had sent him to Holmes, it likely was not long before Lee wished that Magruder was near at hand on the Long Bridge Road, because the real fighting of the day occurred near the Glendale crossroads with Longstreet and Hill taking on nearly half of the disjointed Union army by themselves.

It is altogether fitting for this week of battles that Longstreet's initial attack occurred as a result of a misunderstood order. Lee had left Longstreet at 3:00 P.M. to go scout the River Road, and when he returned shortly after 4:00 P.M., he found Longstreet's division engaged in battle. But it was not the result of the coordinated attack with Huger and Jackson as Lee had hoped. Instead, one of Longstreet's new brigade commanders too eagerly tried to silence a Union battery that had been showering Longstreet's troops with shells. Micah Jenkins, a young colonel from a prominent South Carolina family, was commanding a brigade in battle for the first time because of a new and temporary command arrangement on June 30. Reflecting his growing trust in the energetic and heavily bearded 41-year-old general nicknamed "Old Pete," Lee had named Longstreet commander of a pseudocorps consisting of his and A. P. Hill's divisions. Longstreet then appointed Richard H. Anderson to take over as division commander, and the 26-year-old Jenkins took over Anderson's brigade. Jenkins's South Carolina brigade straddled the Long Bridge Road, which meandered northeast to Glendale. Three quarters of a mile in front of him, bisected by the road, was a line of batteries supported by Yankee infantry. Nearest to Jenkins was Captain James H. Cooper's Battery B, 1st Pennsylvania Light Artillery. Around 4:00 P.M., Longstreet ordered Jenkins to silence the battery, by which he likely thought that Jenkins would send the Palmetto Sharpshooters forward to pick off the gunners, "thus ridding us of that annoyance."[30] He thought Jenkins understood that he was not to bring on a general engagement yet. But the zealous Jenkins misunderstood Longstreet's command and sent his whole brigade forward to muzzle the batteries. "Only too anxious for a dash at a battery," as Longstreet put it, Jenkins charged into a hornet's nest of artillery and infantry, precipitating the general engagement that Longstreet had not yet sought.[31]

Jenkins's brigade charged across the field at Cooper's battery and the regiments of General Truman Seymour's brigade of McCall's division. The fire was withering, and the South Carolinians charged three times before finally reaching the guns and engaging in hand-to-hand combat with the defenders. One Union soldier historian wrote, "No pen will ever write the details of this strife, in which bayonet and butt were freely used."[32] The South Carolinians finally forced Seymour's brigade and the artillerymen to withdraw, leaving their guns on the field. But Colonel Seneca Simmons (who had taken over for the captured John Reynolds) ordered part of his reserve brigade forward and forced the South Carolinians to abandon their prizes. One Pennsylvania soldier wrote to his wife amazed that he lived through it: "If there was one Ball Whistled past my devoted head that day there was thousands . . . It appeared to me they flew in every Square inch of air around me except the little Space I stood in."[33] Jenkins also seemed favored by a divine providence that day, as his life was spared despite being conspicuous on horseback throughout the fight. He had his sword, bridle rein, saddle cloth, and overcoat hit by bullets and shell fragments, while he had two horses killed under him and was peppered in the shoulder and chest by spent shrapnel. He would not meet his end this day at the hands of the Yankees, but instead nearly two years later on May 6, 1864, accidentally shot by Confederates at the battle of the Wilderness. Jenkins's brigade, however, was dealt a severe blow by the Yankees in their opening fight, losing more than 500 of the 1,200 men in the brigade, with the Palmetto Sharpshooters being decimated in the multiple attacks, losing 254 of 375 men engaged, or 68 percent of their unit.[34]

Longstreet had not intended his order to Jenkins to start the battle, but he soon realized that the fight was on nonetheless. He ordered his other brigades to launch their attacks, which they did around 5:00 P.M. Thirty-nine-year-old General James Kemper's Virginia brigade was on Jenkins's right, southeast of the Long Bridge Road. Having been held in reserve at Gaines Mill, Kemper's men were anxious for their first major battle. So ready and eager were they that when Kemper ordered his men forward, they rushed to close with the enemy and lost their disciplined ranks as they charged through 1,200 yards of woods and clearings. They charged at the double-quick despite Kemper's orders to the contrary. They burst out onto a field near the house of a man named Whitlock, about half a mile southeast of the Long Bridge Road and three-fourths of a mile west of the Willis Church Road, the lifeline for the Union army that Lee hoped to cut. The Whitlock house also happened to be a key point in the Union line, for it was the far left flank of McCall's line, which was nearly half a mile in advance of Hooker's division off to his left. Kemper had stumbled upon a weak spot in the Union defense. The gap between McCall and his support was large enough that a force might be able to penetrate to the Willis Church Road. Reinforcements could possibly hold it, and five Union divisions would be cut off from the rest of the army.

Kemper's brigade met two Union batteries and two regiments of Seymour's brigade in a makeshift fortification around Whitlock's log farmhouse. Kemper's men braved the "incessant" artillery fire to close on the farmhouse redoubt. One Virginian remembered, "It looked like sure death to cross that field . . . but there was no stopping, and on we had to go, taking chances who should be shot down."[35] They closed so fast on the farmhouse that they actually reached the batteries under Captains John Knieriem and Otto Diederichs before Jenkins's men ever reached Cooper's battery. The German artillerists abandoned their guns before the Virginians reached them and the infantry fled when it appeared Kemper's men would surround this position. Many of these men fled south where they breached Hooker's line, prompting the angry Hooker to infuriate General McCall by declaring: "Conduct more disgraceful was never witnessed on a field of battle" than that exhibited by McCall's division.[36]

Kemper had actually moved so quickly that no other unit had been able to keep up with him. Branch's brigade of A.P. Hill's division was on Kemper's right, but they were not prepared or authorized to attack at the same time as Kemper. When they were finally ordered to attack, they drifted from Kemper's right to his rear. Kemper and his men realized they were unsupported far out in front and about to be counterattacked. Under McCall's orders, Simmons took two of his brigade's regiments along with another regiment from a different brigade and led the charge against Kemper. Kemper had been considering a withdrawal when he was attacked. Kemper's soldiers, spent from their sprint to the cannon, were driven back through the woods from which they came, leaving more than 400 of their 1,400 soldiers behind on the field or in enemy hands.

However, as Kemper's brigade fell back, they met Branch's brigade, which was finally moving forward. Branch decided to regain the ground around the Whitlock house that Kemper had vacated. At the same time, Colonel Eppa Hunton, who was in charge of the wounded George Pickett's brigade even though he was very ill himself, led his men diagonally across Branch's rear. Hunton had once been to the left and behind Jenkins, but while that brigade attacked northeast along the Long Bridge Road, Hunton led his men due east crossing behind Branch and coming into battle on his right. Hunton was too sick to keep up and passed command to Colonel John B. Strange, who led the brigade into battle riding alongside Captain Charles Pickett, George's brother. Pickett carried the flag until he was wounded and left behind, but the attack kept progressing until both Branch's and Hunton's brigade appeared in the Whitlock clearing. They burst into the clearing amid some confusion as to who was friend or foe, but soon got their bearings and charged the Union defensive line at the Whitlock house. Captains Knieriem and Diederich had just managed to get their men back to their guns, but only fired a few shots before the artillerymen broke and ran again. As the officers tried to rally their men, Colonel Simmons was mortally wounded and General Seymour was thrown heavily to the ground by his wounded horse. Dazed and likely concussed, Seymour would wander away from the battlefield toward White Oak Swamp.[37]

The Union line melted in the face of the yelling rebels and raced back across the fields. Branch and Strange followed them and approached to within a few hundred yards of the Willis Church Road. They scattered some weak resistance that had been set to block their way and appeared to be about to break the Union line. As Union batteries fired desperately to slow the Confederate advance, reinforcements arrived in the form of Sedgwick's division, which had been in reserve across the Willis Church Road. The brigades of Napoleon Dana and Alfred Sully, which had been sent to Franklin in the early afternoon, had just marched back as fast as they could to react to this attack. Sweating and breathless from their march, the regiments were fed into the battle as they arrived, just in time to stop the Confederate progress. Branch and Strange tried to hold their ground at first, but when Hooker sent some troops from General Cuvier Grover's brigade to attack Strange's right, the retreat began. Slowly, the two brigades were forced back to the Whitlock clearing. They had come close, but thanks to Sedgwick and Grover, they had been unable to break the Union line.

While all this was occurring, another bitter struggle was taking place to the northwest, to the left of Jenkins's original line. Cadmus Wilcox sent his Alabama brigade into the fight only after Hunton's brigade had attacked off to the right. Wilcox advanced up the Long Bridge Road. He could see Jenkins's brigade in its fight around Cooper's battery, so two of his regiments crossed east of the road to help out. West of the road, he ordered two other regiments along with a portion of Jenkins's troops who had been left behind, to attack Battery E, 1st U.S. Regulars under Captain Alanson Randol, which was supported by Meade's Pennsylvania brigade. They got within 50 yards of the guns in their first charge before having to fall back. When they did so, three regiments of Meade's brigade, Randol's infantry supports, sprang up and charged past the guns after the retreating foe despite Randol's shouts to stay back. When the Confederates reformed and delivered a volley into the faces of the Pennsylvanians, Meade's men lost their discipline and fled back to their own lines, going right through

Randol's battery and preventing him from firing on the Alabamians hot on their tail. By the time the Union troops cleared the guns, the Confederates were only 30 yards away, and Randol could only fire once, causing a lot of damage but not stopping the Southern tide. Randol and his men fled their guns. Meade was wounded in the attack and had to go to the rear. Union reserves were scraped together and charged the rebels around the guns, leading to a prolonged bout of close-quarter combat. The rebels eventually gave ground, leaving more than 250 casualties from Wilcox's two regiments on the field. Randol also fell back, leaving 12 guns in the no-man's land between the lines. McCall's already depleted division— Meade alone had already suffered 1,000 casualties at Gaines Mill—was completely used up. Every unit had broken and ran at least once, and every battery had been either forced to retreat or left guns on the field. But the next attack mercifully was not going to McCall's thin line, but to Kearny's on his right. Sedgwick's division was moving forward to plug the gaps as well during the brief lull in the fighting in the center, until A. P. Hill's reserves came forward.[38]

The next Confederate brigade to attack was General Roger Pryor's, who attacked as Wilcox was giving ground. He advanced to Wilcox's left, heading toward another battery, which was supported by General John C. Robinson's brigade of Kearny's division. Pryor had a more difficult time getting to the front because the heavily wooded terrain broke all sense of brigade order. He ended up having to feed his regiments into the battle one at a time. They were torn up by canister and rifle fire from Thompson's battery and Robinson's brigade. One Yankee lieutenant wrote, "I never saw such a slaughter . . . The head of the column seemed to sink into the ground." The men of the 14th Louisiana agreed, referring to Glendale ever after as "The Slaughter House."[39] Pryor was stymied and could not advance further, so he had his men take cover and hold their position while he called for help from General Winfield S. Featherston's brigade. He asked Featherston to attack on his left to relieve his flank. A quick scan of the Union line, however, showed the former Mississippi lawyer and politician that if he went in his left flank would be open to attack by the more numerous men of Kearny's division. He took a supporting position on Pryor's flank, about halfway between the Long Bridge and Charles City Roads, but did not launch an attack. The two sides exchanged fire from these positions for the rest of the day; Featherston was wounded in this exchange.[40]

As round one of the afternoon's fighting ended with Pryor's stalled attack, round two began as reinforcements from both sides arrived. To participants, there was no discernible lull as the fighting seemed to progress continually in an ebb and flow manner. A Minnesota officer described the long afternoon's musketry as "incessant, one terrific roar, no cessation or pause anywhere."[41] Over on the far left of the Confederate line, General Maxcy Gregg's brigade was sent to extend the flank of Featherston and Pryor, but encountered the same terrain difficulties and a stronger defensive force prepared to receive him. Gregg got one regiment into line to join Featherston's and Pryor's men in engaging in some rather hot and prolonged firing from a hundred yards distance, but found it futile to mount any sort of attack. At dusk, men of Robinson's brigade attacked Pryor and engaged in hand-to-hand combat, forcing the Southerners back a few yards, but nothing more.

To Pryor's right, as Wilcox's men fell back from their bitter fight for Randol's battery, General Charles Field's brigade of A. P. Hill's division entered the fray. The Virginians headed toward Randol's and Cooper's batteries. McCall had formed a ragged line with an assortment of scattered commands. As he was trying to put some of Kearny's regiments into this line, Kearny rode up to him. Both generals knew this was the critical moment of the battle. Kearny began arranging the defensive line and told McCall, "If you can bring on another line in a few minutes, I think we can stop them."[42] McCall rode off toward Glendale to find that other line. McCall found about 500 men from different units gathered there and brought them forward through the trees to the front lines. What McCall did not know was that while he was gone, Field's brigade had overrun Randol's battery and occupied much of the fields and woods he had just vacated. When McCall rode forward to find the best spot for his new line, he blundered into a group of soldiers he could not readily identify in the smoky dusk. He learned quickly that they belonged to Field's brigade. McCall, whose horse's bridle was seized by a private in the 47th Virginia, later admitted to his wife that he "was a prisoner before I knew where I was."[43] McCall was then taken to Longstreet, an old comrade from the 4th Infantry in the prewar army, who instinctively extended his hand in greeting to his old friend. Longstreet humorously recalled years later: "At the first motion, however, I saw he did not regard the occasion as one for renewing the old friendship," and instead he gave McCall an escort to prison in Richmond.[44]

Kearny nearly met the same fate as McCall at the same time. When riding to where he thought McCall's troops would be on his left flank, he found himself in the midst of Field's brigade. When a Southern captain saluted the general and asked what he should do next, the gruff Kearny, who knew he was in a tight spot, snarled, "Do, damn you, why do what you have always been told to do," and then sauntered off the way he had come leaving the bewildered captain even more confused. Kearny escaped with his bluff this time, but under almost the exact same circumstances two months later at Chantilly, Virginia, he would be shot and killed trying to escape.[45]

While part of Field's brigade captured Randol's battery, the right flank regiments recaptured Cooper's battery. Field's men charged bayonets and engaged in more close-quarters fighting forcing the Yankees to flee. The Rebels were able to maintain control of these guns for the remainder of the battle. At the end of the day, the Confederates captured and carried away 14 guns from Randol's, Cooper's, and Knieriem's batteries. Like Kemper before him, Field pursued the retreating Federals toward the Willis Church Road, allowing his men to get far out in front of their supports, opening themselves up to flank attacks. They were eventually attacked on their left flank by a unit near the Long Bridge Road. This attack stopped Field's momentum, and his men hunkered down in the darkness in a defensive position. The mystery brigade that stopped the attack was General George W. Taylor's New Jersey brigade of Slocum's division. Kearny had asked Slocum for a brigade to help fill a gap between him and McCall. Since Slocum was not being threatened by Huger, he felt safe in detaching Taylor's brigade. As Taylor's men marched to the field, Kearny showed them where to go. After waiting in the darkening woods, they found the right moment to make Field's brigade aware of their presence. Realizing a strong force was on his flank—primarily by the hundreds of muzzle flashes in the dim light—Field halted his men and pulled back to a safer position. When Field gave up the fight, fighting slowly ground to a halt for the night on the Confederate left, save for instances of blind firing.

While Field was having success driving the Union forces beyond the batteries, General William Dorsey Pender was leading his brigade into the fight on Field's right. It was not a continuous line, however, and Pender did not know Field was so close. Pender pushed his men through some scattered Yankee forces and advanced well past the Whitlock house. But he came across strong resistance in the Union army's last defensive line near the Willis Church Road. These were Sedgwick's men, plugging the gap left by McCall's shattered division. The fighting here was very hot. In the 22nd North Carolina regiment, the flag was shot to pieces and six color bearers went down. In the face of heavy fire in his front and right, Pender pulled back at dusk, unaware that Field was even further forward on his left flank. General James Archer took his brigade in at the same time as Pender on the latter's right and had some success, until he brushed up against Hooker's division on his front and right flank. His attack stalled, but his men held their position well to the south of the

Whitlock house and in front of Hooker's men. At the height of twilight, A. P. Hill decided to send his last brigade of General J. R. Anderson up the Long Bridge Road along the same general path that Jenkins and Field had taken. But difficulty telling friend from foe in the confused, smoke-clouded, dark forests prevented any successful action.[46]

Once the firing ended, the woods and clearings were again haunted by the groans of the wounded and their pitiful cries. "It was the saddest night I ever spent," wrote one Massachusetts soldier. "We could hear calls for Mississippi, Georgia, and Virginia, mingled with those for Michigan, New York, and Massachusetts." Tallying up the casualties is a difficult task because many units did not itemize their casualties by battle, but only totaled them for the whole campaign. Scholars have deduced through various calculations that the Confederates lost nearly 3,700 men in the fight while the Federals suffered approximately 3,800 casualties. The Union forces also lost 18 pieces of artillery, a heavy toll for any defending force, and nearly the same number lost at Gaines Mill, which was an admitted defeat.[47]

Glendale was not a clear victory for either side. The Confederates had driven the Union lines back and captured much of the battlefield, but they had not accomplished what they set out to do—breach the Willis Church Road and cut off part of the enemy army. Although they came close on several occasions, a little better organization, concert of action, or the support of a few more reserves may have succeeded. In the fight, Longstreet's and Hill's divisions were totally used up and not combat effective for the near future. At Gaines Mill and Glendale, Longstreet had lost more than half (4,600) of his 9,000 men, and in three hard fights, Hill lost nearly a third of his division—4,000 out of 14,000 men. On the Union side, McCall's division was exhausted, losing more than 3,000 of his 9,000 men in his five days of the campaign.

That evening around 8:30 P.M., as the firing died down in the last throes of the final Confederate attack, McClellan and his entourage rode up to Porter's headquarters at Malvern Hill. Refreshed from his trip and fine dinner on the *Galena*, McClellan arrived at the very end of the battle to check on the outcome of this dangerous day. Without knowing the result, he had sent a message to Washington saying, "We are hard pressed by superior numbers," and vowing once again: "If none of us escape we shall at least have done honor to the country. I shall do my best to save the Army," before requesting more reinforcements.[48] It was at once heroic, morose, and disingenuous. McClellan had not been present at the fight to save the army, and he left them with a leadership void by not designating a commander of the field. As it turned out, he also did not face overwhelming numbers. Since Huger, Jackson, and Magruder did not get into the fight, fewer than 20,000 Confederates ended up fighting more than 23,000 defenders.

That night, without any communication from McClellan, the Union defenders of Glendale pulled back from their lines and continued the march south to the James. McClellan claimed to his staff that he was surprised by this move, but he had made it clear all week that they were seeking to reach the James River as quickly as possible. In the absence of any specific orders to the contrary, his corps commanders were merely following the plan they expected McClellan to approve. Once more, the tired Union soldiers engaged in another night march. They moved in such a confused manner that some pickets were accidentally left behind to be captured, and "Baldy" Smith, who had fallen asleep, almost met the same fate. They trudged south along the Willis Church Road, though few knew or cared. As a Yankee lieutenant wrote, "What the road was . . . I cannot recall . . . I know simply that it was darkness and toil, until we began climbing a hill and were greeted with advancing dawn."[49] The hill they crossed was Malvern Hill, a little over two miles south of the Glendale crossroads, and it would be the scene of the last desperate battle in this exhausting week.

* * *

As darkness descended on the Confederate lines, Lee tried to understand why his plan had failed again. It had seemed such a golden opportunity. Years later, E. Porter Alexander was still haunted by the failure: "When one thinks of the great chances in General Lee's grasp that one summer afternoon, it is enough to make one cry to give the story of how they were all lost."[50] Alexander placed most of the blame on Jackson, but there was plenty of blame to go around. Longstreet and A. P. Hill, who did all of the fighting, and Magruder, who simply obeyed all seven orders he received through Lee's auspices, can be largely absolved of blame. Nor can Holmes be faulted, for his puny division was never able to take Malvern Hill. Huger and Jackson have already been singled out for their particular failures this day, which were great. But if Lee wanted to honestly find the source of what went wrong this day, he had only to look in the nearest mirror. There had been another serious lack of communication, and though Huger and Jackson should have been more forthcoming with their problems, Lee could have sent a courier to discover what delayed them. Lee chose to ride with Longstreet, perhaps because of his growing partiality to this stalwart fighter, but Lee considered Huger's assault to be the linchpin of the day's activity—the catalyst of the battle. Since Longstreet was waiting on Huger to start the battle, Lee could have joined Huger to make sure he got the battle going in a timely manner. The fact that he did not—in fact, Huger is the only division commander Lee did not personally speak to on June 30—is all the more perplexing given Lee's bitter disappointment with Magruder's failure to engage the enemy in a timely manner the day before. Huger sent Lee a note at noon saying he was delayed by obstructions. Lee could have ridden over then to inspect to see if he needed to alter his plan, or at least could have sent a staff officer he trusted to get more specifics on Huger's dilemma. The same is true for Jackson. If Lee wanted to make sure that all his separate elements were going to perform their assignments, then he could have micromanaged a little more effectively, sending couriers to get regular updates on progress and difficulties. After all, he did consider this day to be his best chance to win the battle he was seeking.

The one part of the battlefield that Lee did personally inspect was the least important. Lee rode to Holmes's sector at 3:00 P.M. to see Union troops on Malvern Hill guarding the passing supply wagons. Lee seemed to be of mixed mind on what to do. He did not tell Holmes to prepare for an assault on that virtually impregnable hill, but did order Magruder to move his divisions to the River Road to prepare for just such an undertaking. When Magruder communicated with Holmes to coordinate their alignment, Holmes was both testy and clueless about any proposed assault because Lee had never told him.

This indicates that Lee perhaps got greedy, thinking he could try to bag everyone at once. He assumed that the action at Glendale would cut off the Union rearguard without Magruder's presence being necessary, and decided to try to capture Malvern Hill as well. But for Lee, the engineer and veteran scout, to look at the Malvern Hill position—with its high crest, dominating artillery, and no reasonable route for attack—and think it could be taken by storm reveals poor military judgment. Holmes was in no danger, as Lee already had realized McClellan would not be the aggressor. Magruder's men would have been much better utilized serving as a reserve force for Longstreet and Hill and could have been in position on the Long Bridge Road by late afternoon with several hours of daylight left. As it was, any attack at Malvern Hill would have to be a twilight assault. This is the most difficult decision of Lee's to understand. He knew that, soon after he returned to Longstreet and witnessed the fighting there, Longstreet would need support, which is why he sent back for half of Magruder's division to march to Longstreet. He likely even realized that he had made a mistake in diverting Magruder, but by then it was too late—the damage had been done.

Therefore, through a combination of failures by Huger and Jackson, a lack of communication, and surprisingly poor judgment by Lee, Glendale failed to be the decisive battle Lee had thought it would be. Much of this was simply growing pains for a new commander. As Brian Burton argues, Lee "had not yet honed his army into a coordinated fighting force," and he also had not developed his own battle management skills, yet.[51] He had demonstrated a gift for crafting clever plans, but had not yet learned how to insure the proper execution of those plans. This would come in time, but unfortunately for the Confederates that day would not be the next day, Tuesday, July 1. For a great many of Lee's soldiers, it would be their last day in this world.

6

⎯⎯◦≪◦⎯⎯

Malvern Hill, July 1

Dawn of July 1 broke hazy, hot, and humid, but with the promise of a slight breeze on the plateau of Malvern Hill. The Union army was arranged in a loose, inverted horseshoe, with the bend facing north in the direction from which the Confederates would emerge. The Willis Church Road bisected the plateau on its way south. Confederate scouts examining the Union line that dewy dawn would have found George Sykes's division holding the west side, topping Malvern Cliffs and covering the River Road. His division had turned away Theophilus Holmes the day before. George Morell's division guarded the north side of the line, extending from Sykes's division east to the Willis Church Road. His position bent around one of the two main landmarks on the battlefield—the Crew House. The other notable structure was the West House, a few hundred yards to the east, across the Willis Church Road. General Charles Griffin's brigade was in a field north of the Crew House, with a few slave cabins scattered among the lines. The brigades of Generals John H. Martindale and Daniel Butterfield were behind and east of Griffin, with Butterfield's right flank touching the road. General Darius Couch's division of Keyes's IV Corps extended the Union line east of the road. Couch—a thin, wiry New Yorker of delicate health just three weeks shy of 40, who had graduated 11 places behind McClellan at West Point in 1846—arranged his three brigades of Generals Innis Palmer (minus two regiments), Albion Howe, and John Abercrombie in depth, facing north, just in front of the West House. Their right abruptly stopped in some thick woods surrounding a ravine, through which flowed a small stream called Western Run. Behind Couch's line and facing east were Sumner's II Corps and Heintzelman's III Corps. Franklin's VI Corps was even further south, guarding the eastern approaches of the River Road.

The infantry manning the lines on the high ground made the line a very formidable one, but the artillery crowning the plateau is what made the position especially daunting. All of the army's artillery—268 regular pieces including 26 siege pieces—was in the vicinity guarding the approaches from every direction. On the narrow northern front, facing the direction from which the Confederate attacks would eventually appear, seven batteries of 31 guns spread across the Willis Church Road under the leadership of Griffin, a former artillery officer. Further to the east, guarding the approaches from the east and northeast were 10 batteries, or 60 guns. Another 52 guns were in reserve around Malvern House, along with 16 heavy guns of McClellan's siege train, all under the capable leadership of Colonel Henry J. Hunt, who would play an instrumental role on this day locating artillery and moving units to the front to keep up a steady fire. According to Porter, who had already fought behind strong positions at Beaver Dam Creek and Gaines Mill, the Malvern Hill area was "better adapted for a defensive battle than any with which we had been favored."[1]

Despite the favorable nature of the position, the army's commander did not intend to share the battle with his soldiers. McClellan rode around the lines that morning to hearty cheers from his soldiers and then rode off to Haxall's Landing where he sent several telegrams. Then, accompanied by General William Franklin, McClellan boarded the *Galena* to steam downriver to inspect the Harrison's Landing site, which he had chosen as the army's ultimate destination. He even napped for a couple of hours during the journey. After the inspection he returned by river to Haxall's Landing and rode up to Malvern Hill in mid-afternoon, shortly before the battle began. After Porter expressed his confidence in holding the position facing north, he suggested McClellan tend to the eastern side, where the corps of Sumner and Heintzelman were located. Little Mac did so, and as a result took no substantial part in the battle, acting more as an observer than a commander.

The only potential weakness of this position was the narrowness of the northern front. It was only 1,200 yards wide, with two divisions and 31 guns guarding that approach. Yet, the ravines on either side funneled the Confederates into their approach over open terrain, making a perfect killing field. If Lee was to break this line through frontal assault, it would take a great deal of skill and coordination. A successful assault not only

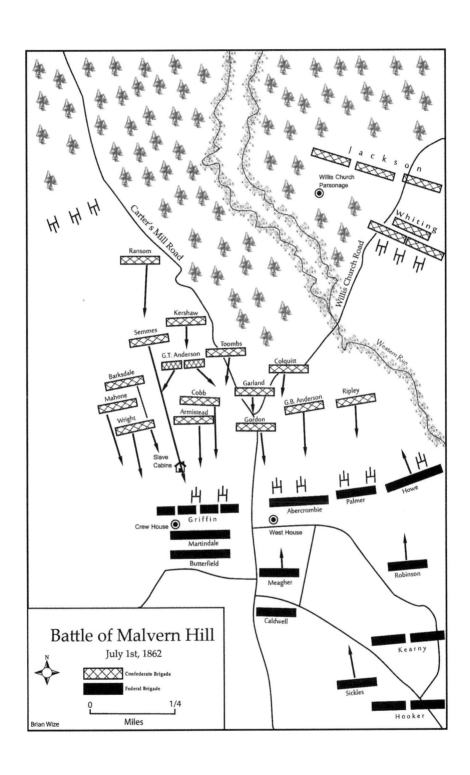

Battle of Malvern Hill

July 1st, 1862

N

⬡⬡⬡⬡ Confederate Brigade

███ Federal Brigade

0 ——————— 1/4

Miles

Brian Wize

Jackson

Willis Church
Parsonage

Whiting

Carter's Mill Road

Ransom

Willis Church Road

Kershaw

Semmes

Toombs

G.T. Anderson

Western Run

Barksdale

Cobb

Garland

Colquitt

Mahone

Armistead

Gordon

G.B. Anderson

Ripley

Wright

Slave
Cabins

Griffin

Abercrombie

Palmer

Howe

Crew House

West House

Martindale

Robinson

Butterfield

Meagher

Caldwell

Kearny

Sickles

Hooker

would suffer heavy casualties, but would also have to overcome the depth of the Union position, where several divisions were available to be rushed forward to plug gaps. It would be a remarkable achievement if Lee could break McClellan's army here. He would have to be at the top of his game.

However, on this day, at the end of a frustrating and disappointing week, Lee was not at his physical best. He had not slept long or well on any night of the week, and he felt fatigued and generally ill. The bitter disappointment over the last two days' failures had not ameliorated his condition. In fact, he felt so out of sorts that he asked Longstreet, whose division was to remain in reserve with A.P. Hill's men, to accompany him that day, in case "Old Pete" had to assume command of the army. While D.H. Hill and Longstreet both claimed that Lee remained composed in light of all the army's misfortunes, he was not able to entirely mask his exasperation. When General Jubal Early, just recovered from a wound he had received nearly two months earlier, reported to Lee for assignment that morning and commented that McClellan might elude them, Lee snapped uncharacteristically, "Yes, he will get away because I cannot have my orders carried out!"[2]

Lee and Longstreet rode south in the direction of the recently fled Yankees until they came to Willis Methodist Church, where they met D.H. Hill who had been doing some scouting after his division had crossed the White Oak Bridge. Hill had been chatting with a chaplain from the area as to what the ground looked like at Malvern Hill and he did not like what he heard. He learned that Malvern Hill was an imposing position and he repeated the chaplain's warnings to Lee, suggesting, "If General McClellan is there in strength, we had better let him alone." At this, Longstreet chuckled and bantered, "Don't get scared, now that we have got him whipped." Hill undoubtedly did not appreciate this remark, but apparently did not retort.[3]

Though Longstreet had lost half his division during the week, he was convinced the Union army was demoralized and retreating in a hurry. Thousands of blankets, knapsacks, and weapons were scattered all over the fields and the Willis Church Road. It indicated that McClellan's army was shattered in spirit and ripe for the taking if they were pressed hard. Lee wanted badly to believe that as well and he moved his army into position to try to hit the retreating Federals one last time in order to demolish them. D.H. Hill later confirmed, "It was this belief in the demoralization of the Federal army that made our leader risk the attack."[4]

During the early daylight hours, Jackson's army crossed White Oak Swamp and moved south through Glendale. As he came to the intersection with the Willis Church Road, the leading elements of his troops met skirmishers from Magruder's command. Magruder and Jackson soon met up and rode to meet Lee, whom they found on the Willis Church Road. Lee had decided that today's attack would be conducted by the troops of Magruder, Jackson, and Huger, because they had seen no significant fighting the previous day. Lee spoke to Magruder and Jackson directly about their roles. Jackson was to lead with his army down the east side of the Willis Church Road, while Magruder would follow Jackson down the same road and position his men to the west of the road. The main problem with Lee's instructions was that he referred to the Willis Church Road as the Quaker Road, because that was how it was labeled on all of his maps. However, there was another Quaker Road about two miles to the west that led from Long Bridge Road southwest to an intersection with River Road. This was yet another example of confusing maps that plagued Lee's army the entire campaign. It would have bad consequences, as Magruder employed three local guides to lead his troops down the Quaker Road, and they would dutifully take him toward the real Quaker Road and not the Willis Church Road as Lee intended. Also missed by the mapmakers was another road about a mile east of the Willis Church Road that ran largely parallel to it. It had been taken by Keyes's and Franklin's wagons, and would have possibly provided a better flanking avenue for Jackson's troops.

While Jackson and Magruder left to conduct their troops in opposite directions, Lee dispatched Longstreet to ride over to scout the west side of the Willis Church Road while he personally scouted the east. Lee wanted to see if there was a fruitful opportunity for attacking McClellan's army. Longstreet saw real possibilities as he emerged onto the north end of the clearing facing the Union's Malvern Hill position. Longstreet arrived where two of Huger's brigades had already appeared. These two brigades, under Generals Armistead and Wright, had been sent by Huger on a flanking attack that morning, 12 hours too late to help the Confederates on the Glendale battlefield. They found Union troops gone and Confederates everywhere. Armistead encountered Lee on the Long Bridge Road that morning and the commander had sent him down the Carter's Mill Road, which ran southeast from Long Bridge Road about a mile west of Glendale and intersected the Willis Church Road just a few hundred yards north of the Malvern Hill plateau. Following orders, Armistead with Wright behind him had emerged on a plateau that equaled Malvern Hill in height. Between the two was a 60-foot valley that sloped up nearly 1,000 yards to the Union position.

Longstreet scouted the position and thought the plateau was the key to winning the day. Longstreet believed that the Rebels could fit 60 artillery pieces on the plateau behind Armistead. Longstreet reasoned that if a similar position existed east of the road—and indeed, Confederate artillerists had found one—then massing artillery at both locations would catch the Union army in a powerful and demoralizing crossfire. A strong infantry attack on the heels of this cannonade could carry the Union position and perhaps apply the coup de grace Lee had been seeking.[5]

As he was scouting the plateau, Longstreet encountered Magruder, who had ridden to the same terrain to observe the field. While they agreed on the placement of artillery, Longstreet noticed with disbelief that Magruder's men were marching away from the battlefield. Magruder sensed this too, but his guides were certain they were going to the only Quaker Road in the area. Magruder was sensitive to disobeying Lee's orders, and since Lee had told him to march down the Quaker Road that's what he would do. Yet, he offered to turn around on Longstreet's order. Longstreet was not prepared to override Lee, so Magruder continued his errant march. Longstreet sent a message to Lee reporting the possibility of using artillery to great effect and also of Magruder's mistaken march. Lee wrote back agreeing with Longstreet's artillery plan and sent pioneers to help clear a path for the guns. He also sent his aide, R. H. Chilton, to show Magruder the proper path. In the meantime, Longstreet had decided to ride after Magruder to change his march. Ultimately, he and Chilton arrived at the same time and convinced Magruder to turn around. Meanwhile, Longstreet was supposed to locate batteries to send to Armistead's plateau to take their part in the artillery barrage.[6]

While Magruder's troops were retracing their steps, Jackson's troops were filing into position and Lee was scouting on the left. He decided that a plateau near the Poindexter farm on Jackson's side would serve as an excellent position for a "grand battery" to complement the one Longstreet suggested on the right. Lee ordered Longstreet to place batteries on the right and he ordered Jackson to do the same on the left. After Chilton had returned from his errand to Magruder, Lee explained the attack plan to him and authorized him to draft an order to all his lieutenants. Chilton, however, continued his trend of drafting imprecise orders. Sometime before 1:00 P.M., Chilton wrote the following order: "Batteries have been established to act upon the enemy's line. If it is broken as is probable, Armistead, who can witness effect of the fire, has been ordered to charge with a yell. Do the same."[7]

There are many problems with this ambiguous order. There was no time listed on the order, so no one would know precisely when it was authorized. It placed the burden of launching the army's attack on the shoulders of one brigadier general, who was leading his brigade into battle for the first time. The "yell" that was to be the signal for the attack would never be heard across the entire battlefield over the cacophony of rifle and cannon fire. For an attack that was perhaps his last chance to accomplish his goal, Lee should have drafted the key order himself, or at the very least proofread the order to minimize confusion. But he did not and there is no clear reason why. Some historians argue that exhaustion clouded Lee's judgment. At one point in the afternoon, Lee fell asleep and President Davis, on the field again, prevented anyone from disturbing him.[8]

Perhaps Lee meant the order to be discretionary, contingent only on the clear success of the artillery barrage. If a major attack was to be launched, Lee should have been the one to decide when. If his order was exactly as he intended (and Longstreet suggested that it was), then his place was with Armistead, so that Lee could personally observe the effect of the fire and decide if and when an attack was warranted. The fact that Lee later rode off to the Confederate left looking for other possibilities implies that Lee did not consider the order to be binding, but rather contingent on artillery success. To top it off, the order was sent only to division commanders, so Armistead never received a copy and was completely unaware of the pivotal role that he was to play in the attack.

Lee's attack would not occur after a successful artillery barrage. In fact, the unsparing D. H. Hill characterized the artillery's performance as "most farcical." The lack of adequate numbers, poor communication, and even poorer military judgment by the local commanders resulted in the artillery's poor performance. It also did not help that the Confederates acknowledged that their artillery was of inferior size and quality to the Union artillery. Jackson faced a shortage of batteries near at hand. D. H. Hill's artillery had exhausted its ammunition in the useless barrage at White Oak Swamp the previous day. Therefore, his seven batteries would not be available for this fight. That left 10 remaining batteries, but these were divided throughout Jackson's remaining three divisions. They could not all be brought forward quickly because of their widely scattered nature.[9]

Miscommunication also played a role. Lee had an artillery reserve of six batteries under General William N. Pendleton. However, there is no record that Lee ever sent for Pendleton to bring his guns up, even though it would have been most logical for the creation of two grand batteries. Pendleton, for his part, spent much of the day trying to track down the army's commander to see where he could best be utilized. He never found the general and his batteries remained idle all day. Additionally, there were several available batteries of Longstreet's, A. P. Hill's, and Magruder's commands that were never brought forward into the battle.[10]

Any artillery commander could see the enemy's numerous cannon on the plateau half a mile away and knew that only massed artillery could possibly challenge massed artillery. Opening fire with a single battery or two on the massed Union cannons would only invite retaliation and destruction of the individual batteries. However, Jackson believed that his orders were to move quickly, and he therefore did not wait until he could mass his batteries, but ordered his guns to fire on the enemy as they arrived. When Jackson ordered General Whiting to open fire with his three batteries (only 16 guns) once they were in position in the Poindexter wheat field, Whiting balked. "They won't live in there five minutes," Whiting protested. Jackson crossly barked, "Obey your orders, General Whiting, promptly and willingly." Whiting, equally in a foul temper and unimpressed with Jackson's performance thus far, retorted, "I always obey my orders promptly, but not willingly under such circumstances."[11] With that exchange concluded, Whiting reluctantly sent his batteries into the field. Jackson pointed them to the position he wanted them, and they ventured on to the high ground of the wheat field and unlimbered. As soon as they did so, the 31 Union cannons 800 yards away turned on them and blistered them with a destructive fire, hitting gunners and horses and wrecking the guns.

While the Confederates did some minor damage to the Union line, they were no match for the well-served Federal cannon and had to withdraw, though they had lasted longer than the five minutes Whiting predicted. Three more batteries would suffer the same fate. Because of a lack of coordination, Jackson's guns opened long before Longstreet had gotten the right grand battery into action; thus, there was no crossfire on the Union guns. While Longstreet and Lee had been persuaded that nearly 100 guns could be put into action in the two batteries, the 16 of Whiting's that opened the barrage was the largest concentration on the day. While Longstreet's grand battery did open when Jackson's guns were still hanging on, they were not able to mass either, and therefore were ineffective. As each battery came forward, it was sent into action separately and was overwhelmed by the superior Federal guns. Only six batteries ever got into action on the right, and they did so individually. No more than eight guns ever got into action at the same time. Thirty-five batteries were available, but never got into the fight. Nearly 100 Confederate artillerymen were casualties on this day for practically no gain. One reason for Union artillery superiority on this day was that most of the enlisted men and noncommissioned officers in the Union batteries had been in the army since before 1861, suggesting that they had had much more practice at their craft—and artillery in particular took a lot of time of experience to master—than the relatively recently formed Confederate artillery units.[12]

The Union fire also inflicted numerous casualties on the infantry soldiers nearby supporting the artillery and very nearly took out some of the Southern high command. One shell landed right in front of Jackson's horse as he was riding and talking with General Ewell; Ewell grabbed the bridle of Jackson's horse and steered him away only a few seconds before the shell exploded. On the same part of the field, D. H. Hill was sitting with his back against a tree writing an order when a Union shell landed close enough to bowl him over, cake him in dirt, and tear his uniform coat. Hill stood up and dusted himself off, but then sat on the opposite side of the tree before resuming his activity. He remarked calmly to his stunned nearby staff, "I'm not going to be killed until my time comes." Undoubtedly, for a few seconds, he must have believed that time had arrived on July 1.[13]

Sometime in mid-afternoon, probably around 3:00 P.M., after the Confederate artillery had been testing the range for an hour, Lee recognized that the original plan was not going to work. Still, he was determined to find a way to hit McClellan one more time before he reached the James. Lee asked Longstreet to join him and the two of them rode off to the east to scout that area hoping to find a way to attack the Union right flank. Lee thought he saw an opportunity to hit the Union right, and he decided to move Longstreet's and Hill's reserve divisions to the Confederate left to prepare for an assault that would have to occur the next day. General Branch received an order to move his brigade to the right just as the fighting started at Malvern Hill, which essentially cancelled the order. Lee possibly expected McClellan to remain at Malvern Hill, as it was close enough to the James for the gunboats to aid him—in fact some of these shells had hit Confederates behind the front lines already—and Little Mac's army defended a very strong, elevated position. Lee also assumed that since the artillery had not disrupted the Union lines, there would be no attack on July 1. But thanks to the confusing, untimed order written by Chilton that had never been cancelled by Lee, there would indeed be fighting on that Tuesday afternoon.

There is confusion about the sequence of events that occurred in the early afternoon hours of July 1, especially regarding what Lee's exact plan was and when Chilton's order was written. Stephen Sears suggested that Lee had the order written soon after he and Longstreet discussed the idea of the two grand batteries, and that the order reflected Lee's intended battle plan for the day. Brian Burton dissents, implying that Lee had the order written right about the time the guns began firing, and used Armistead as the signal because Armistead's troops had already advanced to a forward position, about 400 yards from the Union line (because he had been chasing away Union sharpshooters), and therefore could see the effect of the Confederate fire most clearly.[14]

Regardless of Lee's intentions, some facts are undeniable. At some time after noon, Lee did decide to establish two grand batteries to try to soften the Union defenses, and he did authorize Chilton to draw up an order stipulating as much. Lee may or may not have proofread Chilton's order, but if Lee ever decided that the artillery attack was a failure, he never cancelled Chilton's order or sent an updated one. Longstreet speculated, "Under the impression that his officers realized the failure and abandonment of his original plan, General Lee failed to issue orders specifically recalling the appointed battle."[15] His generals on the field remained ready to obey Chilton's untimed order, as soon as the shout was given from Armistead's side of the field.

Shortly after 3:00 P.M., Magruder arrived on the field with his brigades. Lee may have been off scouting to the east at this time, but he more than likely was behind the lines conferring with Huger or others. His presence is not exactly known at this crucial moment, but it is clear from the subsequent events that occurred almost simultaneously that he was not in a position to observe the battlefield. On arrival, Magruder quickly appraised the tactical situation, saw Armistead had advanced, saw the daunting Union line ahead of him, and undoubtedly experienced some of the artillery pounding that subdued the right grand battery. The tired Magruder then dutifully sent an aide, Captain A. G. Dickinson, to report to Lee, stating that he had arrived with his command and that Armistead had driven a body of the enemy—Berdan's sharpshooters who had been picking off his men from behind shocks of wheat.

As Dickinson set off to find Lee, some Union batteries started retiring from the firing line. Several batteries had nearly expended their ammunition during their several hours of firing that day and were falling back to restock. Some had already fired as many as 750 rounds![16] Other batteries came forward to take their place. However, when General Whiting, who was still angry at Jackson and wanted to believe that his artillery had given as much damage as they received, saw the first Union batteries withdraw, he erroneously believed that they had been driven away by Confederate artillery fire and were retreating. He sent a message stating as much to Lee. This messenger and Captain Dickinson found Lee at nearly the same time. Lee, unable to see the battlefield, relied on his two commanders' judgment and decided that the artillery must have had a demoralizing effect on the enemy. Lee decided to initiate the attack after all, hoping to rout the retreating Federals. He gave Dickinson an order to give to Magruder, and Dickinson wrote it down to make sure he got it right: "General Lee expects you to advance rapidly. He says it is reported that the enemy is getting off. Press forward your whole line and follow up Armistead's success."[17]

This was the moment that Lee had been hoping for and it seemed almost too good to be true. But for whatever reason, Lee did not ride to the front to observe the enemy's line for himself. He could not have been more than a 10-minute ride away from the front. He had seen the Union line and knew how formidable it was. Before ordering tens of thousands of his soldiers to charge across half a mile of open field into a strong defensive line, Lee should have checked to make absolutely sure the enemy was retreating. Instead, despite his own judgment that the artillery had failed, he accepted the word of Whiting that it was succeeding, and of Magruder that Armistead had already started driving the enemy. It would be a costly mistake.

As Dickinson was returning to Magruder with Lee's orders, Magruder finally received Chilton's undated order for the first time. He assumed it had just been written, and he endeavored to obey it by placing some more batteries to give greater crossfire on the Union position. Magruder sent Major Brent to bring forward Mahone's and Ransom's brigades and their batteries, but Brent learned from those officers that Huger, who was upset that his brigades had been placed without his knowledge, had given explicit orders to Ransom and Mahone not to move unless by his personal command. Brent reported this to Magruder, who was incredulous. He sent Brent back with the unconditional command to bring at least one up. In the meantime, Lee ordered Huger to give Mahone to Magruder, so Mahone followed Brent, but Huger arrived at Ransom's location and ordered him not to move. It was petulant behavior by Huger, who seemed to be expressing his authority out of spite because others had moved his brigades without consulting him. It did not apparently matter that the army's commander had been the one that ordered Armistead and Wright to travel down the Carter's Mill Road that morning to their front line position.[18]

At around 5:00 P.M., while Brent was dealing with Huger's brigadiers, Captain Dickinson reached Magruder with Lee's peremptory order to "press forward your whole line" rapidly. Two orders from Lee in a short span of time convinced Magruder that it was imperative that he attack immediately. He estimated that he had about 15,000 men present, but not all were in position to attack yet. Magruder rode to the front and observed the field with Armistead and Wright. Their units would lead the

assault. Armistead's brigade was split—three regiments were forward having driven off the sharpshooters and three regiments were behind under
the cover of the woods. Armistead was concerned because the latter three
regiments were not battle tested. Magruder decided to send General
Howell Cobb's brigade in with those regiments to keep them in line. All
would follow the path Armistead had started. Ambrose Wright would also
advance to the right of Armistead, heading directly for the Crew House.
Due to poor direction and leadership on the scene, Wright only had three
regiments embark on the attack, fewer than 1,000 men. Behind Wright
was Mahone's brigade, which had arrived on the field by this time.

Thus, at around 5:30 P.M., Wright's men sounded a shout and began
moving across the field, taking heavy fire as they went. They got to within
300 yards of the Union line before stopping and taking shelter in a dip
in the terrain. One irony of the battle for the emerging Confederates was
that, due to the undulations of the ground, it was often safer to advance
closer to the Union guns where ravines and gullies provided defilades that
sheltered the men from the artillery. The fire seemed so heavy to one
Georgia soldier that he wrote, "It is astonishing that every man did not
fall."[19] Mahone's men following behind Wright went through the same
murderous fire, and eventually joined Wright's men in the depression that
offered only limited concealment. There, the men were still subject to
the fire of Berdan's sharpshooters, who had taken a new position off to
the west, hidden behind shocks of wheat in the field. Around the Crew
House, regiments of Griffin's and Martindale's brigades shifted to meet
the Confederate advance.

Just to the left of Wright, Armistead's men, who had advanced to a
forward position earlier in the day, cheered on Wright's men. With new
orders and new motivation, Armistead's regiments rose and charged to
within 75 yards of the Union line—toward Griffin's brigade—where they
paused and exchanged fire. After a couple of rounds, the partial brigade
charged the Union cannon, but were immediately stopped by a withering
fire and counterattacked by Griffin's infantry who moved in front of the
guns in order to repel the rebel advance. They forced Armistead's men
to retreat. Cobb's brigade and Armistead's remaining regiments were following Armistead's lead regiments and launched a second charge on the
Union line, forcing the Northerners to fall back behind the cannon and
capturing 25 Yankees who did not retreat fast enough. They pressured the
Union line, even causing some bluecoats to be hit by fire from their own
men who worked to secure the line. But, the firing of canister right in the
faces of Cobb's troops was too much and the Confederate line broke and
fell back in a disorganized fashion.

This flirtation with success had emboldened Wright and Mahone to try to charge their opponents again. One difficulty was that they had to charge up a rather steep ravine to reach the Union position around the Crew House on the crest of the bluff. Wright's and Mahone's brigades got to within 200 yards before enemy fire and difficult terrain defeated them. They experienced "as terrible a fire of grape, canister and Minie balls as ever was rained and poured about mortal man," wrote one of Wright's soldiers. Proving his point, the six guns of Company A, 5th U.S. Artillery, under Lieutenant Adelbert Ames, which was located in the center of Morell's line, west of the Willis Church Road, fired 1,392 rounds of shell and canister at the charging gray line in the afternoon! The Confederates could not advance any closer into this destructive fire, and spent the rest of the evening hugging the ground and firing up the hill. It had been brief and intense, but for all intents and purposes, except for a few scattered charges by the remnants, the four brigades of Mahone, Wright, Cobb, and Armistead were out of the fight.[20]

D.H. Hill's division was just getting into the fight. Hill had been preparing to encamp his men for the night and was surprised to hear the signal for the attack. Three and a half hours had passed since Hill had received Chilton's order, and he assumed no attack would be forthcoming given the failure of the artillery. But at 5:30 P.M., he heard the clear "yell" coming from Armistead's direction and the even clearer sounds of battle. Hill shouted, "That must be the general advance!" He ordered his gathered brigadiers: "Bring up your brigades as soon as possible and join in it."[21]

That order reveals a weak point on the Confederate assault plan. In order to have any chance at a breakthrough similar to Gaines Mill, Confederate forces would have to launch a coordinated mass assault, just like they managed to do at the end of the day on June 27 around Boatswain's Swamp. But that would not happen on July 1 on the gentle slopes of Malvern Hill. D. H. Hill had intended to launch a coordinated assault, but the terrain made it difficult. His men were lined up in the woods and swampy ground between the Willis Church Road and Carter's Mill Road. As they advanced, the woods broke up their alignment, causing some units to wander astray altogether. They attacked as they emerged from the woods, rather than wait and realign under the fire of the Union cannon dotting the hill. As they emerged, General Robert Rodes's brigade, under the command of Colonel John B. Gordon because Rodes was sick, was on the right of Hill's line, straddling the Willis Church Road. General Samuel Garland's brigade lined up behind Gordon. General George B. Anderson commanded the brigade to Gordon's left, though Anderson would quickly be wounded and command fell to Colonel C.C. Tew. On the far left was General Roswell Ripley's brigade, including the thin regiments of the 44th Georgia and 1st North Carolina, who had been decimated at Ellerson's Mill. Their experience at Malvern Hill would not be any more successful or pleasant.

As Hill's men were stepping off in the late afternoon sun, the Union commanders were reinforcing their line. Reinforcements from Butterfield relieved regiments in Griffin's brigade who were nearly out of ammunition. On the Union right, the Confederates were heading to Couch's division. Porter requested help from Sumner's corps, and that general reluctantly parted with one brigade, which Porter sent to support Couch's line. But fellow corps commander Heintzelman, who was present when Sumner read Porter's call aloud, remarked, "By Jove! If Porter asks for help, I know he needs it and I will send it," and he ordered a battery and a brigade to go to Porter.[22] Porter was legitimately concerned that a massed Confederate attack could work as it had at Gaines Mill. At the height of the fighting, fearing that he might be captured, Porter ripped apart his diary and dispatch book, "scattering the pieces to the winds." Of course, he later regretted losing such memoranda of the campaign.[23]

The Union line extended beyond Ripley's left flank, and the result was predictable. Ripley's men reached the crest of a rolling hill and were struck with a "furious fire of shot, shell, and musketry." Ripley claimed that his men's fire compelled a Union battery to fall back, but the devastating Yankee rifle fire into their exposed left flank proved too much and the brigade broke back down the hill in a scattered fashion.[24] Things were no better for Gordon and Tew who marched into as terrible a fire as any had ever seen. One Union soldier noted, "We murdered them by the hundreds but they again formed and came up to be slaughtered."[25] One of Tew's North Carolina soldiers confirmed this, though halving the number: "The enemy mowed us down by fifties," despite repeated gallant charges.[26] Though after the war D.H. Hill claimed that his brave soldiers had breached the Union lines briefly, he was mistaken. No Confederate troops would penetrate any part of the Union line on this day. Gordon's and Tew's men only got within 200 yards of the Union line. The 3rd Alabama of Gordon's brigade lost six color bearers killed in the advance and their flag was shredded. Gordon himself suffered several near misses and glancing blows, losing his pistol, canteen, and having several bullets rip holes in his coat, but he survived physically unscathed. Realizing that they could go no further, Gordon ordered his men to lie on the field to escape the flying lead.[27]

Behind Gordon, Garland was unable to advance any closer than 400 yards to the Union line. He called for reinforcements. General Alfred

Colquitt's brigade was nearby, but only one regiment managed to come to Garland's aid. Colquitt's brigade still suffered 200 casualties, primarily from long-range artillery fire throughout the day. D.H. Hill's division was done for the day, wrecked by nearly 2,000 casualties out of 8,000 engaged. Hill was angry at the results of a charge he never felt should have occurred, and wrote of his experience at Malvern Hill bitterly: "It was not war—it was murder."[28]

His anger on the battlefield was obvious, too. Searching for reinforcements to aid his division, he came upon disorganized Georgians under General Robert Toombs. Toombs, who was supposed to advance on Howell Cobb's right, had lost his way in the woods and emerged at the junction of Carter's Mill Road and the Willis Church Road instead. Between the shelling of Union artillery and a contradictory series of orders, the Georgians had paused, unsure of where to go. "It was a perfect scene of confusion at the time we were ordered in, and nobody seemed to know where they were going or what they were going to do," wrote one Georgia soldier.[29] At this moment, Hill rode up and tried to organize them for an attack with little success. When Hill later encountered Toombs, he turned his legendary temper on the former Confederate secretary of state whose military abilities he held in contempt, yelling at him: "For shame! Rally your troops! Where were you when I was riding up and down your line, rallying your troops?" Toombs was so insulted, he later challenged Hill to a duel, but nothing came of it. Plenty of rumors circulated to suggest that Toombs had trouble leading because he had been drinking too much. It was just another in a long line of confused occurrences on this bloody battlefield.[30]

As Hill's and Toombs's troops were being savaged by Union artillery and rifle fire, Colonel George T. "Tige" Anderson's brigade of General D.R. Jones's division tried to go in on Toombs's right, but the disorienting woods, the blinding tempest of lead, and shouts from multiple leaders confused their attack. As Anderson tried to get his five regiments straightened out after they emerged from the woods, Magruder rode up to the right three regiments and ordered them to attack along the path that Wright and Mahone had traveled earlier. They set off immediately, leaving Anderson to lead his remaining two regiments personally along the path Armistead had taken. They likely did not get past the intersection of the Willis Church Road and Carter's Mill Road before pulling back, and the right-hand regiments advanced no further than Wright's position before withdrawing.

As the sun was setting, Magruder moved about his lines sending brigades into action as they arrived on the field. Next to Anderson was Colonel

William Barksdale's brigade of Magruder's own division, emerging on the field near the path that Wright's brigade had taken. He attacked across the same path Wright had traveled, angling toward the slave cabins and a barn north of the Crew House. Barksdale's Mississippians put pressure on the Union position and prompted some line-shifting and requests for reinforcements, but they never came close to reaching the Yankee line, and suffered one-third of their 1,200 men as casualties.[31]

Magruder next sent in Ransom's brigade after Lee had finally ordered Huger to send that unit to the front to participate. Ransom's regiments were separated and sent into battle one at a time and were able to do nothing to assist the effort to dislodge the Union line. As darkness approached, Magruder sent word to Lee for reinforcements, as it became apparent that his and Huger's men were not enough to take the line. Lee was with General Lafayette McLaws's division when word arrived from Magruder, and he personally advanced with McLaws's division and ordered Magruder to send them in further to the right, beyond the Crew House and the Union left flank. McLaws's two brigades under Paul Semmes and Joseph Kershaw, who had done the bulk of the fighting at Savage Station two days earlier, attacked on the Confederate right, following the path of Wright and Barksdale, but they were not able to get even half of their men into the attack in the descending darkness where the field was becoming more and more illuminated by muzzle flashes. Semmes claimed that "a misconception of orders, the difficulties of the ground, and the lateness of the hour" prevented him from getting all of his soldiers into the fight.[32] That notwithstanding, it is very likely that Semmes's men advanced farther than any Confederate that Tuesday, getting to the slave cabins about 50 yards from the Union line and using them as cover, before finally being driven back by a Union counterattack just before it was too dark to see.[33]

Semmes's and Kershaw's inability to get all of their men into the fight was emblematic of Magruder's problem that day. His men had marched more than 20 miles in the hot sun the day before and had not camped until the wee hours of the morning. Then, he had marched and countermarched all morning (because of the misunderstanding over the location of the Quaker Road) before finally getting his men on the field, many of whom had to struggle through thick woods to begin their attack. As a result, several thousand soldiers had fallen out of the ranks. Though Magruder probably had 12,000–13,000 men on his rolls active for duty that day, only about 7,000 ended up charging with their units. As Sears aptly claimed, "Every road and every grove behind Magruder's front was filled with his stragglers."[34]

While Magruder was racing the darkness to get men into the fight on the west side of the road, D. H. Hill was worried that he would be unable to hold off a Union counterattack on his side of the road, because his division had been dealt with so severely. He sent word to Jackson for reinforcements, and Jackson ordered Charles Winder's and Richard Ewell's divisions forward to support Hill. However, in the growing darkness, these divisions had difficulty advancing to the front because the fields, roads, and woods were clogged with the thousands of wounded and stunned soldiers making their way to the rear and impeding forward movement. The reinforcements struggled to get forward and darkness fell before any of them could get into position to attack. Only three more regiments managed to advance down the east side of the Willis Church Road before being driven back.[35]

General Isaac Trimble's brigade finally reached the field as darkness settled over the landscape, and that eager elder commander decided to launch an attack on Couch's division, guided primarily by muzzle flashes, thinking he could turn Couch's flank. When Jackson rode by and discovered what he was preparing to do, Stonewall stopped him by declaring, "I guess you had better not try it. General Hill just tried it with his whole Division and had been repulsed. I guess you better not try it, sir."[36] There would be no more attacks, though the firing continued on both sides until long after it was too dark to see anything other than the streaks and explosions of artillery shells across the night sky. One Confederate soldier recalled, "The pyrotechnic splender was grander than any view of 'the lightnings red glare painting hell in the sky.'"[37] When this fireworks show ended, fighting was over for the day.

* * *

The end of the fighting brought the slow discovery of the enormous casualties. By the time the accounting was all done, Confederates had suffered more than 5,000 casualties, whereas the Union army suffered fewer than 3,000 (historians who claim more than 3,000 are factoring in Union stragglers who were captured during the continued retreat the next day). It is impossible to be exact on either side with the casualty figures, but it was clear to everyone that the Confederates had received the worst of it. Well, almost everyone. Longstreet rode over the field the next day looking at the carnage on both sides. When he reported to Lee that morning, Lee asked him what he had concluded from his scouting. Longstreet replied optimistically, "I think you hurt them about as much as they hurt you." The less sanguine Lee replied sardonically, "Then I am glad we punished them well, at any rate," for there was no disguising the fact that Lee's army had been soundly thrashed on July 1.[38]

During the night of July 1, Lee tried to understand how this disastrous battle had been set in motion, after he had personally observed the failure of the two grand batteries to soften the Union defenses. When he rode to Magruder's headquarters, he asked, "General Magruder, why did you attack?" Magruder responded without a moment's hesitation, "In obedience to your orders, twice repeated."[39] This was true and Lee knew it. He had authorized Chilton to send out the first order; he had ordered Magruder to attack when he received Magruder's message that Armistead had advanced; and late in the evening, Lee had personally ordered Magruder to move McLaws's men more to the right flank to attack. He had never called off the attack or cancelled any orders. There was nothing to do but accept that the army had been defeated by a strong, well-defended force.

The defeat was so complete that many Confederate commanders were convinced that McClellan would take advantage of his victory and launch a counterattack the next day. Jackson's division officers were concerned about that logical development and woke Jackson in the middle of the night to find out how he wanted them to deploy their forces to meet the expected attack. To their surprise, the drowsy Jackson stated, "McClellan and his army will be gone by daylight," and fell back to sleep practically in their presence. Many left that short conference dissatisfied and further convinced that Jackson was not himself, but Jackson was right. By the time the fog and mist lifted off the battlefield at dawn on July 2, nothing remained but the dead, dying, and wounded from both sides covering the field, the bodies marking the crest of the Confederate wave from the previous day.[40]

If one visits the battlefield today, one will see a bucolic landscape that seems absolutely incongruous with the grim and destructive scene that occurred that long ago Tuesday afternoon. One can walk multiple paths from the Confederate lines toward the Union line, and try to imagine what was going through the minds of those men who marched those paths in the face of blistering artillery fire on July 1, 1862. On multiple trips to the battlefield over the years, this author has heard the plaintive cry of mourning doves, a haunting and appropriate refrain, as if they are singing a perpetual dirge to all the men who died on these fields. Such a lament was undoubtedly shared by all those men who had to see the carnage of the battlefield on July 2.

From almost the moment the battle ended, interested observers began placing blame for the defeat. D. H. Hill noted that all the units were fed into battle piecemeal, rather than in a massed wave, which was correct;

but he also claimed that Magruder hardly did any fighting at all on his side of the field, which was patently false. Magruder had the casualties to prove it and his men had gotten closest to the Union lines near the Crew House. Hill had simply been too engrossed in the fighting on his section of the field to notice what was occurring elsewhere. Every Confederate general has been subject to criticism and blame for his role at the battle. Jackson was blamed for not sending his troops to the fight, but he did send in Hill's division and he was bringing more divisions forward when darkness put an end to the fight. The attack simply began too late in the day for Jackson to get all of his men into the fight over the narrow plains of Malvern Hill. Huger was petulant and uncooperative, which did not help matters, but in the end three of his four brigades brought their full weight into the fight. Two, under Armistead and Wright, even led the attacks that evening. Clifford Dowdey places a lot of blame on Longstreet for overly influencing Lee that two grand batteries could drive off the Union forces and then failing to do much to bring enough batteries forward on his side of the field to ensure success. But Lee saw the ground and believed that the two grand batteries could work. Dowdey also accuses Longstreet of lying when he said that Lee investigated turning the Union right flank. But Lee did make such an investigation and sent orders to Branch's brigade to begin moving that way. Nothing came of it because the battle was joined at that moment.[41]

Finally, Magruder receives much blame for sending his troops off in the wrong direction and thus delaying his arrival on the battlefield by several hours, then launching ill-advised assaults. But there is no indication that attacking earlier in the day would have changed the result. And when he did finally arrive on the field, Magruder obeyed his orders—one from Lee through Chilton and one directly from Lee by way of Magruder's aide—to rapidly attack the enemy. Not wanting to be rebuked for his lack of aggression as he had been on June 29, Magruder promptly obeyed Lee's orders the moment he received them. It was a confusion of circumstances that led to an attack that Lee had not wanted.

As with the earlier battles, the final responsibility for the Malvern Hill debacle rests with the army's overall commander. Lee allowed Chilton to send out a poorly worded order that set the advance of one brigade as the signal. He did not place himself in the most advantageous location so that he could see the results of the artillery crossfire, and thus take responsibility for launching the attack himself. When he decided the artillery was ineffectual, he rode away from the front, first to the Confederate left and then behind the main lines, without canceling the earlier order. When word arrived from both Whiting and Magruder in the late afternoon that the Union army was retreating and that Armistead had advanced, Lee did not ride to the front to observe for himself and confirm the events (which he had reason to doubt), but instead peremptorily ordered Magruder to attack. When he got to the front and saw it was a more difficult task than he had been led to believe, he did not order the attacks to cease, but instead sent in McLaws's division and instructed Magruder to shift his attack further to the right. These were all Lee's decisions, and the ultimate outcome resulted from his actions (orders given) and inactions (not canceling orders and not going to the front).

Lee was fatigued, frustrated, and feeling ill on July 1. He asked Longstreet to accompany him as a hedge against his own incapacitation. He even took a nap at a key moment in the afternoon with none other than President Davis standing watch over him. Lee was not at his physical or mental best on that day, and the decisions he made reflect as much. Events of July 1, much like the events of the entire week, did not turn out the way that Lee had wanted them to. But on July 1, as on June 26, 27, 29, and 30, much of the blame for the poor outcome belongs to Lee himself and his developing command style. Perhaps more frustrating to Lee than anything else was the fact that he likely knew this to be true.

* * *

McClellan had not seen the victory as the potential starting point of a decisive counter offensive against a bloodied, bruised, and weakened army, but rather a temporary check of the Confederate hordes that he claimed were pursuing him. Many of his commanders, including his loyal friend Fitz-John Porter, tried to persuade Little Mac that they should launch a counterattack from their strong position, but McClellan would not consider it. He ordered the army's retreat to continue. From Haxall's Landing, it was eight miles by the River Road to Harrison's Landing, the spot McClellan had personally chosen as his new base. Nothing, not even victory, could deter him from his decision to move his army to that place of sanctuary.[42]

The order to retreat perplexed and angered many enlisted men and officers. One junior officer wrote, "The idea of stealing away in the night from such a position after such a victory, was simply galling." When General Phil Kearny learned of the order, he exploded. Kearny could not berate the commander personally this night, as he had on the evening of June 27, because McClellan was already aboard the *Galena* heading toward Harrison's Landing. But he did rail against the Young Napoleon long and loudly for all of his fellow officers in the III Corps to hear. Kearny protested the retreat order and declared vociferously, "I say to you all, such an order can only be prompted by cowardice or treason."[43]

It is tempting to agree with Kearny, but McClellan was not committing treason; in fact, he fancied himself the only person who could save the nation. McClellan would be accused of cowardice on this day by several people, especially two years later in the presidential election of 1864 when his critics castigated his absence from the battlefield at Malvern Hill. But there was no sudden onset of cowardice on July 1. McClellan had also been absent from the main fighting at each of the other battles, and most egregiously at Glendale. Rather, McClellan was insisting on following the plan he devised the moment Lee launched his attack north of the Chickahominy and McClellan lost his will to fight. He argued that the Confederates outnumbered his army; he assumed that even after the week's casualties they still numbered near 180,000 and had plenty of fresh troops. Although it is hard to believe that McClellan could have honestly believed his own numbers at first, perhaps he had convinced himself of Lee's massive superiority by now. After all, how could Lee attack him on five out of six days unless he had a much larger force than McClellan?

McClellan's retreat was not a product of strictly "rational" generalship as his most recent defender would have us believe; rather, it was a product of a character flaw in his generalship.[44] The Young Napoleon, unlike the authentic Napoleon, was inflexible. He could not readily adapt to changed circumstances or alter his plan when new developments disrupted it. He intended to besiege Richmond and did not expect the enemy to interfere. Yet, once Lee attacked and McClellan realized that Jackson was on his right flank, he decided that the only course of action for him was to abandon the entire campaign and retreat all the way to the safety of the James River. When favorable outcomes in individual battles spurred his subordinates to suggest that the circumstances had changed and warranted an attack, McClellan overruled them. He could not deviate from his new plan of retreat. He was rarely on the fields of battle to develop his own sense of the enemy's condition. He simply continued to imagine they were much stronger than him. It was not fear for his own life—personal cowardice—that prompted McClellan's withdrawal, it was fear of losing his army, risking national defeat, and ruining his own idealized reputation that prompted him to order his army to leave a victorious battlefield and continue its retreat. McClellan was a broken commander, and the decisive crack had come all the way back on the evening of June 26.

The last retreat for the Union army was perhaps the worst. They had not marched very far before the heavens opened up again and a downpour quickly turned the road into nearly impassable mud channels. Weary soldiers trudged on, dispirited and demoralized. Thousands of them discarded their gear—chucking aside everything from knapsacks to tents to rifles during the hard slog. Wagons were abandoned by the roadsides, as was much of the equipment carried in them. The Confederates would find tons of material strewn along the path from Malvern Hill to Harrison's Landing in the next few days. The weather made Confederate pursuit impossible for a couple of days. The Union army finally reached Harrison's Landing and the remaining 90,000-man force, complete with tens of thousands of horses, mules, and cattle, crowded into a four-square mile space and set up camp. By the time Lee was able to get his army close enough to observe the new Union position on July 4, he wisely decided that there was no opportunity to win any decisive victory here. The Union defenses were too strong and the gunboats protected the entirety of the perimeter. Lee ordered the bulk of his army back to camps near Richmond where they could rest, refit, and recover. The Seven Days' Campaign was officially over.[45]

7

—⧉—

Consequences and Lessons

The battle was over and the Confederate capital had been saved for the moment, as McClellan's army had been driven 35 miles away from the city. But the cost had been high. Lee began his offensive with roughly 90,000 soldiers in his army and suffered slightly more than 20,000 casualties to achieve his victory; McClellan had begun with an army of more than 100,000 men and suffered approximately 16,000 casualties in his retrograde movement to the James.[1] He had preserved his army, an accomplishment for which he was rather proud. He issued a decree to his soldiers on July 4 that inflated their deeds, spun their retreat as if it had been a successfully calculated plan, and boasted to his men: "Your conduct ranks you among the celebrated armies of history."[2] Not every soldier in the army shared his view of the matter, and certainly none of his superiors in Washington took similar pride in the retreat.

President Lincoln left Washington on July 7 and traveled to Harrison's Landing to examine the Army of the Potomac for himself. During the trip, Lincoln met with McClellan and received from him a lengthy and unsolicited letter detailing to the president how to proceed with the war—at least according to McClellan's principles. In the letter, McClellan argued for a limited war and strongly opposed the policies of confiscation of Southern property or emancipation of Southern slaves. Lincoln read the letter in McClellan's presence without comment, which frustrated Little Mac who had hoped for a positive reaction. He complained to his wife that Lincoln was incapable of rising to meet the challenges of the times. Lincoln was thinking the exact same thing about his commander. The president had already moved on from the more conservative mindset that he had shared with McClellan in 1861, and was probably dismayed, though not surprised, to see that McClellan was still fighting last year's war. Times had changed and McClellan's failure at Richmond had helped change them. While Lincoln was at Harrison's Landing, Congress was putting the finishing touches on a more stringent Confiscation Act, and Lincoln had already begun drafting an Emancipation Proclamation, which he read to select cabinet ministers for the first time on July 13. McClellan's military failures had convinced Lincoln that "the nation could no longer pursue a 'forbearing policy.'"[3]

Lincoln had tried to understand his commander, but undoubtedly still wondered what motivated McClellan's actions. If Lincoln had been a psychiatrist inclined to put Little Mac on the couch for an extended session, he would have discovered that McClellan was a man who was too predisposed to take counsel of his fears and to see worst possible outcomes as probabilities rather than just possibilities. McClellan's recurring nightmare was one of total defeat. He was very protective of his stellar reputation and constantly feared that a defeat would ruin it. Most of the military actions he took were reactionary and designed to prevent a disastrous defeat. As a result, McClellan convinced himself that he had accomplished great things by preserving his army. Ironically, it was this very caution that ruined his reputation. McClellan was convinced that history would absolve him. However, he did not take into account that historians would be privy to more accurate sources than just McClellan's intelligence reports or his personal views. Historians are the ones who turned him into a caricature—the timid general, too nervous to risk a trial, too eager to retreat.

McClellan felt both a keen sense of duty to preserve the Union and also an enormous responsibility, as he believed he had been chosen as the nation's savior. This was a heavy load—one that he relished and wilted under. If he was the sole embodiment of all the hopes of the nation, then he could not make a mistake. The scrutiny was so intense and the odds so enormously high that he could not risk failure. As he built his army up, he determined, even if subconsciously, that the best way to avoid failure was to not risk failure by engaging in pitched battle. Whenever he felt that he was ready to finally engage the enemy on his terms, something always occurred to rough up the smoothness of his plans.

McClellan admitted no mistakes and always blamed others, particularly his superiors in the War Department and the Lincoln administration, for his failures. This continued after he reached Harrison's Landing, as the general wrote a series of telegrams and letters to friends and loved ones suggesting that the "heartless villains" in Washington denied his army what it needed to win. He convinced himself that Stanton and Lincoln wanted him to lose. He crafted ever more outlandish scenarios in which the administration wanted disunion to succeed, and he began rationalizing his defeat as if it was for the best in order to prevent this. "If I had succeeded in taking Richmond," he wrote to his wife, "the fanatics of the North might have been too powerful & reunion impossible."[4] This was a general who had lost all sense of perspective. In a candid summation of the campaign that McClellan probably did not intend to be read by historians the way that it has been, he wrote to his wife on July 10: "I have honestly done the best I could; I shall leave it to others to decide whether that was the best that *could* have been done." Historians have generally agreed that it was probably the best that he could do, but certainly not the best that could have been done under a more flexible and responsive commander.[5]

On his July circuit of the army, Lincoln also met with McClellan's five corps commanders and sounded them out about the army's prospects. The fact that two of the five—including McClellan's loyal friend, William B. Franklin—recommended that the army retreat did not instill Lincoln with much confidence of a possible victory from this location. The other three commanders argued instead that a retreat would be too demoralizing. Lincoln returned to Washington on July 10, convinced that McClellan was not capable of leading the army to victory, but he did not make the final decision to replace him immediately. Instead, he sent General Henry Halleck, whom he had just recalled from a successful campaign in the western theater and appointed as general-in-chief, to Harrison's Landing to form his own opinion of McClellan and the army. Lincoln gave Halleck the power to relieve McClellan of command, rather than take the burden of making that decision himself.[6]

Lincoln must have been unsure of his own judgment in military matters. If he did not believe the irrational numbers that McClellan attributed to the Confederate army, and if he thought the army was strong enough to win from the James River, then he should have exercised his powers as commander-in-chief and replaced McClellan with someone he thought more capable.[7] William Swinton, a *New York Times* reporter embedded with the army, wrote in his history of the Army of the Potomac in 1866 that McClellan's army was a greater threat to Richmond from the James than it had been at the Chickahominy a week earlier. "Yet, so potent is the sway that general results have over the imaginations of men," he lamented, "the North was stunned with grief and despair at the thought that the army that was the brave pillar of its hopes was thus struck down."[8] But in fact, Lincoln had made a move in the direction of replacing McClellan and offered Little Mac's job to General Ambrose Burnside, based on that general's success conquering much of the North Carolina coast during the spring. Burnside declined, however, arguing that he was not up to the task (a prediction that would be proven all too true at Fredericksburg five months later).

On July 25, Halleck met with McClellan and listened to the army commander elaborate on a new plan to move the army south of the James River and attack Petersburg, a vital railroad junction that fed supplies to Richmond. Halleck was highly distrustful of the plan, largely because of McClellan's own projections that 200,000 Confederates were in Richmond. If that was anywhere near accurate, then the plan was too risky. That massive Confederate army could defeat General John Pope's recently created 40,000-man army north of Richmond, and then return to annihilate McClellan's 90,000 men south of the city. Halleck told McClellan that he either had to attack Richmond from the north side of the James or abandon the peninsula altogether. McClellan asked for reinforcements and Halleck promised him 20,000 (largely from Burnside's force arriving from North Carolina); McClellan declared that would be sufficient. However, when Halleck returned to Washington a day later, he found that McClellan had returned to form and declared that he needed approximately 60,000 more troops in order to have a chance. An exasperated Halleck decided that Lincoln was right that McClellan would not fight. In early August, he issued the telegram to McClellan that called for the withdrawal of his army.[9]

* * *

While McClellan was bitterly disappointed with the order to abandon the campaign, Lee was disappointed that he had left McClellan any army to extract from the peninsula. Despite the accolades he received from the Southern press, who argued that he had "amazed . . . his detractors by the brilliancy of his genius," Lee felt that his army could have achieved a victory that was so much more significant. He complained to his wife that his victory was not "as great or complete as we should have desired." When he wrote his final report on the battles, he declared, "Under ordinary circumstances the Federal Army should have been destroyed." Yet, Lee did not write that report until March 1863, after he had won two major battles (Second Manassas and Fredericksburg) and fought a stalemate against great odds at Antietam. He was reading his own eventual success back into his first campaign as commander of the army. Undoubtedly, he felt that if he had the well-oiled machine that he possessed in March 1863—the same army that would defeat a Union army twice its size two months later at Chancellorsville—then he would have won a more decisive victory at Richmond.[10]

The simple military fact of the matter, however, is that without the difficulties encountered and mistakes made during the Seven Days, Lee would not have been the commander he was during those later battles. He made a great many mistakes during the Seven Days, but he learned from those mistakes, even if he never publicly admitted any of them. Lee frequently constructed plans that were too complex to carry out over miles of wooded terrain. He misunderstood the size of the enemy forces in places, such as at Gaines Mill when he thought far more enemy were present than actually were and Savage Station when he thought far fewer were present than there were. He also granted his subordinates too much leeway, without checking behind them. Though micromanaging is rarely considered a positive attribute today, in his opening campaign as commander of the Army of Northern Virginia, one of Lee's greatest flaws was that he did not micromanage enough. He needed to maintain firm control over the reins of battle, making sure that his subordinates carried out their parts of his plans. In the future, Lee would develop crisper, less complicated plans. He would assert direct control over the battles more firmly, and he would in essence act as his own chief of staff, making sure that the orders that emerged from his headquarters were clearly what he desired. In fact, in his next campaign, at Second Manassas in August 1862, Lee demonstrated a much firmer grasp on his army and managed the battle, which was a resounding victory, much more effectively.[11]

Lee's actions after the battle demonstrate that he must have felt that his subordinates were responsible for much of the failure of the campaign (and hagiographic historians have supported him in this interpretation). Within just a few days after the campaign, three of his major commanders were no longer with the army. John B. Magruder, who had been offered command in the Trans-Mississippi region before the Seven Days' battles began, could not leave the army fast enough. He only remained around Richmond long enough to defend himself from fellow officers' erroneous charges of dereliction of duty at Malvern Hill. Magruder had not been pleased with his experience under Johnston's or Lee's command, and Lee, tellingly, did not try to persuade Magruder to stay. Theophilus Holmes was trundled off unceremoniously to the Trans-Mississippi region as well. Benjamin Huger was removed from field command and named as inspector of artillery and ordnance.[12]

Lee reorganized his army into a more manageable two-corps format. James Longstreet emerged from the campaign as the general in whom Lee felt he could most rely. He shuffled brigades around and expanded Longstreet's command to include 28 brigades. Conversely, Lee never publicly (or even privately, as far as we know) criticized or rebuked Stonewall Jackson for his poor performance during the campaign. However, he did reduce the number of brigades in Jackson's command from 14 to 7. From these actions, Douglas Southall Freeman perceptively deduces, "If Jackson was to return to independent command, his great abilities could of course be trusted, but if he was to remain with the Army of Northern Virginia and was to prove recalcitrant, his power to thwart the general strategy of the army was to be limited."[13]

Though Freeman understands that Lee's faith in Jackson was tempered, he fails to understand the flaws of Lee. Instead, Freeman blames the lack of complete success on a variety of factors that seem to be out of Lee's control. He censures Lee's staff, claiming: "The campaign will always remain a tragic monument to defective staff work." He points out the flaws of each young officer, who he declares "functioned simply as the inexperienced staff of the average division commander might have done."[14] He further blames bad cavalry, bad maps, and subpar subordinates—dedicating much of the first volume of Lee's Lieutenants to pointing out how their individual stars did not shine as brightly as their leader's. Freeman writes as if he does not recognize that Lee was ultimately in control of the army.[15]

Lee's victory outside Richmond guaranteed that the war would take on a whole new shape. Gone were the days of conciliation and the belief of treating the South with kid gloves in order to foster a harmonious reunion. The Second Confiscation Act passed within days of the end of the campaign, ushering in a harsher treatment of Southern property, particularly slaves. A little more than two months after the Union army retreated from Malvern Hill, President Lincoln issued the preliminary Emancipation Proclamation, dramatically altering the complexion of the war and raising the stakes of the contest. Lee's repeated attempts to win the decisive battle that might lead to independence, which he felt required aggressive campaigns (such as Antietam and Gettysburg), led to hundreds of thousands more casualties in both armies before the broken Army of Northern Virginia eventually surrendered at Appomattox on April 9, 1865. Along the way, the Southern states suffered massive damage to infrastructure, farmland, and property. Southerners on the home front felt the invasiveness of their own government, with tax-in-kind laws, impressment laws, conscription, and the suspension of habeas corpus. The prolonged conflict and its resulting human and physical destruction left scars that lasted decades. The nation that emerged from the Civil War was not the same nation that likely would have emerged if McClellan's Army of the Potomac had defeated Lee's Army of Northern Virginia and captured Richmond in July 1862. Instead, a new war that began in that hot summer led to a new national identity. "For," as Clifford Dowdey eloquently wrote, "at the Seven Days, when the Army of Northern Virginia was born, the old America died, and the Union Lincoln and McClellan tried to restore became as lost in time as the traditional society Lee sought to preserve."[16]

Notes

CHAPTER ONE

1. Stephen W. Sears, ed., *The Civil War Papers of George B. McClellan: Selected Correspondence, 1860–1865* (New York: Da Capo Press, 1992), 383–384.

2. Stephen W. Sears, *George B. McClellan: The Young Napoleon* (New York: Ticknor & Fields, 1988), 1–68.

3. Clifford Dowdey, *The Seven Days: The Emergence of Lee* (Boston: Little, Brown, 1964), 20.

4. Ibid., 23.

5. Shelby Foote, *The Civil War: A Narrative*, 3 vols. (New York: Random House, 1958), 1:110.

6. Ibid., 1:143.

7. George B. McClellan, "The Peninsular Campaign," in *Battles and Leaders of the Civil War*, 4 vols., ed. Robert Underwood Johnson and Clarence Clough Buel (New York: The Century Co., 1884–1888), 2:164.

8. Stephen W. Sears, *To the Gates of Richmond: The Peninsula Campaign* (New York: Ticknor & Fields, 1992), 4–9.

9. Sears, *George B. McClellan*, 7.

10. Sears, *To the Gates of Richmond*, 16–18.

11. Ibid., 25.

12. Dowdey, *Seven Days*, 39–43.

13. Ibid., 45.

14. Kevin Dougherty with J. Michael Moore, *The Peninsula Campaign of 1862: A Military Analysis* (Jackson: University Press of Mississippi, 2005), 82.

15. Brian K. Burton, *Extraordinary Circumstances: The Seven Days Battles* (Bloomington: Indiana University Press, 2001), 6.

16. Wilmer L. Jones, *Generals in Blue and Gray: Davis's Generals* (Westport, CT: Praeger Publishing, 2004), 57.

17. Sears, *To the Gates of Richmond*, 11–14.

18. Ibid., 48.

19. Ibid., 46–48.

20. Russell Weigley, *The American Way of War: A History of United States Military Strategy and Policy* (Bloomington: Indiana University Press, 1973), 82–84, 95–96, 133–135.

21. For more on conciliation and its failure, see Mark Grimsley, *The Hard Hand of War: Union Military Policy toward Southern Civilians, 1861–1865* (New York: Cambridge University Press, 1995), 23–92.

22. Sears, *To the Gates of Richmond*, chapter 4.

23. Burton, *Extraordinary Circumstances*, 15–17.

24. Sears, *To the Gates of Richmond*, 100.

25. Sears, *Civil War Papers of McClellan*, 309.

26. John B. Jones, *A Rebel War Clerk's Diary*, ed. Earl Schenck Miers (New York: A.S. Barnes & Company, Inc., 1961), 76; Burton, *Extraordinary Circumstances*, 6.

27. Dowdey, *Seven Days*, 63–83.

28. Ibid., 79.

29. Sears, *To the Gates of Richmond*, 97.

30. See Peter Cozzens, *Shenandoah 1862: Jackson's Valley Campaign* (Chapel Hill: University of North Carolina Press, 2008).

31. Edward Porter Alexander, *Fighting for the Confederacy: The Personal Recollections of General Edward Porter Alexander*, ed. Gary W. Gallagher (Chapel Hill: University of North Carolina Press, 1989), 85.

32. Dowdey, *Seven Days*, 4.

33. For a fuller description of Seven Pines, see Dowdey, *Seven Days*, 84–127, and Sears, *To the Gates of Richmond*, 117–145.

CHAPTER TWO

1. Sears, *Civil War Papers of McClellan*, 293.

2. Sears, *To the Gates of Richmond*, 57.

3. Douglas Southall Freeman, *R.E. Lee: A Biography*, 4 vols. (New York: Charles Scribner's Sons, 1934), 2:76.

4. Ibid., 80.

5. Jones, *Rebel War Clerk's Diary*, 82–83.

6. Alexander, *Fighting for the Confederacy*, 91.

7. Clifford Dowdey and Louis H. Manarin, eds., *The Wartime Papers of Robert E. Lee* (New York: Da Capo Press, 1961), 184.

8. Freeman, *R.E. Lee*, 2:86.

9. Ibid.

10. Dowdey and Manarin, *Wartime Papers of Lee*, 192.

11. Sears, *To the Gates of Richmond*, 167–174; Ezra J. Warner, *Generals in Blue: Lives of the Union Commanders* (Baton Rouge: Louisiana State University Press, 1964), 89–90.

12. Sears, *To the Gates of Richmond*, 153; Freeman, *R.E. Lee*, 2:95–96.

13. Dowdey and Manarin, *Wartime Papers of Lee*, 194.

14. For a good analysis of the relationship between Jackson and Dabney, see Wallace Hettle, *Inventing Stonewall Jackson: A Civil War Hero in History and Memory* (Baton Rouge: Louisiana State University Press, 2011), chapter 2.

15. Robert K. Krick, "Sleepless in the Saddle: Stonewall Jackson in the Seven Days," in *The Richmond Campaign of 1862: The Peninsula and the Seven Days*, ed. Gary W. Gallagher (Chapel Hill: University of North Carolina Press, 2000), 66–70.

16. Dowdey, *Seven Days*, 148.

17. Peter S. Carmichael, "The Great Paragon of Virtue and Sobriety: John Bankhead Magruder and the Seven Days," in *The Richmond Campaign of 1862: The Peninsula and the Seven Days*, ed. Gary W. Gallagher (Chapel Hill: University of North Carolina Press, 2000), 96–120.

18. Sears, *To the Gates of Richmond*, 175–177; Burton, *Extraordinary Circumstances*, 36–39; Dowdey, *Seven Days*, 148–152.

19. Dowdey, *Seven Days*, 196–201.

20. Sears, *George B. McClellan*, 61.

21. Dowdey and Manarin, *Wartime Papers of Lee*, 189.

22. Krick, "Sleepless in the Saddle," 69.

23. Wallace Hettle argues that Dabney spent a long time trying to redeem himself for his poor performance. Hettle, *Inventing Stonewall Jackson*, chapter 2.

24. Burton, *Extraordinary Circumstances*, 52–55.

25. Sears, *Civil War Papers of McClellan*, 288.

26. Ibid., 299.

27. Ibid., 295, 309.

28. Burton, *Extraordinary Circumstances*, 24.

29. Dowdey, *Seven Days*, 162.

30. Sears, *Civil War Papers of McClellan*, 303, 305.

31. Sears, *To the Gates of Richmond*, 183.

32. Burton, *Extraordinary Circumstances*, 46–51.

33. Sears, *Civil War Papers of McClellan*, 301.

34. Sears, *To the Gates of Richmond*, 188.

35. Ibid., 190.

36. Sears, *Civil War Papers of McClellan*, 309–310.

37. Ibid., 310.

38. Ibid., 312.

39. Ibid., 315.

40. Sears, *To the Gates of Richmond*, 191–194.

41. A review of many marches in several campaigns demonstrates that a large body of troops could only march an average of nearly two miles per hour in reasonably good conditions. Anything faster than that would frequently leave large numbers of stragglers behind and reduce a unit's fighting effectiveness.

42. Sears, *To the Gates of Richmond*, 199; Burton, *Extraordinary Circumstances*, 52–62.

43. Sears, *To the Gates of Richmond*, 201.

44. Burton, *Extraordinary Circumstances*, 64–65.

45. Ibid., 71.

46. Sears, *To the Gates of Richmond*, 199.

47. Burton, *Extraordinary Circumstances*, 71.

48. Sears, *To the Gates of Richmond*, 206.

49. Ripley's Official Report reprinted in Matt Spruill III and Matt Spruill IV, *Echoes of Thunder: A Guide to the Seven Days Battles* (Knoxville: University of Tennessee Press, 2006), 34.

50. Ibid.

51. Burton, *Extraordinary Circumstances*, 74.

52. Judkin Browning, "All for One Charge: The 44th Georgia Infantry," *Columbiad* 1 (Winter 1998): 36–39.

53. Sears, *To the Gates of Richmond*, 207.

54. Daniel Harvey Hill, "Lee Attacks North of the Chickahominy," in *Battles and Leaders of the Civil War*, 4 vols., ed. Robert Underwood Johnson and Clarence Clough Buel (New York: The Century Co., 1884–1888), 2:352.

55. Sears, *To the Gates of Richmond*, 208; Burton, *Extraordinary Circumstances*, 74.

56. Sears, *To the Gates of Richmond*, 208.

57. Sears, *Civil War Papers of McClellan*, 317.

CHAPTER THREE

1. Burton, *Extraordinary Circumstances*, 80.

2. Ibid.; Fitz John Porter, "Hanover Court House and Gaines Mill," in *Battles and Leaders of the Civil War*, 4 vols., ed. Robert Underwood Johnson and Clarence Clough Buel (New York: The Century Co., 1884–1888), 2:336.

3. Sears, *To the Gates of Richmond*, 57.

4. National Park Service marker at Watt House on Gaines Mill battlefield, Virginia.

5. Sears, *To the Gates of Richmond*, 214.

6. Ibid., 214–215.

7. Ibid., 216.

8. Freeman, *R.E. Lee*, 2:136.

9. Burton, *Extraordinary Circumstances*, 83–84; Dowdey, *Seven Days*, 205; Sears, *To the Gates of Richmond*, 218–219.

10. Foote, *Civil War*, 1:488; Sears, *To the Gates of Richmond*, 219–222.

11. Sears, *To the Gates of Richmond*, 223–224.

12. Historians disagree over what Lee thought was happening at Gaines Mill when Gregg discovered Porter's position on the afternoon of June 27. Stephen Sears argues that Lee believed that McClellan was committing to a "showdown" battle north of the Chickahominy and that Lee "accepted the challenge." But it is unlikely that Lee thought as much at first. He only came to that conclusion when Hill's attack was met so severely. Brian Burton is more likely correct when he says that Hill attacked because he thought he was driving Porter's men east and that Jackson and D.H. Hill would feast on them. Sears, *To the Gates of Richmond*, 223.

13. As stated in the introduction, I created a composite of the battle narratives from Burton's *Extraordinary Circumstances*, Sears's *To the Gates of Richmond*, Dowdey's *Seven Days*, Freeman's *R.E. Lee*, volume 2, and Spruills's *Echoes of Thunder*. I also read each of the Official Reports for the battle and made my own determination as to what I believe is the most accurate location and sequence for the individual unit attacks.

14. Dowdey, *Seven Days*, 227; Alexander, *Fighting for the Confederacy*, 102 (quote).

15. Burton, *Extraordinary Circumstances*, 95.

16. Sears, *To the Gates of Richmond*, 226.

17. Burton, *Extraordinary Circumstances*, 100.

18. Ibid., 109; Sears, *To the Gates of Richmond*, 230.

19. Burton, *Extraordinary Circumstances*, 109.

20. Sears, *To the Gates of Richmond*, 227.

21. Burton, *Extraordinary Circumstances*, 116.

22. Sears, *To the Gates of Richmond*, 236.

23. James Longstreet, *From Manassas to Appomattox: Memoirs of the Civil War in America* (Philadelphia: J.B. Lippincott Company, 1896), 127.

24. Sears, *To the Gates of Richmond*, 238.

25. Ibid., 238–239.

26. Ibid., 240.

27. Ibid.

28. E. M. Law, "On the Confederate Right at Gaines's Mill," in *Battles and Leaders of the Civil War*, 4 vols., ed. Robert Underwood Johnson and Clarence Clough Buel (New York: The Century Co., 1884–1888), 2:363.

29. Sears, *To the Gates of Richmond*, 241.

30. Law, "On the Confederate Right at Gaines's Mill," 2:363.

31. Sears, *To the Gates of Richmond*, 241.

32. Ibid., 242.

33. Hill, "Lee Attacks North of the Chickahominy," 2:355.

34. Sears, *To the Gates of Richmond*, 247.

35. Ibid., 245.

36. Ibid., 249–250.

37. Burton, *Extraordinary Circumstances*, 136–137.

38. Alexander, *Fighting for the Confederacy*, 103.

39. Daniel H. Hill, "McClellan's Change of Base and Malvern Hill," in *Battles and Leaders of the Civil War*, 4 vols., ed. Robert Underwood Johnson and Clarence Clough Buel (New York: The Century Co., 1884–1888), 2:395.

40. Sears, *To the Gates of Richmond*, 250.

41. Burton, *Extraordinary Circumstances*, 148–149; Warner, *Generals in Blue*, 259 (for Winfield Scott quote).

42. Sears, *To the Gates of Richmond*, 251; Foote, *Civil War*, 1:493.

43. Sears, *To the Gates of Richmond*, 251.

CHAPTER FOUR

1. Jones, *Rebel War Clerk's Diary*, 87.

2. Paul E. Steiner, *Disease in the Civil War: Natural Biological Warfare in 1861–1865* (Springfield, IL: Charles C. Thomas, 1968), 139.

3. Sears, *To the Gates of Richmond*, 257.

4. National Park Service marker on Gaines Mill battlefield, Virginia.

5. Freeman, *R.E. Lee*, 2:162.

6. Burton, *Extraordinary Circumstances*, 155.

7. Sears, *To the Gates of Richmond*, 255–256; Burton, *Extraordinary Circumstances*, 157–159.

8. Burton, *Extraordinary Circumstances*, 159–160, 163–164.

9. Dowdey and Manarin, *Wartime Papers of Lee*, 206.

10. Burton, *Extraordinary Circumstances*, 179.

11. Sears, *To the Gates of Richmond*, 262–265.

12. Robert Knox Sneden, *Eye of the Storm: A Civil War Odyssey*, ed. Charles F. Bryan Jr. and Nelson D. Lankford (New York: Free Press, 2000), 69.

13. Burton, *Extraordinary Circumstances*, 200–201.

14. W.B. Franklin, "Rear-guard Fighting during the Change of Base," in *Battles and Leaders of the Civil War*, 4 vols., ed. Robert Underwood Johnson and Clarence Clough Buel (New York: The Century Co., 1884–1888), 2:371.

15. Sears, *To the Gates of Richmond*, 267.

16. Ibid., 257–260.

17. Carmichael, "Great Paragon of Virtue and Sobriety," 106–107.

18. Ibid., 108.

19. Sears, *To the Gates of Richmond*, 267.

20. Burton, *Extraordinary Circumstances*, 208–209.

21. Alexander, *Fighting for the Confederacy*, 105.

22. Sears, *To the Gates of Richmond*, 269.

23. Ibid., 268.

24. Franklin, "Rear-guard Fighting," 2:373.

25. Sneden, *Eye of the Storm*, 75.

26. Burton, *Extraordinary Circumstances*, 191.

27. Sneden, *Eye of the Storm*, 75.

28. Burton, *Extraordinary Circumstances*, 221; Sears, *To the Gates of Richmond*, 272–274. These authors have different casualty numbers, reflecting the estimated range listed in the text.

29. Carmichael, "Great Paragon of Virtue and Sobriety," 108.

30. Ibid.

31. Burton, *Extraordinary Circumstances*, 223.

32. Ibid., 223–225.

33. Ibid., 228–229.

CHAPTER FIVE

1. Sears, *To the Gates of Richmond*, 283.

2. Ibid., 280.

3. Sneden, *Eye of the Storm*, 84.

4. Sears, *To the Gates of Richmond*, 81.

5. Ibid., 281. Brian Burton claims that McClellan did not lack personal courage, but perhaps "lost his will to command"; yet, he concludes, "It is impossible to be sure." Burton, *Extraordinary Circumstances*, 244.

6. Sears, *To the Gates of Richmond*, 283.

7. Alexander, *Fighting for the Confederacy*, 110.

8. It is actually unclear whether he met with Magruder or Jackson first that morning; historians disagree.

9. Burton suggests that it may have been Lee who drew the map with his shoes and did the talking, but all other authors are convinced it was Jackson.

10. Dowdey, *Seven Days*, 292. Burton, unlike every other historian, never mentions this episode, which is strange given the comprehensive nature of his history.

11. Sears, *To the Gates of Richmond*, 283.

12. Ibid., 286.

13. Burton, *Extraordinary Circumstances*, 257.

14. Sears, *To the Gates of Richmond*, 288.

15. Foote, *Civil War*, 1:505.

16. Sears, *To the Gates of Richmond*, 288.

17. Burton, *Extraordinary Circumstances*, 258.

18. Sears, *To the Gates of Richmond*, 289.

19. James Longstreet, "'The Seven Days,' including Frayser's Farm," in *Battles and Leaders of the Civil War*, 4 vols., ed. Robert Underwood Johnson and Clarence Clough Buel (New York: The Century Co., 1884–1888), 2:402.

20. Burton, *Extraordinary Circumstances*, 263.

21. Dowdey, *Seven Days*, 308; Sears, *To the Gates of Richmond*, 289; Burton, *Extraordinary Circumstances*, 263; Freeman, *R.E. Lee*, 2:199.

22. Hill, "McClellan's Change of Base," 2:389; Burton, *Extraordinary Circumstances*, 263.

23. Franklin, "Rear-guard Fighting," 2:381.

24. Burton, *Extraordinary Circumstances*, 265–266.

25. Ibid., 266–267.

26. Freeman, *R.E. Lee*, 2:181–182.

27. Longstreet, "The Seven Days," 2:400; Longstreet, *From Manassas to Appomattox*, 134.

28. Burton, *Extraordinary Circumstances*, 269.

29. Ibid., 271.

30. Longstreet, "The Seven Days," 2:401.

31. Longstreet, *From Manassas to Appomattox*, 135.

32. Burton, *Extraordinary Circumstances*, 279.

33. Sears, *To the Gates of Richmond*, 295.

34. Burton, *Extraordinary Circumstances*, 277.

35. Ibid., 282.

36. Sears, *To the Gates of Richmond*, 295.

37. Burton, *Extraordinary Circumstances*, 284–286.

38. Sears, *To the Gates of Richmond*, 298–299.

39. Ibid., 302.

40. Burton, *Extraordinary Circumstances*, 291–293.

41. Ibid., 299.

42. Ibid., 295.

43. Ibid.

44. Longstreet, "The Seven Days," 2:402.

45. Sears, *To the Gates of Richmond*, 303; John Hennessy, *Return to Bull Run: The Campaign and Battle of Second Manassas* (New York: Simon & Schuster, 1993), 449–450.

46. Sears, *To the Gates of Richmond*, 304–306.

47. Ibid., 307.

48. Sears, *Civil War Papers of McClellan*, 326.

49. Sears, *To the Gates of Richmond*, 309.

50. Alexander, *Fighting for the Confederacy*, 109.

51. Burton, *Extraordinary Circumstances*, 300.

CHAPTER SIX

1. Burton, *Extraordinary Circumstances*, 309; Keith S. Bohannon, "One Solid Unbroken Roar of Thunder: Union and Confederate Artillery at the Battle of Malvern Hill," in *The Richmond Campaign of 1862: The Peninsula and the Seven Days*, ed. Gary W. Gallagher (Chapel Hill: University of North Carolina Press, 2000), 217–241.

2. Dowdey, *Seven Days*, 326.

3. Hill, "McClellan's Change of Base," 2:391.

4. Ibid.

5. Ibid., 2:403.

6. Burton, *Extraordinary Circumstances*, 314–316.

7. Sears, *To the Gates of Richmond*, 317; Freeman, *R.E. Lee*, 2:207.

8. Burton, *Extraordinary Circumstances*, 326.

9. Sears, *To the Gates of Richmond*, 318; Bohannon, "One Solid Unbroken Roar of Thunder," 222–223.

10. Burton, *Extraordinary Circumstances*, 321–323.

11. Bohannon, "One Solid Unbroken Roar of Thunder," 223.

12. Ibid., 223–225, 237–238; Burton, *Extraordinary Circumstances*, 321.

13. Burton, *Extraordinary Circumstances*, 320.

14. Sears, *To the Gates of Richmond*, 317, 325–326.

15. Longstreet, *From Manassas to Appomattox*, 144.

16. Burton, *Extraordinary Circumstances*, 329.

17. Ibid., 330.

18. Ibid., 330–332.

19. Sears, *To the Gates of Richmond*, 325.

20. National Park Service marker, Malvern Hill battlefield, Virginia; Burton, *Extraordinary Circumstances*, 333–337 (quote on p. 334).

21. Sears, *To the Gates of Richmond*, 326.

22. Ibid., 327.

23. Fitz John Porter, "The Battle of Malvern Hill," in *Battles and Leaders of the Civil War*, 4 vols., ed. Robert Underwood Johnson and Clarence Clough Buel (New York: The Century Co., 1884–1888), 2:421.

24. Ripley's official report quotes in Spruill and Spruill, *Echoes of Thunder*, 218.

25. Burton, *Extraordinary Circumstances*, 339.

26. Sears, *To the Gates of Richmond*, 326.

27. Hill, "McClellan's Change of Base," 2:393; Burton, *Extraordinary Circumstances*, 338–339.

28. Burton, *Extraordinary Circumstances*, 340; Hill, "McClellan's Change of Base," 2:394 (quote).

29. Burton, *Extraordinary Circumstances*, 342.

30. Sears, *To the Gates of Richmond*, 329.

31. Burton, *Extraordinary Circumstances*, 342–345.

32. Sears, *To the Gates of Richmond*, 331.

33. National Park Service marker, Malvern Hill Battlefield, Virginia.

34. Sears, *To the Gates of Richmond*, 331.

35. Burton, *Extraordinary Circumstances*, 347–349.

36. Ibid., 356.

37. Ibid., 357.

38. Sears, *To the Gates of Richmond*, 340.

39. Burton, *Extraordinary Circumstances*, 358.

40. Sears, *To the Gates of Richmond*, 337.

41. Dowdey, *Seven Days*, 330–331.

42. Porter, "Battle of Malvern Hill," 2:423.

43. Sears, *To the Gates of Richmond*, 337–338.

44. Ethan S. Rafuse, "Fighting for Defeat? George B. McClellan's Peninsula Campaign and the Change of Base to the James River," in *Civil War Generals in Defeat*, ed. Steven E. Woodworth (Lawrence: University

of Kansas Press, 1999), 92. For a fuller defense of McClellan, see Rafuse, *McClellan's War: The Failure of Moderation in the Struggle for the Union* (Bloomington: Indiana University Press, 2005).

45. Sears, *To the Gates of Richmond*, 339–341.

CHAPTER SEVEN

1. Burton, *Extraordinary Circumstances*, 386; Sears, *To the Gates of Richmond*, 343–345.

2. Sears, *To the Gates of Richmond*, 346.

3. Eric Foner, *The Fiery Trial: Abraham Lincoln and American Slavery* (New York: W.W. Norton & Company, 2010), 217.

4. Sears, *To the Gates of Richmond*, 347.

5. Burton, *Extraordinary Circumstances*, 391.

6. Sears, *To the Gates of Richmond*, 350–351.

7. Howard M. Hensel, *The Anatomy of Failure: Major General George B. McClellan and the Peninsular Campaign* (Montgomery, AL: Air Command and Staff College, 1985), 23.

8. William Swinton, *Campaigns of the Army of the Potomac* (New York: Charles B. Richardson, 1866), 165.

9. Sears, *To the Gates of Richmond*, 352–353.

10. Burton, *Extraordinary Circumstances*, 391; Freeman, *R.E. Lee*, 2:231.

11. Hennessy, *Return to Bull Run*.

12. Freeman, *R.E. Lee*, 2:246.

13. Ibid., 248.

14. Ibid., 234.

15. Ibid, 237, 239; Douglas Southall Freeman, *Lee's Lieutenants: A Study in Command, Volume 1* (New York: Charles Scribner's Sons, 1942).

16. Dowdey, *Seven Days*, 358.

Bibliographic Essay

The relevant literature on the Seven Days' campaign is large and varied, in both content and quality. For those seeking books dedicated to the campaign, Stephen W. Sears's *To the Gates of Richmond: The Peninsula Campaign* (New York: Ticknor & Fields, 1992) is still the best narrative of the campaign. It places General George McClellan at the center of the story, takes the focus off the Confederates exclusively, and situates the campaign in its broader national context. Brian K. Burton's *Extraordinary Circumstances: The Seven Days Battles* (Bloomington: Indiana University Press, 2001) is as solid as Sears's and is not only the most recent, but also an exhaustive and very detailed analysis of the campaign. Burton presents a nuanced perspective of the battles that is much deeper and closely argued than any previous work. Joseph P. Cullen's *The Peninsula Campaign, 1862: McClellan and Lee Struggle for Richmond* (Harrisburg, PA: Stackpole Books, 1973) is a broader overview of the campaign that does not go into as much detail on the individual battles. Clifford Dowdey's *The Seven Days: The Emergence of Robert E. Lee* (Boston: Little, Brown, 1964) is a very entertaining examination of the campaign. Dowdey's prose is crisp, flowing, and extremely witty, and he is as kindly toward Lee as he is devastating toward Lee's subordinates.

Several valuable collections of essays have been dedicated exclusively to the greater Peninsula campaign of which the Seven Days was a part. Gary W. Gallagher edited *The Richmond Campaign of 1862: The Peninsula and the Seven Days* (Chapel Hill: University of North Carolina Press,

2000), which presents a variety of excellently argued perspectives on the campaign. William Miller's edited essays on the campaign, *The Peninsula Campaign of 1862: Yorktown to the Seven Days* (Campbell, CA: Savas Woodbury Publishers [vols. 1–2] and Savas Publishing [vol. 3], 1993–1997) offer a wide variety of perspectives on McClellan's Peninsula campaign, with only a very few essays on the Seven Days and several personal narratives of soldiers in the campaign. Two of the earliest histories of the campaign are also worth consulting. Alexander S. Webb, a low-ranking Union officer during the campaign, presents a rather critical examination of McClellan's failures in *The Peninsula: McClellan's Campaign of 1862* (New York: Charles Scribner's Sons, 1881). William Swinton, a *New York Times* reporter who covered the campaign, wrote *Campaigns of the Army of the Potomac* (New York: Charles B. Richardson, 1866), which is a much more forgiving analysis of the Union army and its commander during the campaign.

One can learn much about the campaign through the biographies of the major participants involved. There are simply too many biographies to recount, but some of the more important ones are listed here. Stephen W. Sears's *George B. McClellan: The Young Napoleon* (New York: Ticknor & Fields, 1988) is the best biography on McClellan to date, easily readable with a deft blend of narrative and analysis of the general and the reasons for the decisions he made. While Sears is sharply critical of McClellan, other scholars have tried, though not with great success, to redeem McClellan. Ethan Rafuse's *McClellan's War: The Failure of Moderation in the Struggle for the Union* (Bloomington: Indiana University Press, 2005) focuses on McClellan's actions as a reflection of his philosophy of waging war, and as a result paints a much more positive portrait of the general. Not everyone will be convinced by his tortured defense of McClellan's actions during the Seven Days, however. Another positive interpretation of McClellan can be found in Warren W. Hassler's *George B. McClellan: Shield of the Union* (Baton Rouge: Louisiana State University Press, 1957). For a much more negative, unbalanced portrait of McClellan, one need only consult Edward H. Bonekemper's screed, *McClellan and Failure: A Study of Civil War Fear, Incompetence, and Worse* (Jefferson, NC: McFarland Press, 2007). John C. Waugh's *Lincoln and McClellan: The Troubled Partnership between a President and his General* (New York: Palgrave Macmillan, 2010) is a lucid analysis of the complex and counterproductive relationship between McClellan and his commander-in-chief.

When one looks for biographies of Robert E. Lee, the list of titles is seemingly endless, though not all deal in any meaningful way with his actions during the Seven Days. Emory Thomas's *Robert E. Lee: A Biography*

(New York: W.W. Norton & Company, 1995) offers a balanced and thoughtful study of Lee's role in the battles. In Michael Fellman's *The Making of Robert E. Lee* (New York: Random House, 2000), the author offers a psychological analysis of what drove Lee to make the military decisions that he made. A more positive view of Lee can be found in Joseph L. Harsh's *Confederate Tide Rising: Robert E. Lee and the Making of Southern Strategy* (Kent, OH: Kent State University Press, 1998). Harsh gives Lee much credit for his strategic decisions, but does point out mistakes in Lee's tactics. Looking at the same campaign, but interpreting Lee's action in a more negative light is Alan Nolan's *Lee Considered: General Robert E. Lee and Civil War History* (Chapel Hill: University of North Carolina Press, 1991). However, if an extensive biography of Lee is what one seeks, then one need look no further than Douglas Southall Freeman's *R.E. Lee,* 4 vols. (New York: Charles Scribner's Sons, 1934–1935), the classic and extremely detailed biography in which nearly the entire second volume is dedicated to Lee's performance in the Seven Days. Freeman casts Lee is the most flattering light possible, but writes a cogent narrative that thoroughly, if not dispassionately, recounts the story of the battles. Soon after completing his biography, Freeman published a three-volume study of Lee's subordinate officers, entitled *Lee's Lieutenants: A Study in Command* (New York: Charles Scribner's Sons, 1942–1944). The first volume of that series is dedicated to analyzing the positive and many negative characteristics of Lee's subordinate officers of the campaign.

In addition to biographies of the commanding generals, there are innumerable biographies of the subordinate officers. Stonewall Jackson has had more than his fair share, and they all take a stance on Jackson's performance in the Seven Days. For one that gives Jackson every positive consideration, see James I. Robertson Jr., *Stonewall Jackson: The Man, the Soldier, the Legend* (New York: Macmillan, 1997). For one that is more critical of Jackson's performance, see Frank E. Vandiver, *Mighty Stonewall* (New York: McGraw-Hill, 1957). A recent work that deftly examines the mystique that has built up around Stonewall and examines his role in the campaign is Wallace Hettle's *Inventing Stonewall Jackson: A Civil War Hero in History and Memory* (Baton Rouge: Louisiana State University Press, 2011).

There are plenty of specialized studies of the campaign as well. Nothing gives an interested party a better sense of the scope and scale of a battle than actually visiting the battlefields and walking the grounds. If one wishes to do so, one should take along Matt Spruill III and Matt Spruill IV's *Echoes of Thunder: A Guide to the Seven Days Battles* (Knoxville: University of Tennessee Press, 2006), which is also the most recent book on the campaign. It is a thorough guide for those wishing to literally walk the battlefields and visualize what occurred at each battle. The book is full of official reports of many officers of the units involved in the battle, and gives an excellent step-by-step accounting of the individual battles. While in my reading of the primary sources, I interpreted the location and attack routes of certain units differently than the Spruills, I found their guide to be a fresh and innovative way to experience the battlefield. However, a word of warning from my own personal experience—be careful when the guide directs you to private property. Although they may have received permission from the owners to allow access to private roads and land to view the battle, the owners of certain properties have changed hands and may no longer be as gracious and accommodating. The interested reader should stick to the lands owned by the National Park Service.

Kevin Dougherty's (with J. Michael Moore) *The Peninsula Campaign of 1862: A Military Analysis* (Jackson: University Press of Mississippi, 2005) and Howard M. Hensel's *The Anatomy of Failure: Major General George B. McClellan and the Peninsular Campaign* (Montgomery, AL: Air Command and Staff College, 1985) are thin books that examine the tactical and strategic decisions of the battles. Neither book places the campaign in a broader context, but for those interested in looking at the battle through purely military perspectives, these works are useful.

There are a great many printed primary sources that shed light on the Seven Days' battles. The largest and best source is U.S. War Department, *The War of the Rebellion: The Official Records of the Union and Confederate Armies,* 127 vols. (Washington, D.C.: Government Printing Office, 1880–1901), specifically series 1, volume 11, parts 1–3, which deal with the fighting outside Richmond in 1862. For Northern soldier views of the campaign, see the *Papers* of the Military Order of the Loyal Legion of the United States (MOLLUS), 66 vols. and 3-vol. index (Wilmington, NC: Broadfoot, 1991–96). There is also much in the way of Confederate reminiscences of the war in the *Southern Historical Society Papers,* ed. J. William Jones et al., 52 vols. (1876–1959; reprint, with 3-vol. index, Wilmington, NC: Broadfoot, 1990–1992). Additionally, Robert Underwood Johnson and Clarence Clough Buel edited *Battles and Leaders of the Civil War,* 4 vols. (New York: The Century Co., 1884–1888), in which many prominent Union and Confederate officers related their experiences during the war, often in a hybrid style of essay that was part official report and part reflective recollection. Much of volume two in that series deals with the Peninsula Campaign and the Seven Days' battles.

Many memoirs emerged after the war from participants in the campaign. George B. McClellan wrote his own not entirely truthful account,

McClellan's Own Story (New York: Charles L. Webster, 1887), while Stephen W. Sears edited *The Civil War Papers of George B. McClellan: Selected Correspondence, 1860–1865* (New York: Ticknor & Fields, 1989), which is an excellent source. Clifford Dowdey and Louis H. Manarin edited *The Wartime Papers of Robert E. Lee* (Boston: Little, Brown, 1961), which is an equally invaluable tool. James Longstreet's *From Manassas to Appomattox: Memoirs of the Civil War in America* (Philadelphia: Lippincott, 1896) takes similar liberties with the truth as McClellan, but is important. A much more candid and critical memoir is Edward Porter Alexander's *Fighting for the Confederacy: The Personal Recollections of General Edward Porter Alexander*, ed. Gary W. Gallagher (Chapel Hill: University of North Carolina Press, 1989). In his lifetime, Alexander published *Military Memoirs of a Confederate: A Critical Narrative* (New York: Charles Scribner's Sons, 1907), which conveys many of the same themes as the later work.

For memoirs of low-ranking officials, see Robert Knox Sneden's *Eye of the Storm: A Civil War Odyssey*, edited by Charles F. Bryan, Jr., and Nelson D. Lankford (New York: Free Press, 2000). Private Sneden provides both a candid appraisal of the campaign and a perceptive and highly critical contemporary account of McClellan. For an account from a Richmond government official, see John B. Jones, *A Rebel War Clerk's Diary*, edited by Earl Schenck Miers (New York: A.S. Barnes & Company, Inc., 1961). For an account from a female resident of Richmond, who related the effects of the battle on the city as the wounded swamped the city's hospital facilities, see Sallie Brock Putnam's *Richmond during the War: Four Years of Personal Observation* (1867; reprint, Lincoln: University of Nebraska Press, 1996).

Several broad, comprehensive histories of the Civil War have dealt with the campaign in great detail as well. Bruce Catton produced two trilogies of the war. In *Mr. Lincoln's Army* (New York: Doubleday, 1951), the first volume of his Army of the Potomac trilogy, and *Terrible Swift Sword* (New York: Doubleday, 1963), the second volume of his American Civil War trilogy, Catton discusses the peninsula campaign in broad context and elaborates the consequences of the campaign, focusing specifically on the Union army's performance. Shelby Foote delved into much greater detail on the campaign in the first volume of his three-volume history of the war, *The Civil War: A Narrative* (New York: Random House, 1958). Foote presents a Southern-tinctured view of the war, but is an excellent storyteller and is less pronounced in his biases than is Dowdey. In contrast to Foote's slight Southern bias is Allan Nevins's slight bias toward the Union in his magisterial eight-volume history of the war, *Ordeal of the Union* (New York: Charles Scribner's Sons, 1947–1971). In volume three, *War Becomes Revolution, 1862–1863* (1961), Nevins examines the campaign and its consequences for the war. Nevins has a strong command of the narrative format and writes in a clear, if occasionally moralizing, prose. Herman Hattaway and Archer Jones present an excellent analysis of the larger ramifications of the campaign and how it changed the nature of the war in *How the North Won: A Military History of the Civil War* (Urbana: University of Illinois Press, 1983). Finally, for the Internet-savvy reader, many of the older books mentioned in this essay can be accessed via online portals, such as Google Books. Thus, it is incredibly easy for the interested reader to discover more about the campaign than is captured in this brief work.

Index

About the Author

JUDKIN BROWNING is an associate professor of history at Appalachian State University in Boone, North Carolina. He is also the author of *Shifting Loyalties: The Union Occupation of Eastern North Carolina* (2011) and *The Southern Mind under Union Rule: The Diary of James Rumley, Beaufort, North Carolina, 1862–1865* (2009).